WITHDRAWN

A

An tional
ex les in
A₁ erican
fic s that
th

• those

•
•
•
•

A₁ ich as
D , who
w₁ emer-
ge 'roulx,
D it into
bᵢ action
bᵢ s, this
vᵢ erican
literature and culture and late-twentieth-century fiction.

Contributors include: Timothy Aubry, Alex E. Blazer, Kasia Boddy,
Stephen J. Burn, Andrew Dix, Brian Jarvis, Suzanne W. Jones, Peter
Knight, A. Robert Lee, Stacey Olster, Derek Parker Royal, Krishna Sen,
Zoe Trodd, Andrew Warnes and Nahem Yousaf.

Jay Prosser is Senior Lecturer in American Literature and Culture at the
University of Leeds. He is author of *Second Skins: The Body Narratives of
Transsexuality*, *Light in the Dark Room: Photography and Loss*, and co-editor of
Palatable Poison: Critical Perspectives on The Well of Loneliness.

American Fiction of the 1990s

Reflections of history and culture

Edited by Jay Prosser

Routledge
Taylor & Francis Group

LONDON AND NEW YORK

First published 2008
by Routledge
2 Park Square, Milton Park, Abingdon, OX14 4RN

Simultaneously published in the USA and Canada
by Routledge
270 Madison Ave, New York, NY 10016

Routledge is an imprint of the Taylor & Francis Group, an informa business

Typeset in Baskerville by
Taylor & Francis Books
Printed and bound in Great Britain by
TJ International Ltd, Padstow, Cornwall

British Library Cataloguing in Publication Data
A catalogue record for this book is available from the British Library

Library of Congress Cataloging in Publication Data
American fiction of the 1990s : reflections of history and culture /
edited by Jay Prosser.
p. cm.
Includes bibliographical references.
1. American fiction–20th century–History and criticism. 2.
Literature and society–United States–History–20th century. 3. History
and literature–United States–History–20th century. 4. History in
literature. 5. Social problems in literature. 6. Emigration and
immigration in literature. 7. Race relations in literature. 8. Nineteen
nineties. I. Prosser, Jay.
   PS374.S7A45 2008
   813'.5409353–dc22

                                        2008004058

ISBN 13: 978-0-415-43566-6 (hbk)
ISBN 13: 978-0-415-43567-3 (pbk)
ISBN 13: 978-0-203-09104-3 (ebk)

Contents

Contributors

Timothy Aubry is Assistant Professor of English at Baruch College, City University of New York. His essays on contemporary American fiction have appeared in *Modern Fiction Studies*, *Iowa Journal of Cultural Studies* and *Critical Matrix*.

Alex E. Blazer is Assistant Professor of English at Georgia College and State University, where he teaches American literature. He has published articles on Barrett Watten, Bret Easton Ellis, and the Matrix trilogy. His book, *"I Am Otherwise": The Romance between Poetry and Theory after the Death of the Subject*, was published in 2007.

Kasia Boddy is Lecturer in English at University College, London. She is the author of *Boxing: A Cultural History* (2008) and co-editor (with Ali Smith and Sarah Wood) of *The Virago Book of Twentieth-Century Fiction* (2000). Her essays on American literature have appeared in many journals and essay collections, including the *European Journal of American Culture*, *Critical Quarterly*, *The Yale Journal of Criticism*, *The Journal of American Studies*, and *The Review of Contemporary Fiction*. She has also published interviews with many writers, including Raymond Carver, Grace Paley, Kathy Acker, John Ashbery, Lynne Tillman, and Dennis Cooper.

Stephen J. Burn is an Associate Professor of English at Northern Michigan University. He is the author of *David Foster Wallace's Infinite Jest: A Reader's Guide* (2003), *Jonathan Franzen at the End of Postmodernism* (2008), and co-editor of *Intersections: Essays on Richard Powers* (2008).

Andrew Dix is Lecturer in American Studies in the Department of English and Drama, Loughborough University. He is the author of *Beginning Film Studies* (2008) and co-editor, with Jonathan Taylor, of *Figures of Heresy: Radical Theology in English and American Writing, 1800–2000* (2006). His essays in journals and collections include work on Mark

Twain, John Steinbeck, contemporary Native American fiction and the travel writing of Jonathan Raban.

Brian Jarvis is Senior Lecturer in American Literature and Film in the Department of English and Drama at Loughborough University. He is author of *Cruel and Unusual: Punishment and US Culture* (2003) and *Postmodern Cartographies: The Geographical Imagination in Contemporary American Culture* (1998), which was reviewed in the *Times Literary Supplement* as "path-breaking ... shows how valuable the findings of a new literary geography could be." His essays on contemporary American literature and culture have appeared in various places, including *The Yearbook of English Studies, Crime, Media, Culture: An International Journal*, and another collection by Routledge (*Urban Space and Cityscapes*, ed. Christoph Lindner [2006]).

Suzanne W. Jones is Professor of English at the University of Richmond. Her book *Race Mixing: Southern Fiction since the Sixties* was published in 2004. She is the editor of two collections of stories, *Crossing the Color Line: Readings in Black and White* (2000) and *Growing Up in the South* (1991), and the editor of three collections of essays, *Writing the Woman Artist* (1991), *South to a New Place* with Sharon Monteith (2002), and *Poverty and Progress in the US South since 1920* with Mark Newman (2006). Her articles on the US South and on race and gender in American literature have appeared in many essay collections and journals, including *American Literature, Critical Survey, Journal of American Studies, Journal of Modern Literature, Masculinities, Southern Literary Journal, Southern Quarterly, Southern Studies*, and *Women: A Cultural Review*. Her current research is on the reappearance of the racially mixed figure in the contemporary American imagination.

Peter Knight is Senior Lecturer in American Studies at the University of Manchester. He is the author of *Conspiracy Culture: From the Kennedy Assassination to "The X-Files"* (2000), and *The Kennedy Assassination* (2007). He has edited two further works, *Conspiracy Nation: The Politics of Postwar American Paranoia* (2002) and *Conspiracy Theories in American History: An Encyclopedia* (2004). His articles have been published in various collections and journals, including *Modern Fiction Studies* and *Cultural Studies*.

A. Robert Lee, formerly of the University of Kent at Canterbury, is Professor of American Literature at Nihon University, Tokyo. He has held visiting appointments at Princeton, the University of Virginia, the University of Colorado and the University of California at Berkeley. His recent books include *Designs of Blackness: Mappings in the Literature and Culture of Afro-America* (1998); *Postindian Conversations*, with Gerald Vizenor

(1999); *Multicultural American Literature: Comparative Black, Native, Latino/a and Asian American Fictions* (2003), which won the 2004 American Book Award; *Japan Textures: Sight and Word*, with Mark Gresham (2007), and *Gothic to Multicultural: Idioms of Imagining in American Literary Fiction* (2008). He has also been responsible for a large number of essay collections, among them *Other British, Other Britain: Contemporary Multicultural Fiction* (1995), *The Beat Generation Writers* (1996), the four-volume *Herman Melville: Critical Assessments* (2001), and *China Fictions/English Language: Literary Essays in Diaspora, Memory, Story* (2008).

Stacey Olster is Professor of English at the State University of New York at Stony Brook. Her book publications include *The Trash Phenomenon: Contemporary Literature, Popular Culture, and the Making of the American Century* (2003) and *Reminiscence and Re-Creation in Contemporary American Fiction* (1989), the latter a classic work on contemporary American literature, particularly on models of history in fiction. She has also recently edited *The Cambridge Companion to John Updike* (2006). Her essays on con-temporary American fiction and culture have appeared in many places, including *Modern Fiction Studies*, *The Review of Contemporary Fiction*, *Critique*, and *Critical Inquiry* as well as in many essay collections.

Jay Prosser is Senior Lecturer in American Literature and Culture at the University of Leeds. He is the author of *Second Skins: The Body Narratives of Transsexuality* (1998), *Light in the Dark Room: Photography and Loss* (2004) and co-editor of *Palatable Poison: Critical Essays on The Well of Loneliness* (2002). His essays have appeared in journals and collections including *PMLA*, *Modern Fiction Studies*, and *The Cambridge Companion to John Updike* (2006).

Derek Parker Royal is Associate Professor of English and Director of Liberal Studies at Texas A&M University-Commerce and Founding Executive Editor of the journal *Philip Roth Studies*. He is the editor of *Philip Roth: New Perspectives on an American Author* (2005) and is currently completing a manuscript, *More Than Jewish Mischief: Narrating Subjectivity in Philip Roth's Later Fiction*. His essays on American literature have appeared in a variety of journals and collections, including *Contemporary Literature*, *Modern Fiction Studies*, *MELUS*, *Studies in the Novel*, *Poe Studies/ Dark Romanticism*, *Modern Drama*, *Shofar*, *Studies in American Jewish Fiction*, and *The Cambridge Companion to Philip Roth* (2007).

Krishna Sen is Professor of English at the University of Calcutta. She is author of *Negotiating Modernity: Myth in the Theatre of Eliot, O'Neill and Sartre* (1999) and *Narrative: Form and Theory* (2000). Her edited collections of essays include *Colonial and Postcolonial Shakespeares* (2002), *Revisiting the Raj*

(2004), *Tagore and Modernity* (2006), *Colonial and Postcolonial Perspectives* (2007) and *Narrating the (Trans)Nation* (2008). She has also produced annotated editions of contemporary Indian fiction, such as Amitav Ghosh's *The Calcutta Chromosome* (1999), as well as editions and critical introductions in India of American and European literature, such as Ibsen's *A Doll's House* (2005). She has published over thirty-five essays in international journals, including *South Asian Review*, *Victorian Periodicals Review*, and *Nineteenth-Century Literature in English*, and in book collections, most lately *A New Companion to James Joyce* (2008). Her essay on "glocalization" in the literature of American dreaming appeared in *Studies in American Literature*, and an essay on Mukherjee's earlier fiction in the *Indian Journal of American Studies*. She has been a Fulbright NEH Scholar in the USA, a Commonwealth Scholar and Leverhulme Visiting Professor in the UK, and an invited speaker internationally, including the Universities of Shanghai, Singapore, and Salzburg.

Zoe Trodd is a member of the History and Literature Tutorial Board at Harvard University, where she lectures on American protest literature. Her books include *Meteor of War: The John Brown Story* (2004), *American Protest Literature* (2006), *To Plead Our Own Cause: Narratives of Modern Slavery* (2008), and *The Long Civil Rights Movement, 1945-73* (2008). She has also published numerous articles on American literature, history, and photography, including on Civil Rights protest literature.

Andrew Warnes is Lecturer in American Literature and Culture at the University of Leeds. He is author of *Hunger Overcome? Food and Resistance in Twentieth-Century African American Literature* (2004) and *Richard Wright's Native Son* (2007). His essays on food, music, and diaspora have appeared in *Moving Worlds*, *Popular Music* and *Journal of American Studies*. His next book, *Savage Barbecue: Race, Culture and the Invention of America's First Food*, will appear in summer 2008.

Nahem Yousaf is Professor and Head of English at Nottingham Trent University. He is author, editor or co-editor of a number of books about modern and contemporary literature, including *Chinua Achebe* (2003), *Critical Perspectives on Pat Barker* (2005), *Apartheid Narratives* (2001). He is co-editor of the Manchester University Press series of monographs on Contemporary American and Canadian Writers. His articles have appeared in journals such as *Journal of American Studies*, *Journal of Commonwealth Literature*, *Critical Survey*, and *Wasafiri*.

1 Introduction

Jay Prosser

"How innocent can you be, at the age of thirty-nine, in the year 1999?" (Updike 2000: 256). In "Rabbit Remembered," John Updike resurrects his protagonist Rabbit through reunited descendants to focus on turn-of-millennium hopes dashed into disappointments, comically dramatized in the family missing the New Year while caught in a traffic jam. If the novels in the Rabbit tetralogy (Updike 1995) each staged a decade since World War II, this final novella, firmly set in 1999, is about the 1990s. *American Beauty* jokes about a president getting a blow job ("slick Willie"), the Y2K bug, Tomb Raider, global warming, an Egyptian pilot committing suicide by downing his entire plane, *The Vagina Monologues*, Mrs. Clinton running against Giuliani for New York Senator, Alan Greenspan, Boolean, Net surfing, *The Simpsons*, Valley Girls, Lisa Kudrow on *Friends*, Elián González, lo-cal frozen yoghurt, AIDS, teeth implants, San Pellegrino mineral water, *The Art of Happiness* by the Dalai Lama and an American doctor: Into this short form Updike packs the memorable news items, media events, cultural practices, public figures and idiomatic vocabulary of the decade. Innovator of not only period fiction but also new forms from putting period into fiction, Updike—reproducing emails of Rabbit's grandson minus apostrophes but with smileys—brilliantly captures what was distinct about the decade. His fiction reflects, or refracts, America's history and culture.

The end of innocence that Rabbit's illegitimate daughter ties to the end of the millennium runs through the decade in America and its fiction. The fall of the Berlin Wall in 1989 and with it Communism for some commentators signaled the triumph of liberalism, the end of history's driving dialectic (Fukuyama 1993). Culturally America was truly global: AOL, Microsoft, MTV, Starbucks—the large corporation seemed everywhere and indispensable. Domestically the USA was uplifted with the hopes of the Clinton era, after the 1992 election win from Bush Sr. promised a liberal renewal, following twelve years of Republicanism, of welfare, education and health, a restoration of the public state. Clinton radiated energy, eloquence, ease—and a guilelessness that didn't hide that he was a cultured president, whose declared favorite reading was the sophisticated African-American "Easy Rawlins" detective novels by Walter Mosley, who played saxophone, and whose Southern roots and demographic support led Toni Morrison to call him America's first black president. Yet the decade under Clinton was in reality marred by civil unrest—racial and cultural tensions which seemed to return to pre-progressive 1960s, increased gun violence and immigration controls, a defensive entrenchment of conservative America in the "Culture Wars," and the home-grown terrorism of the Oklahoma City and Una-bombers. Various high-profile race- and sex-related trials would climax in the President's own impeachment hearings in 1999 over the Monica Lewinsky sex scandal ensuring that the Democrats would be sandwiched as they lost to the second Bush in 2000. The post-Communist redefining of America saw the emergence of what Bush Sr. proclaimed a New World Order, with America as world policeman intervening, in sequence, in Iraq during the Gulf War, in Somalia, Haiti, and Bosnia, so that some were led to see America as a new form of postimperialist empire (Hardt and Negri 2000). Backlash against this increased American presence abroad was one way of understanding 9/11, an event that marked the end of the American Century and any innocence that went with it. And America had in common with the developed world anxieties about the germs of millennial apocalypse, from the Y2K bug to global warming.

American fiction published during the 1990s is vital, energized, and prolific in good part from being hooked into the decade—from reflecting and refracting American culture and history. Major novelists of post-1950s American literature produced their most ambitious work by engaging with the time or the genealogy of their time: Thomas Pynchon tells in *Mason & Dixon* (1997) about the origins of the American empire; Don DeLillo's *Underworld* (1998) compares nuclear apocalypse and consumer waste; and Philip Roth, in the American trilogy (1997, 1998, 2000), wrote three consecutive historical novels about late-twentieth-century America. African-American writers who began their careers in the 1970s and 1980s redefining the canon became central to it and set trends for their times. Morrison won the Nobel Prize for Literature in 1993, consummate chronicler of American history. Aided by the increasingly popular reading groups and book clubs, Terry McMillan was a national bestseller telling the private lives of the burgeoning affluent middle-class black women (McMillan 1992, 1996). Latino/a-American and Asian-American fiction were among the fastest-growing literary fields, the dissemination of this work transferring from grassroots presses to mainstream publishing houses in reflection of the cultural concerns of immigration and assimilation some address. And emerging were new writers—Sherman Alexie (1993, 1995), Chang-rae Lee (1995), E. Annie Proulx (1993, 1995), David Foster Wallace (1996), Jonathan Franzen (2001), Jonathan Lethem (1999), Dave Eggers (2000)—whose voices and styles would be influential in the next decade.

Formally and aesthetically the fiction is multifaceted. Old genres continue, detective, sci-fi, thriller, family drama, the coming-of-age novel, and old modes, realism and postmodern play, but alongside new genres, from mainstream or pop culture comics or the graphic novel, and memoir, for some characteristic of the age (Miller 2002), blurred with fiction. The distinctions between categories, and high and low culture, are increasingly crossed. Along with post-postmodernism, classics from the American canon are rewritten, *The Scarlet Letter, Lolita*. New combinations appear, notably earnestness alongside irony with *McSweeney's*, Eggers's publishing house and literary journal which made a point of publishing only works rejected by other magazines, hence starting many young writers—Foster Wallace, Jonathan Lethem, Michael Chabon, T. C. Boyle. To describe the big ambitious novel that some of these writers pursued at all costs, combining high pitch with the everyday, James Wood, in an essay in the *New Republic*, coined the term "hysterical realism" (Wood 2000). The sense is, even from British critics such as Wood, that "the triumph of the postwar novel decisively belonged to the Americans, not the British" (Wood 2004). In Britain, Lisa Jardine protested that the opening of the Man Booker Prize to American writers would make British fiction look "parochial" in comparison: "With someone like Roth at his best, I can't see how an Amis or McEwan would touch them" (Chrisafis 2002). In their books about American fiction from around the decade, eminent critics Jay Clayton (1994), Robert Durante (2001), Arthur Saltzman (2000), and Marc Chénetier (1996) confirm the richness of aesthetic design.

While subjects include Nicholson Baker's *Box of Matches* (2003), fiction of the period embeds in large issues, concerned with the wider meanings of events. In spite of the problems of periodization recognized by Fredric Jameson (1988), certain themes can be noted, which provide the subheadings for the collection: transnational borders, race cathexes, historical narratives, sex images, postmodern technologies. These themes have deep roots in American literature and culture—in motifs from the landscape (Gidley and Lawson-Peebles 1995) and frontier (Turner 1935) to the machine in the garden (Marx 1964). But the 1990s saw the emergence of approaches that question the mythologization surrounding old ideas such as America as pastoral and the function of the frontier to advance history. New American Studies, as they came to be known and practiced by scholars such as John Carlos Rowe (2002) and George Lipsitz (2001), as well as in journal special issues, in *PMLA* (Kadir 2003), and new journals such as *Comparative American Studies*, read radically and interrogatively across several kinds of contexts: national, taking account of the international and global dimension of American literature and culture; disciplinary, acknowledging literary as intertwined with other modes of production; and historically, examining how the contemporary tells the foundation and evolution of history. New American Studies questions American innocence—ideals of America and the contemporary as exceptional—by showing connections between America and the world and the continuation of history into the present. Angular and international, our essays here are not only by top scholars in the field but advance the New American Studies.

Part I: Transnational borders

In the Soviet Union's dissolution, the nation-state is reconfigured, drawing attention to the border as contemporary trope. The border, the *Heath Anthology of American Literature* says, is definitive of postmodern life (Lauter 2005), globalization working through transnational flows and conjuring the possibility of the postnational. America's key place in globalization is now recognized, and some suggest that as an immigrant nation it is global from the start (Sen 2003). "Floating" for the characters of Bharati Mukherjee is the figure for what it means to be American in global New York at the end of twentieth century (Mukherjee 1988). The border of Gloria Anzaldúa (1987), a bilingual and bicultural ambiguous space between the USA and the Spanish Americas and in the definite form of the USA–Mexican border, comes to seem paradigmatic and, in Cormac McCarthy's *Border Trilogy* (1990), mythologized. Latin America and Mexico dominated US immigration during the 1990s, near doubling in size, and with the differing population growth rates promising to make the USA Spanish-speaking. The quincentenary gathering in Mexico City in 1992 celebrating the discovery of America revises the relation between American hemispheres, as do archeological studies that reveal the first Americans appear in Brazil and Peru, not in North America (Dillehay 2000). A preoccupation to demarcate the USA's cultural and geographical borders can be seen in a series of legal decisions, such as the repatriation of Elián González to Cuba, and various anti-immigrant laws in California, Propositions 227, which required all teaching in schools to be conducted in English, and 187, which denied immigrants public services including education. Immigrant American writers and children of immigrants nevertheless travel in writing back to their ancestral home, Jessica Hagedorn to the Philippines (Hagedorn 1990), Julia Alvarez to Dominica (Alvarez 1991). The essays here identify the relation of national and geographical border crossing to intertextuality and the multidimensional narrative structures in some of the fiction about transnational America.

A. Robert Lee (Chapter 2) writes on the southern border with Latin America to show its enriching of the American English canon, language, genres, and geography. *Las lineas* are several, and the idea behind coverage is to convey depth and breadth. The border is symbolic and internal as much as geographic and, with narratives crossing, also formal. Nahem Yousaf's chapter (Chapter 3) on new immigrant fiction follows a range of figures, from white Europeans in E. Annie Proulx to Haitians in Edwidge Danticat, Vietnamese in Lan Cao and Dominicans in Junot Diaz. In the new narratives, an old story of transnationalism and globalization emerges, as fictions question the assimiliationist American dream and negotiate crossing borders more successfully than the social commentary critical of cosmopolitanism. Moving the metaphors of immigration from bridge between places and generations (the border as join), Krishna Sen in Chapter 4 holds the "diaphor" as one figure of multiple and discontinuous translation in Bharati Mukherjee's *Holder of the World*. This narrative of reverse immigration translates an American to India, and America, via Mukherjee as an Indian immigrant author, is seen in the context of the history of several empires as having long global connections, from the origins never exceptional. In patterns of hybridity that raise interesting contemporary questions about the relation between America and the postcolonial (Singh and Schmidt 2000), America is crucially transnationalized through a process of intertextuality.

Part II: Race cathexes

Part II, "Race Cathexes," investigates race relations, of violence, of desire and of identification, grouped under the Freudian term for investments of psychic energy. A new interethnic approach to writing about race and its representations attended to the relations between ethnicities, to transcultural crossings. In fiction Gish Jen's *Mona in the Promised Land* (Jen 1997) moves a Chinese-American teenager to a New York Jewish suburb. At the same time, in Roth's *The Human Stain* (2000), a protagonist is caught between Jewish and black. The term "interracialism" (meaning interracial relationships as well sometimes mixed-race or "biracial" characters) gains prominence (Sollors 2000) as individuals are able to identify themselves as mixed race for the first time in the US census of 2000, allowing an engagement with the interstitial that is not tragic. Symptomized in the new whiteness studies, there emerges an awareness of whiteness as raced, of how white constructs itself through other races, notably in Morrison's *Playing in the Dark* (1992), a short, profound, classic study of the literature.

Deep differences within communities are voiced in the emphasis of ethnic nonrepresentativity, sometimes antipathetically, as, for example, in the Asian-American community with *Charlie Chan Is Dead: An Anthology of Contemporary Asian American Fiction* (Hagedorn 1993). In the introduction, Hagedorn says that Asian-American literature is too confining. Chang-rae Lee (Lee 1995) achieved various awards—the Hemingway Foundation/PEN, American Book Award—for *Native Speaker*, about a Korean-American but again knocking up against other ethnicities in New York and in interracial marriage. Humor is to be found in stereotypes, in Sherman Alexie's (1993, 1995) and Paul Beatty's (1996) comic novels on life, respectively, in the Indian reservation taking on stereotypes of the silent Indian and alcoholism, and in the ghetto, on inner-city violence and gun culture. At the same time, racial conflicts dominate the media and public spheres, with the police beating of Rodney King and the subsequent Los Angeles disturbances, the O. J. Simpson trial, and debates about reparations and apologies for slavery and Native American genocide—all thoroughly mediated. Returning to W. E. B. Du Bois's color line at the end of twentieth century, Henry Louis Gates wonders how much had changed (Percival 2002).

In Chapter 5, Andrew Dix considers triangular relationships in the fiction of Sherman Alexie in which American Indians and African Americans are complicit but also connected in white subordination of each other. There are no transcultural bridges here but rather troubling reaffirmations of racial separatism. Yet Alexie's forms crucially borrow from another, African-American tradition. Andrew Warnes, in Chapter 6, selects two African-American novels and reads them as returning to history as a way of converting, condensing in cathexis the violence of the present, both idealizing and working through the past. In a mode appropriate to the pointillist style of Morrison and Johnson, Warnes foregrounds imagery to connect one novel to another and both to context. In Chapter 7, Suzanne W. Jones examines the mixed-race protagonist who, after largely disappearing from literature of the Civil Rights, returns in fiction in the context of the legal and demographic recognitions. Three novels in which the protagonists' biracialism rewrites the tragic mixed-race story become tests for the nation's legacy of race, showing the shortfalls of identity politics of the 1970s and 1980s and yet also that narratives of social construction are distressing.

Part III: Historical narratives

Part III, "Historical Narratives," examines questions of the nation's memory and the narrativization techniques of memorialization. In spite of the imminence of the future and the end of history, a preoccupation with the past characterizes the period. There is hyperconsciousness of history, "hypermnesia," as Roger Luckhurst and Peter Marks note: "the thickness of time and temporality in the contemporary world" (Luckhurst and Marks 1999: 10), when the contemporary is caught up with past times, particularly in the form of public memorials and *lieux de mémoire* (Nora 1984–92). At the same time, the past is doubted, the accuracy of remembering and representing history distrusted. Following New Historicism (Veeser 1989) and the work of Hayden White (1987), history is not an innocent recording but a narrativization, with techniques similar to fiction. We see a concern with traumatic memory, the Holocaust paradigmatic. America opens a museum devoted to the memory of the Holocaust in 1993. *Schindler's List* (dir. Steven Spielberg, 1993) appears the same year, the lability of memory shown when this film based on novel based on an episode in World War II becomes the reference point for the Holocaust. Critics complain of a "Holocaust industry" (Finkelstein 2000) and the Americanization of the Holocaust (Novick 2000). As Morrison writes, with "no bench by the road," there do not yet exist equivalent public memorials to more indigenous American events, such as slavery or the war against American Indians (Morrison 1989). Holocaust fiction shows itself often comically self-conscious about representing traumatic memory, with *Maus II* (Spiegelman 1993), *After* (Bukiet 1997) and *Operation Shylock* (Roth 1993). The issues of the ownership and political uses of memory are also at stake in Recovered Memory Syndrome, in which the authenticity of stories of childhood abuse are debated in the media, from Debbie Nathan in *LA Weekly* calling for the retrials of those convicted of child abuse (Nathan 1989), to a *60 Minutes* program on false/recovered memories on PBS in 1995, to Geraldo Rivera apologizing for promoting recovered memory in his talk show; several novels, including Jane Smiley's *A Thousand Acres* (1992), address incestuous memories. In psychoanalysis, there are comparable but more academic memory battles. Frederick Crews published *Memory Wars: Freud's Legacy in Dispute* (1997), based on essays originally published in the *New York Review of Books* in which he alleged that recovered memory originates in Freud and damns the whole enterprise of psychoanalysis as pseudoscience.

This section tackles memory in terms of its fraught representation. Stacey Olster, in Chapter 8, reads *Mason & Dixon* as an exploration of fin-de-millennium America traced through its prehistory in eighteenth-century empire, contemporary overlapping with originary memories. The New World Order is shown by Pynchon taking shape at the moment that America becomes a nation. As Olster reveals, the novel has a crucial role in nation-making, and she attends to parody, referencing and cartography through which Pynchon makes America a text. In Chapter 9, Derek

Parker Royal dwells on the writer whose decade's novels systematically engaged history: Roth, who in the three novels of his American trilogy explores how individuals and fiction are captivated by the forces of history. History reveals the pastoral as fiction, again interrogating American innocence. Brian Jarvis (Chapter 10) is concerned with one traumatic historical event which America seems to repeat in the 1990s, with the global military interventions echoing Vietnam. If Tim O'Brien captures the ongoing presence of Vietnam over twenty years, Jarvis shows how his 1990s fiction gives trauma a topography, a geographical as well as a temporal dimension in the "shit field." Building connections in O'Brien's landscape between Asia and colonial America, Jarvis finds America's cryptic indigenous histories buried in Vietnam though a psychoanalytic reading of the traumas of birth and sexual recognition.

Part IV: Sex images

Part IV, "Sex Images," maps the paths of sexuality and gender following achievements of 1970s and 1980s feminism. ACT UP (The Aids Coalition to Unleash Power) is set up in 1987; Queer Nation appears in 1990. The successes of activists for adequate treatment and social destigmatization of those with AIDS and the highly visible performative activism catalyzed in the lesbian and gay community lead the media to dub the decade the Queer Nineties. Queer activism, soon to be intertwined in the academy with queer theory, moves the goals of earlier gay politics from mere acceptance to a confrontation with the idea of normal sexuality and gender. The most visibly queer subject, the butch dyke, the drag queen— camp, the cross-gendered person—comes to dramatize queer performance. In the influential theory of Judith Butler (1990), queer transgender challenges identity essence, the bedrock of gender in sex. A reconfiguration of the family takes place, at least in popular culture, from nonsexual cross-gendered or failing sexual relationships in *Seinfeld*, *Frasier* and *Friends* to the first gay-starring sitcom character in *Ellen*. The period is one of public sexual scandals. In 1998, the same year as "Monicagate," DNA evidence emerges for the rumored, procreative affair between Thomas Jefferson and his slave Sally Hemings (Lewis and Onuf 1999)—America's first presidential sex scandal. Entangled with the phenomenon of Recovered Memory Syndrome, the 1990s also sees charges of sexual abuse in which children were killed—or as in the Long Island Lolita, killed others—staged on television and in newspapers, making the sexuality of children a public subject. Before he could be sworn in as the Supreme Court, Justice Clarence Thomas had to defend himself from charges of sexual harassment made by Anita Hill in 1991. Profound challenges to masculinity are recognized, with men either in crisis or in feminism (Jardine and Smith 1987). Susan Faludi's *Stiffed* (2000) draws to attention what she interprets as the sense of betrayal among American men. And through all gender configurations, popular mediation, the reflection and construction of images, is evident. In the image world, commodification of surface produces an anxiety about the body, the delusive lure of perfection. The hypergendered or hypersexual body is a vehicle for consumerism.

Zoe Trodd's essay (Chapter 11) examines two pieces of queer writing, part autobiography, part fictionalized, transgenerically between passing and coming out. Their postmodern style examples of the new queer movement, the works of Leslie Feinberg and Dorothy Allison, as Trodd shows, nevertheless remember earlier American protest literature and movements, such as those of the Gay Liberation Front of the 1970s, of black civil rights, and indeed the democratic, universal vision of Walt Whitman. Kasia Boddy (Chapter 12) weighs the representation of adolescent sexuality in popular culture and fiction, through rewritings of Vladimir Nabokov's *Lolita* by authors such as A. M. Homes and Emily Prager and drawing on the media-inspired feminism of Camille Paglia. Alex E. Blazer reads the work of two novelists, Bret Easton Ellis and Chuck Palahniuk, in Chapter 13, to show how an image-driven culture colonizes interior consciousness particularly of male protagonists. When image takes over identity and the body is subsumed, primal brutality is one fight back against consumerism and the dominion of good looks.

Part V: Postmodern technologies

Part V, "Postmodern Technologies," addresses fin-de-millennial anxieties. The World Wide Web and the Internet are born in 1992, and the Information Age also sees the move from fax to email, from beeper to mobile phone, with text messaging starting in 1995, and above all the shift in developed economies from the manufacture of industrial goods to the selling of image and brands (Klein 2000). Technologies here means not just postindustrial objects but also the systems of production and dissemination that support technocratic and consumerist society, the large corporation, commodification, the idea of progress—and our key output, waste. The image-screen is crucial, changing our notions of the real into virtual reality, and as war is fought on television as happens when the USA bombed Iraq in the First Gulf War, making war a made-for-television movie: Desert Storm (the Gulf War, as Jean Baudrillard says, didn't happen [1995]). Technology becomes intimately linked to fear and addiction, with terrorists both deploring developed society's addiction to technology (the pastoral manifesto of the Unabomber condemned technology as limiting freedom [Kaczynski 1995]) and used by them—and technology is thus seen by the state as both a surety against terrorism and yet an always-potential source of it. Domestic terrorism (the mail-bombs of the Unabomber, the Oklahoma City bombing, the Waco stand-off), in staging mini-dramas of millennial apocalypse, foreshadowed the terrorism and technology—the terrorism of technology—of 9/11. Work here comes to seem prophetic, and ambivalence in relation to technology is also the tenor of several novels of this decade. Postmodernism is an unsurprising aesthetic for fiction engaging with technology. As Jameson says, postmodernism is the cultural logic of late capitalism and seems to grow out of it (1991). Novels that criticize technology replicate it in their postmodern form, massifying representations, proliferating images, dodging linear plots.

In Chapter 14, Peter Knight takes DeLillo's two big novels, *Mao II* and *Underworld*, and explores how they capture the moment at which the fear of nuclear apocalypse during the Cold War dispersed into a less locatable terror. What, asks the essay, are the aesthetic forms DeLillo creates to net this globalized mass fear? Timothy Aubry (Chapter 15) provides a close textual reading of Foster Wallace's *Infinite Jest*, which in postmodern form dramatizes the addictiveness to the cycle of production and consumption and attention to surface of the new-media technologies. In its humor and appeal for readers' engagement, the novel's postmodernism marks a shift from the distantiating and more flattening narcissism of earlier postmodern fictions, working through a paradoxical sincere irony. Stephen J. Burn, in Chapter 16, traces the end of postmodernism from authors such as John Barth and Robert Coover to the post-postmodernism called for by Wallace, in works in pyrotechnical and metafictional dialogue. Setting waves of postmodern aesthetics in context, this essay serves as a postscript to the 1990s and offers a glimpse of one mode that would come prominently to the fore in American fiction of the next decade. Perhaps the figure for 1990s may be trans: transnational, transhistorical, and transitional, into the next millennium.

References

Alexie, S. (1993) *The Lone Ranger and Tonto Fistfight in Heaven*, New York: Atlantic Monthly.
—— (1995) *Reservation Blues*, New York: Atlantic Monthly.
Alvarez, J. (1991) *How the García Girls Lost Their Accents*, Chapel Hill, N.C.: Algonquin Books.
Anzaldúa, G. (1987) *Borderlands/La Frontera: The New Mestiza*, San Francisco, Calif.: Aunt Lute Books.
Baker, N. (2003) *A Box of Matches*, New York: Random House.

Baudrillard, J. (1995) *The Gulf War Did Not Take Place*, trans. Paul Patton, Bloomington, Ind: Indiana University Press.

Beatty, P. (1996) *The White Boy Shuffle*, New York: Houghton Mifflin.

Bukiet, M. (1997) *After: A Novel*, New York: Picador.

Butler, J. (1990) *Gender Trouble: Feminism and the Subversion of Identity*, London: Routledge.

Chénetier M. (1996) *Beyond Suspicion: New American Fiction since 1960*, trans. Elizabeth A. Houlding, Philadelphia, Penn.: University of Pennsylvania Press.

Chrisafis, A. (2002) "US Authors' Entry to Booker Prize seen as Betrayal," *The Guardian*, 22 May. Online. Available http://books.guardian.co.uk/news/articles/0,719960,00.html#article_continue (accessed January 14, 2008).

Clayton, J. (1994) *The Pleasures of Babel: Contemporary American Literature and Theory*, Oxford: Oxford University Press.

Crews, F. (1997) *Memory Wars: Freud's Legacy in Dispute*, London: Granta.

DeLillo, D. (1998) *Underworld*, London: Picador.

Dillehay, T. (2000) *The Settlement of the Americas: A New Prehistory*, New York: Basic Books.

Durante, R. (2001) *The Dialectic of Self and Story: Reading and Storytelling in Contemporary American Fiction*, New York: Routledge.

Eggers, D. (2000) *A Heartbreaking Work of Staggering Genius*, New York: Vintage.

Faludi, S. (2000) *Stiffed: The Betrayal of Modern Man*, London: Vintage.

Finkelstein, N. J. (2000) *The Holocaust Industry: Reflections on the Exploitation of Jewish Suffering*, London: Verso.

Franzen, J. (2001) *The Corrections*, New York: Farrar.

Fukuyama, F. (1993) *The End of History and the Last Man*, New York: Harper Perennial.

Gidley, M. and Lawson-Peebles, R. (eds) (1995) *Modern American Landscapes*, Amsterdam: VU University Press.

Hagedorn, J. (1990) *Dogeaters*, New York: Random House.

—— (ed.) (1993) *Charlie Chan Is Dead: An Anthology of Contemporary Asian American Fiction*, New York: Penguin.

Hardt, M. and Negri, A. (2000) *Empire*, Cambridge, Mass.: Harvard University Press.

Jameson, F. (1988) "Periodizing the 60s," *The Ideologies of Theory, Essays 1971–1986*, Minneapolis, Minn.: University of Minnesota Press, Vol. II: *The Syntax of History*, pp. 178–208.

—— (1991) *Postmodernism, Or The Cultural Logic of Late Capitalism*, London: Verso.

Jardine, A. and Smith, P. (1987) *Men in Feminism*, New York: Routledge.

Jen, Gish (1997) *Mona in the Promised Land*, New York: Vintage.

Kaczynski, T. (1995) "Industrial Society and Its Future." Online. Available http://en.wikipedia.org/wiki/Theodore_Kaczynski (accessed January 14, 2008).

Kadir, D. (ed.) (2003) *America: The Idea, the Literature*, Special issue of *PMLA* 118.1, New York: Publications of Modern Languages of Association of America.

Klein, N. (2000) *No Logo: Taking Aim at the Brand Bullies*, London: Flamingo.

Lauter, P. (ed.) (2005) *The Heath Anthology of American Literature, Volume E: Contemporary Period: 1945 to the Present*, New York: Houghton Mifflin.

Lee, C. R. (1995) *Native Speaker*, New York: Riverhead.

Lethem, J. (1999) *Motherless Brooklyn*, New York: Doubleday.

Lewis, J. and Onuf, P. (eds) (1999) *Sally Hemings and Thomas Jefferson: History, Memory, and Civic Culture*, Charlottesville, Va.: Virginia University Press.

Lipsitz, G. (2001) *American Studies in a Moment of Danger*, Minneapolis, Minn.: Minnesota University Press.

Luckhurst R. and Marks, P. (eds) (1999) *Literature and the Contemporary: Fictions and Theories of the Present*, Harlow: Longman.

Marx, L. (1964) *The Machine in the Garden*, Oxford: Oxford University Press.

McCarthy, C. (1990) *The Border Trilogy*, New York: Everyman.

McMillan, T. (1992) *Waiting to Exhale*, New York: Viking.

—— (1996) *How Stella Got Her Groove Back*, New York: Viking.

Miller, N. K. (2002) *But Enough About Me: Why We Read Other People's Lives*, New York: Columbia University Press.

Morrison, T (1989) "A Bench By the Road," *The World* 3 (1): 4.

—— (1992) *Playing in the Dark: Whiteness and the Literary Imagination*, Cambridge, Mass.: Harvard University Press.

Mukherjee, B. (1988) "A Wife's Story," in P. Lauter (ed.) (2005) *The Heath Anthology of American Literature, Volume E: Contemporary Period: 1945 to the Present*, New York: Houghton Mifflin, pp. 2694–703.

Nathan, D. (1989) "False Evidence: How Bad Science Fueled the Hysteria over Child Abuse," *LA Weekly*, 7–13 April: 15–18.

Nora, P. (1984–92) *Les Lieux de mémoire*, Paris: Gallimard.

Novick, P. (2000) *The Holocaust and Collective Memory*, London: Bloomsbury.

Percival, D. (2002) *America Beyond the Color Line*, PBS, starring Henry Louis Gates.

Proulx, E. A. (1993) *The Shipping News*, New York; Scribner.

—— (1995) *Accordion Crimes*, New York: Scribner.

Pynchon, T. (1997) *Mason & Dixon*, New York: Henry Holt.

Roth, P. (1993), *Operation Shylock: A Confession*, London: Cape.

—— (1997) *American Pastoral*, Boston, Mass.: Houghton Mifflin.

—— (1998) *I Married a Communist*, Boston, Mass.: Houghton Mifflin.

—— (2000) *The Human Stain*, Boston, Mass.: Houghton Mifflin.

Rowe, J. C. (2002) *The New American Studies*, Minneapolis, Minn.: Minnesota University Press.

Saltzman, A. (2000) *This Mad Instead: Governing Metaphors in Contemporary American Fiction*, Columbia, SC: University of South Carolina Press.

Sen, K. (2003) "From the Global to the 'Glocal': Re-visioning the American Dream," *Studies in American Literature*, Calcutta American Literature Study Circle, 3: 153–64.

Singh, A. and Schmidt, P. (eds) (2000), *Postcolonial Theory and the United States: Race, Ethnicity and Literature*, Jackson, Miss.: Mississippi University Press.

Smiley, J. (1992), *A Thousand Acres*, London: Flamingo.

Sollors, W. (ed.) (2000) *Interracialism: Black-White Intermarriage in American History, Literature and Law*, Oxford: Oxford University Press.

Spiegelman, A. (1993) *Maus: A Survivor's Tale, II: And Here My Troubles Began*, New York: Pantheon.

Turner, F. J. (1935) *The Frontier in American History*, New York: Henry Holt.

Updike, J. (1995) *Rabbit Angstrom: The Four Novels*, New York: Everyman.

—— (2000) *Licks of Love: Short Stories and a Sequel, "Rabbit Remembered,"* London: Hamish Hamilton.

Veeser, H. Aram (ed.) (1989) *The New Historicism*, London: Routledge.

Wallace, D. F. (1996) *Infinite Jest*, Boston, Mass.: Little, Brown and Co.

White, H. (1987) *The Content of the Form: Narrative Discourse and Historical Representation*, Baltimore, Md.: Johns Hopkins University Press.

Wood, J. (2000) "Human, All Too Inhuman," *The New Republic*, 24 July.

—— (2004) "Prize of the Yankees," *New York Magazine*, 14 June. Online. Available http://nymag.com/nymetro/arts/books/reviews/9296 (accessed January 14, 2008).

Part I
Transnational borders

2 Outside in

Latino/a un-bordering in US fiction

A. Robert Lee

> The US–Mexican border *es una herida abierta* where the Third World grates against the first and bleeds. And before a scab forms it hemorrhages again, the lifeblood of the two worlds merging to form a third country—a border culture. Borders are set up to define the places that are safe and unsafe, to distinguish *us* from *them*. A border is a dividing line, a narrow strip along a steep edge. A borderland is a vague and undetermined place created by the emotional residue of an unnatural boundary. It is in a constant state of transition. The prohibited and forbidden are its inhabitants.
>
> (Anzaldúa 1987: 3)

Latino/a. Hispanic. The Browning of America. These terms, even if they arouse reservations, bespeak a US cultural dispensation at once ancestral and hemispheric. Yet, given recent Mexican border and migration controversies, media reportage frequently designates the population now collectively America's largest minority and, however, in fact, longstanding, somehow a "new" demographics. For where the 1960s can be said to have put Afro-America and its history to the forefront in the form of Civil Rights and Black Power, Martin Luther King and Malcolm X, the 1990s and after, almost more than at anytime previously, have pointed to yet another order of North American life and word: *Chicano/a, Nuyorriqueño/a,* Cuban American, alongside cultural geographies originating among others in the Domincan Republic, Chile, Colombia, Peru, El Salvador or Argentina.

Nothing less than a dazzling array of American fiction and other writings in the 1990s confirms this plurality, reflecting histories born of *Nueva España* and the evolving *mestizaje* or mix of Native, Spanish, European, and African peoples, the ongoing momentum of Mexican and other Latin American migrancy south to north, and the different Caribbean horizons. In a US population of 300 million, Hispanics currently number 42.7 million, more than 14 percent of the whole. Those of Mexican descent account for 66.9 percent, Puerto Rican descent 8.6 percent, Cuban descent 3.7 percent, Central and South American descent 14.3 percent, and other Hispanic descent 6.5 percent. An inevitable upshot has been not only the always-evolving patterns of life, with its bi- and multiculturalism, its code-switching and language mix, but also art. Theatre coexists as *actos*, poetry as *poesía*, and novels and stories as *ficciones*, *corridos*, or *cuentos*. In these, accordingly, is to be met not just America but *Las Américas*, a body of writing wholly implicated in the cultural if not literal unbordering of the USA as white canonical society.

That embraces, first, the Hispano-*mestizo/a* southwest once historically Mexico and today's California, Texas, Arizona, Colorado, New Mexico, and Nevada, whose 2,000-mile border has become increasingly iconic (the more so since 9/11), and whose cities include Los Angeles with its "East Los" as *barrio* and *la raza*, San Diego, Albuquerque, Houston, Tucson, and Denver. *Ristras*, the chains of multicolored dried peppers, hang indicatively, whether in pueblo homes, migrant-worker camps, cities, or even the suburbs. The further dynamic is to be found in Manhattan's Spanish Harlem and island origins in El Estado Libre de Puerto Rico, the Miami of Cuban America with its Florida Straits, proximity to Havana, and central thoroughfare of Calle Ocho, and each other Hispanic community.

This so-called "browning of America," the legal citizenry and the estimated 12 million illegals, bears all manner of cross-border or island-to-mainland footfall. Chicano memory readily summons the Treaty of Guadalupe Hidalgo (1848), the César Chávez and the West Coast agricultural worker activism of the Johnson–Nixon decade, and, latterly, the impact of the North American Free Trade Agreement (NAFTA) on Mexican smallholding and immigration into the USA. *Riqueños/as* think of 1898 and the Spanish-American War in which suzerainty passed to America and always the debate between *independentistas* as against those favoring US citizenship under autonomous commonwealth status. Florida's anti-Castroism arises out of the rankling political tapestry of the Batista years (1929–59), the Castro–Guevara revolution (1959), the Mariel Boatlift (1980) with its exportation of 125,000 refugees, the Elián González child-custody affair (1999), and always the speculation and ideologies of "after Fidel."

Generally shared *Latino/a* references can also look to vernacular Catholicism and Pentecostalism, the different inflections of *barrio* culture, language issues, the controversies as to "documented/undocumented" migration. Whatever, too, the degree of assimilation and access to wealth (New Mexico land or Miami business), there persists the class-structure inherent in employment and *la pobreza*. The community calendar can be *fiestas patrias*, Cinco de Mayo or *quinceañeras* (for girls reaching fifteen). Musical heritages include Tito Puente, Los Lobos, the Havana-born Gloria Estefan, and Cuba's re-emerged Buena Vista Social Club.

Filmmaking calls up Edward James Olmos' *Zoot Suit* (1981), with its high-energy musical remembrance of the 1942 hounding of *barrio* youth, or *American Me* (1992) as prison screen epic. Foodways offer their alimentary markers variously of *burritos* and *tamales* and, from Puerto Rico and the islands, *arroz con habichuelas* or root vegetables like yucca and malanga. Television can be both the English-language networks and Univision or Telemundo.

Little wonder this hybridity of migrancy and settlement has seized the literary imagination, worlds-within-worlds yet also cross-worlds with the rest of the USA. English, however much America's "official" language, coexists with a community Spanish of home, street or workplace. As to the literary fiction of the 1990s, it looks to writers both whose bow belongs earlier and to those who bring new voices to bear. Either way, the fictions to hand confirm little short of a treasury.

Rudolfo Anaya's *Bless Me, Ultima* (1972), with its portrait of the artist set in postwar New Mexico, along with Tomás Rivera's "*...y no se lo tragó la tierra*"/*And The Earth Did Not Part* ([1971] 1987) as the story cycle of a migrant-worker year, rightly are credited with having inaugurated a Chicano literary renaissance. Anaya's career, since, has seen a steady output, not least his 1990s Sony Baca Private Eye trilogy of the American southwest—*Zia Summer* (1995), with its cult murder and witch-criminal (or *brujo*) antagonist Raven; *Rio Grande fall* (1996), with its opening of the Albuquerque International Balloon Fiesta, killing and further *brujería*; and *Shaman Winter* (1999), with its ventures into shamanism, supernatural dream-territory and fusion of Native and Mexican fable.

These each delve not only into the one or another crime but the southwest itself as a "mystery," a hybrid American world order, Spanish and Anglo in settlement but only in the wake of the diverse, rich seams of Native population—notably Rio Grande pueblo populations such as Santo Domingo, San Felipe, Isleta, Cochití or Jémez with their networks of people, belief systems, land cultivation, and art and story. Thus, he offers a physical New Mexico of the *llanos* (plain lands), the Sandia and the Sangre de Cristo mountains, the historic Camino Real, adobe architecture, the desert in its sumptuous colors, light, and rock and plant variety, and also Albuquerque with its Central Avenue, Bernalillo County, *barrios* like Barelas, hosting of the annual Gathering of Nations Pow-Wow, and proximity to Roswell of UFO fame and Los Alamos of the atomic Manhattan Project. New Mexico, in Anaya's writing, has ever been the borderland complexity of history and people, a vision that has long situated him at the very forefront of Chicano authorship.

With *Alburquerque* (1992), he characteristically layers New Mexico in symbolic resonance, a labyrinth of ethnic and family borders, inlaid politics, a boxer's quest for his true parentage and a city's Hispano-*mestizo* lineage signaled in the novel's title which restores the original "r" to its place name (legend holds that it was removed by an Anglo postmaster unable to pronounce it correctly). Its central figure, Abrán González, light-skinned Golden Gloves boxing champion and student at the University of New Mexico, finds himself caught in a quest for his true parentage ("He was a child of this border, a child of the line that separated white and brown. La raza called people like him 'coyote'" [Anaya 1992: 38]). As his story unravels, he finds himself not alone, for this is a fable of Albuquerque as endemic *mestizaje*. The local politico Frank Dominic, with his plans to turn the city into a new Venice, a new Las Vegas and for all that he affects his ducal Spanish lineage, in fact is of migrant Italian stock; his rival, the banker-landowner Walter Johnson, is of lost white-Chicago immigrant stock and his wife Vera of hidden Jewish ancestry; and Abrán, fostered-out son to Sara yet the offspring to the then-unmarried Johnson artist-daughter Cynthia and the Hispanic writer Ben Chávez, finally arrives at not only his own identity but that of the very culture about him. For as these personal borders elide and fall, so Anaya unborders Albuquerque, whether Native (notably in the person of Joe Calabasa), Spanish, Mexican, Anglo, Jewish, and African.

Rolando Hinojosa has similarly long weighed for the series he began with *Klail City y sus alrededores* (1976), reissued as *Klail City* (1987), in which the Río Grande Valley of south Texas is made over into the collagist Tex-Mex border kingdom of Belken County. In *Ask A Policeman* (1998), Hinojosa continues his multicultural estate with rare virtuosity, a detective fiction whose violent drugs-and-murder portraits of a warring family is given its unraveling in the figure of Chief Inspector Lieutenant Rafe Buenrostro, As each circle vies, the Lee Gómez-Felipe Segundo Gómez brothers tied into prison escape, cocaine and fratricide, bank fraud, pathological nephew-sons, the killing of the Assistant DA Theo Crixell, the sex-and-party Laura Castañón de Grayson, and an ancillary cast of informers and miscreants, the whole comes under the auspices not only of Buenrostro but his opposite number, Lu Cetina, Director of the Mexican Federal Police Office in Barrones. Two jurisdictions thus hold, the one Napoleonic and the other Anglo in their begetting legal codes, along with two styles of gendered authority. Yet, the Río Grande against which each intrigue or revenge is played out bears witness, literally and figuratively, to both Americas as quite inextricable the one from the other, a live, always plural cross-border of people, estate, language, and, to be sure, crime.

This same "border" impulse equally threads through Sandra Cisneros's *Woman Hollering Creek and Other Stories* (1991), rarely more appositely than in "Tepeyac," a story-memoir of the hillside borough in Mexico City with its

Aztec and San Juan Diego history. Remembrance turns on the narrator's return to Tepeyac and her fond cross-border memory of childhood amid the local world of goods, church, cafés, food, and inhabitants inhabited by her storekeeper grandfather/*abuelo* and religious *abuela* ("it is me who will remember when everything else is forgotten" [Cisneros 1991: 23]). Other vignettes span childhood to maturity or the USA–Mexico borderland as rite-of-passage. "My Lucy Friend Who Smells Like Corn" captures the fidget and word-inversions of childhood. "Mericans," told as the reluctant Mexico-Chicano churchgoing of two grandchildren, takes a slap at Anglo condescension ("But you speak English" says a white woman tourist, "Yeah ... we're Mericans" (Cisneros 1991: 20) replies the brother). "Never Marry a Mexican" tells a woman teacher-artist's love affair with both a father and son which leads her to fantasize a borderland of shifting genders. "Woman Hollering Creek," as the title story, uses the legend of *la llorona*, the weeping woman, to confront a failed cross-frontier marriage. "*Bien Pretty*," on a lighter note, looks to the narrator's affair with Flavio Michoacán ("I'd never made love in Spanish before" [Cisneros 1991: 153]), a story full of winning border idiosyncrasy, love as its own kind of emotional and linguistic *mestizaje* which can cause the world to seem a field of chattering *urracas* or magpies.

Cisneros has been but one voice, albeit a leading one, in a consequential generation of Chicana authorship whose texts echo and expand these perspectives. Roberta Fernández's *Intaglio: A Novel in Six Stories* (1990) tells the lives and rise to consciousness of different southwest border femininities. In sequence, these are the album-keeper ("Andrea"), the seamstress ("Amanda"), the religious bird-keeper ("Filomena"), the card-reader ("Leonor"), the local movie-house beauty ("Esmeralda"), and the memorial war-narrator ("Zulema"). Each closely fashioned portrait interacts with the other to supply a form of intimate Latina sisterhood, border-located women who amid gain and loss arrive at their own life signature.

Ana Castillo, whose *The Mixquiahuala Letters* (1986) won her immediate recognition, continues the blend of real and irreal in *Sapogonia* (1990) and *So Far from God* (1993). The former, in the finally murderous relationship of Máximo Madrigal and Pastora Velásquez Aké, both anatomizes and subverts patriarchy, male sexuality as customary power dominance. *So Far from God*, its title adapted from the celebrated pronouncement of Porfirio Diaz, Mexico's autocratic president from 1876–1911 ("Poor Mexico, so far from God. So near the United States"), portrays two Latina generations both bitterly caught out by that history yet in the case of its main figure put to take possession of that history.

Set in the central New Mexico township of Tome, it tells of lives bleak in their fate yet lively in their living, whether the mother, Sofi (for Sofia) or her four daughters: in turn, Esperanza, a journalist who is tortured and dies as a Middle East hostage; Fe, the conformist, who dies of cancer brought on by toxic chemicals in a weapons factory; Caridad, mutilated in an attack and eventual suicide; and the youngest, La Loca, whose psychic and *curandera* abilities do not prevent her contracting AIDS. Sofi outlives her offspring, founds Mothers of Martyrs and Saints (MOMAS), and becomes a political and community activist. Against evident cost, she transcends her mythic status as *la llorona*, the weeping mother. If Castillo tells a Chicana-feminist fable, she does so with wit, a willing ply of fact and fantasy, the rejection of Hispanic life as American margin in favor of a *latinidad* of hard-won but necessarily sustaining femininity at the very centre of things.

"It's a long story" says Soveida Dosamantes, waitress in the New Mexico restaurant El Farol in Denise Chávez's *Face of an Angel* (1994: 4). So it proves, as the restaurant ("cockroach-ridden, leaky-assed, chile-splattered, greasy-smelling" [1994: 461]) acts as both home and a memory chamber of voices for the four generations of women in the Dosamantes family. These are women who have spent their lives in service, whether as wife/mothers (the break-up of Soveida's parents is given in mutual and parallel column narrative), domestics, cleaners, servants like Chata and Orelia or waitresses like Soveida. The upshot is a female-worker southwest epic, a Book of Service as Soveida calls it (Chávez mines the implications of service to rich effect) and a full-length successor to the story collection *The Last of the Menu Girls* (1986) with its chronicles of Rocío Esquibel's New Mexico young womanhood from hospital orderly to student and teacher. *Face of an Angel*, pledged to female body and spirit within the specific border world of the Dosamantes family history, can be at times antic, roistering, but it is also tender even as it remembers the toughness of Latina women's blue-collar working continuity.

Alejandro Morales's speculative fiction *The Rag Doll Plagues* (1992) invites special esteem: a serial fable that spans Mexico as nineteenth-century autocracy, the America of contemporary Orange County and the AIDS crisis, and a futurist war-zone America called Lamex. Don Gregorio, living in the earlier period, serves as ancestor to Gregory Revueltas MD, a thread of history subject to three distinct waves of pestilence, physiological but also cultural-political and military. Variously, the novel has been termed metatrope, trauma narrative, a hall of mirrors: each applies Mexican into Chicano history, a future shaped by each past, a triptych of dark self-reflection.

Other kinds of history have not gone missing. Daniel Cano's *Pepe Rios* (1991) envisages the Mexican Revolution as both epilogue to dictatorship and prologue to the cultural formation of *Chicanismo*. Arturo Islas's *Migrant*

Souls (1991), the second in his Moma Chona trilogy, turns on literal border in the form of California and Texas but also the internalization of light and dark skin in the figures of Josie Salazar as against the Aunt Jesús María. Demetria Martinez's *Mother Tongue* (1994) blends the north–south politics behind US-supported Salvadoran military repression and the American sanctuary movement into an Albuquerque love story between Mary, the retrospective narrator and José Luis, political refugee. Helena María Viramontes's *Under the Feet of Jesus* (1995) uses the coming-of age love between Estrella and Alejo to refract California farm-worker migrancy and, with it, *la migra*, the toxic effects of fruit-spraying, and worker exploitation. It pitches for a mutual humanity well beyond Mexico and the USA as fixed counter-sites.

The counterculture of the 1960s yields few names more transgressive than John Rechy. It is a career that has continued into *The Miraculous Day of Amalia Gómez* (1991), pitched as its title-heroine's religious vision of a cross in the sky set against the shabbier end of Hollywood, her jealous *copiloto* of a husband, a son edging into gang life, and a daughter at the verge of sexual adventure. This is America's screen capital as class-oppressed hinterland, a species of Chicano dark cinema.

Like other Hispanic writing, Puertorriqueño/a fiction looks to contexts of history and site, rarely more so than in Judith Ortiz Cofer's *Silent Dancing: A Partial Remembrance of a Puerto Rican Childhood* (1990), thirteen story panels in alternating prose and poetry of island girlhood and an America of tenement Paterson, New Jersey, and Esmeralda Santiago's *When I Was Puerto Rican* (1993), another island upbringing of *borinquén* family yet one of fractured kinship with to follow migration into a Brooklyn block. Alongside, and of necessity, has to be the Nuyorican Poets Café, founded in 1973 by the poet Miguel Algarin, situated first on East 3rd and then East 6th Street known as *Loisaida* (the Village's Lower East Side given Spanish adaptation), and always a vitally important multi-cultural literary gathering-place and performance venue.

In Nicholasa Mohr, the tradition has its best-known name who made her bow in acclaimed narratives like *Nilda* (1973), with its portrait of ten-year-old Nilda Ramírez in the *barrio* New York of 1941. Her story telling now extends through juvenile fiction such as *Growing Up Inside the Sanctuary of My Imagination* (1994) and *The Magic Shell* (1995) into the collection *A Matter of Pride* (1997). This develops a gallery of Latinas encountering different borders of self—becoming a bride, a dip into the seeming supernatural, or femininity to be refracted and measured in a visit to a drag-queen show. Mohr cannot be regarded as other than a major literary presence, her tales of rites of passage, individual and community language, densely located sited in the multiethnicity of America's first city.

Puerto Rico takes on virtuoso imagistic form in Judith Ortiz Cofer's *The Latin Deli* (1993), a mural-in-small, which has its follow-up in the twelve-story collection for young readers of *An Island Like You* (1995). Using stories, often in the form of anecdotes, poems, dream sequences, and letters, *The Latin Deli* centers on life in El Building, the Paterson New Jersey tenement block that is the family's successor home to island Puerto Rico. These two worlds span the 1960s to present time but their borders join in the life of its girlhood-to-college teacher narrator. "American History" offers one story touchstone, El Building and its residents as stigma, unwanted lower depth, in the view of the mother of the narrator's fellow-student Eugene and in the wake of the Kennedy assassination. Another lies in "Twist and Shout," with its portrait of heady but risk-laden teenage love, and "Corazón's Café," in which El Building is remembered as "filled with the life energies of generations of other island people" (Cofer 1993: 93). The island itself can be the place of loved, ailing grandparents ("The Witch's Husband") or an old man's near-magical death as he is taken out to sea clinging to dolphins ("Letter from a Caribbean Island"). As she inter-weaves verse and story, the narrator builds a one composite narrative, a juncture of seeming disjuncture. The Puerto Rico of New Jersey and of the Caribbean both carry their contrary yet overlapping pasts into present. This evolution as child, woman, mother, and writer accordingly becomes a spectrum of viewpoint, involving innocence, threat, query, celebration, memory, time, and place, always and coevally the one and the several American life histories.

Ed Vega, albeit that he bristles at the label of Puerto Rican-American writer, was early to win plaudits with *The Comeback* (1985), his satire of too solemn an emphasis on *hispanidad* as ethnicity with its Eskimo-Puerto Rican hockey-player and Freudian shrinks. *Casualty Report* (1991), by contrast, uses its ten stories to explore a ground-level panorama, lives often caught at the margins within the New York of Sixth Street ("Spanish Roulette"), the Port Authority Terminal ("Revenge and Prelude to a Well Deserved Suicide") or the Welfare Department ("The Kite"). Few more trenchantly catch the implosion of being treated as the stereotypical poor-stupid Puerto Rican than the title piece, "Casualty Report." It tracks the planned revenge-terrorism of Sonny Maldonado against an America that has colo-nized the island ("For as long as Puerto Rico was a colony, not one person could hold his head high" [Vega 1991: 47]), New York-ghettoized Puerto Ricans, made him participant in the killing fields of Vietnam, and filled his life with scenes of "people with broken dreams" as against the gilded tid-ings of television commercials. His own life, even with his wife Carmen, has become fractured, life inside a multi-America as may be but one itself the seeming endless casualty report.

Cuban America achieved an almost flamboyant step into American literary consciousness with Oscar Hijuelos's *The Mambo Kings Play Songs of Love* (1989). This was Havana and island music brought to 1940s–1950s New York as a *latinidad* full of life, sexual heat, the fiction-of-fact figure of Desi Arnaz from CBS's *I Love Lucy* (1951–7), and, above all, the mambo as triumphant-sad dance. Hijuelos's subsequent fiction exhibits a shared fullness, rarely more so than in *The Fourteen Sisters of Emilio Montez O'Brien* (1993). Two family geographies join, Irish and Cuban, in the persons of Nelson O'Brien, photographer, and Mariela Montez, his well-born wife, and in their plenitude of daughters born in the Pennsylvania township of Cobbleton ("The house in which the fourteen sisters of Emilio Montez O'Brien lived radiated femininity," [Hijuelos 1993: 2]). The upshot, a genealogical time-map centered mainly in the eldest girl Margarita and the one son, Emilio, who edges his way into Hollywood, might indeed be a photographic album of the US as Hispano/a destiny. Whether second-generation America, with a backdrop running from the Spanish American War through to Castro, or the memory of Ireland and Cuba as snared by two imperialist regimes, the novel rarely loses touch with family as an epic of migrant strands and evolution.

Cristina Garcia's *Dreaming in Cuban* (1992) deftly pitches its story as the Havana and Brooklyn lives of a three-generation woman dynasty. In Celia del Pino, *fidelista*, wife to the long-dead but en-ghosted Jorge del Pino, and memorial letter-writer to a long-ago lover Gustavo, the novel has its matriarch, at once the embodied dream of the revolution and yet its worn, despotically cancerous sick body. Her daughters, Lourdes Puente—who is raped by soldiers of the revolution and eventually sets up her Yankee Doodle Bakery in Brooklyn to become at once capitalist and fiercely anti-Fidel (she fantasizes becoming his assassin)—and Felicia, three times married, mother of twins, and, eventually, the unhinged acolyte of *santería*, throw a contrasting light on Cuba as heritage. As the novel devolves into the life of Lourdes's daughter, Pilar Puente, runaway, art-punk Brooklyn painter, who journeys to Cuba and there meets her dying *abuela*, the elusive border meaning of this dynasty and its counterhistories is made yet more emphatic. "Cuba is a peculiar exile," she observes, "an island-colony. We can reach it by a thirty-minute charter flight from Miami, yet never reach it at all" (Garcia 1992: 219).

A trio of 1990s Cuban American authorship suggests no drop in imaginative vitality. Virgil Suarez's *Havana Thursdays* (1995), set in Miami but sited also in Cuba, Mexico City, and Brazil, depicts the Torres clan—Zacaría, recently dead of a heart attack, his wife Laura, and their disjunctive clan of son, three daughters, Laura's bibulous sister, and arriving grandchildren. The novel envisages America as dynastic loss as against gain within the paradigm of exile and assimilation. Roberto Fernández's *Holy Radishes!* (1995), on another tack, lowers the liveliest satiric boom on Miami as Cuban exile community, oddball figures like the poet rock-star Lisander, Dina the ex-hooker and now owner of a radish-processing factory, and a cadre of all-talk male weekend warriors against Castro even as women like the dreamer Nelly Pardo and her ally the ex-cheerleader Mrs. James B III actually do the real work behind community life.

Achy Obejas's story collection, *We Have Come All This Way from Cuba So You Could Dress Like This?* (1994) and novel *Memory Mambo* (1996) have been dubbed tropical eroticism, Jewish-lesbian close encounter with an eye to the more encompassing gender hierarchies of dynasty spanning Cuba to Chicago. *Memory Mambo*, focused in the life of Juani Casas as an out gay daughter in a family marked by hidden pasts and splits, gives an especially sensitive portrait, at once a given sexuality its own cultural right and its reflective measure of the very shaping of Cuban America. With some justification Abejas speaks of "creating a new syntax from the pieces of our displaced times" (1996: 13).

Dominican American fiction has shown an ever-strengthening hand throughout the 1990s. In an interview for November 1994, Julia Alvarez offers a working perspective: "I am a Dominican, hyphen, American ... As a fiction writer, I find the most exciting things happen in the realm of that hyphen—the place where two worlds collide or blend together" (1994a: 553). *How The García Girls Lost Their Accents* (1991), and its follow-up *¡Yo!* (1997), both vindicate this standpoint, the former as the telling of the García family's flight from the Dominican Republic and gains and set-backs of Americanization, the latter a cleverly reflexive novel in which the family "answers" the story told about them by Yolanda García ("yo" as abbreviation of her name and the Spanish for "I") as celebrated but again wholly imagined fact–fiction author. With *In the Time of Butterflies* (1994b), Alvarez ponders Dominican history, the Trujillo dictatorship (1931–65), and of the heroic three Marabal sisters (*las mariposas*, the butterflies), who played a heroic part in opposition for which they paid with their lives. Told as documentary, fiction and poetry, it makes not only a formidable indictment of US–Dominican political collusion but also a working context for Alvarez's other fiction. In this, it was *How The García Girls Lost Their Accents* that established her name, and with good imaginative reason: for, however upper-echelon the family genealogy it depicts, the novel speaks with rare energy to another hitherto much overlooked US *latinidad*.

Speaking in fractured English, Carlos García, MD and Green Card refugee in the wake of a failed CIA plot against Trujillo, mock-bewails his situation: "I am given up Mami! It is no hope for the island. I will become *un dominican-york*" (Alvarez 1991: 107). It is a comment that underwrites the zigzags of migrancy as enacted in the parentage of Carlos and Laura (Papi and Mami) and their Dominican American daughterhood of Carla, Sandra (Sandi), Yolanda (Yoyo, Joe, Joey, Yo), and Sofia (Fifi). Told as a retrospect of successive times (1989–1972, 1970–1960, 1960–1956), the upshot is a consortium although under the narrative direction of Yolanda, schoolteacher, story-teller and whose own breakdown ("she spoke in rid-dles" [Alvarez 1991: 79]) further confirms that migrant unbordering can be set back or fracture as much as any cliché of always upward and onward American advance. Her journey back to the island in the first chapter, to find, symbolically, the guava she relished in childhood makes for a lived-in landscape as against some postcard Caribbean, just as the last chapter calls up the one-time childhood shadow of voodoo, a dar-kened shed, a mysterious cat, and a one-eyed Haitian maid. Both present and past time, however, she takes on from the vantage point of what her cousin calls "Miss America," a play of benefits and deficits.

This contrast is explored throughout, girlhood and womanhood, Dominican strict Catholic rules as against American secular laxity—dope, contraception, lovers. For Yolanda, as for her sisters, it has indeed signified the divided life. Carla, the eldest, becomes a psychologist and argues for out-and-out assimilation, a "fading into walls." Sandi goes in an opposite direction, inassimilable and psychologically broken by the consequences. Fifi, initially the rebel, has two children by her German lover and, ironi-cally, becomes the good daughter long called for by her father and not least in producing a grandson. As the novel tells the García family's lower and higher ground, "so many husbands, homes, jobs, wrong turns among them" (1991: 11), it shadows Dominican America as at once refuge and hell, always the competing memory.

Dominican American life as tenement, drugs, casual labor, or sexual threat is to be found in Junot Díaz's *Drown* (1996), an eleven-part *barrio* cycle set overlappingly in island Santo Domingo and blue-collar immi-grant New Jersey, and Loida Maritz Pérez's *Geographies of Home* (1999), the memory-fiction of a hard-pressed large family barely able to maintain psychological equilibrium in the American journey which has brought them from the Trujillo-era Dominican Republic to Brooklyn.

Junot Díaz's stories in *Drown*, full of *caló*, or *barrio* vernacular, cast a cool, almost clinical eye upon the Dominican immigrant family history of Ramón and Virta de las Casas and their offspring Rafa and Yunior—his baptismal name Ramón, in whom the stories have their centre. This is the Dominican Republic and blue-collar New Jersey shorn of heroics, a bril-liantly and sparely observed diet of betrayal, cruelties large and small, pinched and furtive sex, and drugs. The father, bigamously married to both Virta and Nilda, often cruel, cheats as though dissembling were intrinsic to survival. His sons can be equally victimizers and victims, respectively in "Ysrael," set in the Dominican hamlet of Ocoa where they stalk and abuse a boy marred by facial defect, and "Fiesta 1980," where the father threatens Rafa for his habitual carsickness and makes both brothers secret witnesses to his philandering with a Puerto Rican woman. Other pieces add to the tenement mosaic—"Aurora" as a portrait of Yunior's drug-dealing and romance amid heroin and theft, "Aguantando" as Yunior's recognition that waiting for his father in the Dominican Republic is all sham, and the title-story "Drown," Yunior's sexual encounter with the gay, college-bound Beto as a glimpse of the vulnerability behind the predatory toughness.

Pérez's *Geographies of Home* likewise eschews any roseate picture of Dominican immigrant life. Told as another family chronicle, that of Papito, Seventh-Day Adventist deacon, his wife Aurelia, also an Adventist but still drawn to island folk belief, and their large sprawl of offspring, the borders are not one but several: migrant, linguistic, sibling, but above all internal and often enough broken. Three daughter/sisters take center stage: Marina, a rape victim who becomes increasingly unhinged; Rebecca, obsessively unable to disconnect herself from an abusive husband; and Iliana, whose destiny is to become the voice of this refugee dynasty. All of their borders, as it were, have traveled with them. Each bespeaks the darker reaches of migration, the will-to-sufficiency or efficacy yet also the spiral of setback, even despair. Iliana, college-educated but a returnee to her family, a writer who "would leave no memory behind. ... All of them were home" with home not so much "a geographical site but ... a frame of mind able to accommodate any place as home" (Pérez 1991: 320). For her, and for the family, the one American border crossing can be said to have begotten others each yet to be fully resolved.

A number of closing perspectives help situate the borders and unborders implicit in these different fictions. Lauro Flores's *The Floating Borderlands: Twenty-Five Years of US Hispanic Literature* (1998), eighty or so contributions of prose, poetry, and artwork—to include cover reproductions from the pioneer journal *Revista Chicano-Riqueña* (founded 1972) and its successor from 1984 *Americas Review*—attests to the ever-burgeoning literary *hispanidad* which has continued into 1990s and beyond.

In Francisco Goldman's *The Long Night of White Chickens* (1992), the archive again extends in range with its chronicle of Roger Graetz, born of a Jewish father and Guatemalan mother, who leaves his comfortable milieu to plunge into a Guatemala ravaged by thirty years of civil war, Reagan-era CIA machinations against the various Marxist cadres, death squads and the eradication of Mayan and other village communities. In his search for Flor de Mayo and her sacrificial politics of child rescue and sanctuary, along with the journalist Luis Moya Martínez, Graetz finds himself involved in an awakening to the hemisphere's power structures and their costly human consequences as any merely spatial north–south border.

The America written into these texts, one of formal border and yet abrim in cultural unborder, has had few better exponents than the performance artist-writer Guillermo Gómez-Peña. Describing himself in *Warrior for Gringostroika* as a "deterritorialized Mexican/American living a permanent border experience" with a commitment to "the territory of intercultural dialogue," he writes, "Today, if there is a dominant culture, it is border culture. And those who still haven't crossed a border will do so very soon. All Americans (from the vast continent of America) were, are, or will be border-crossers" (1993: 46–7).

It is a comment full of both history and prophecy, the multiple Latino/a Americas within the USA as not only longtime human and cultural cross-border but in the 1990s, as at other times, the source of many of its quite most challenging literary fictions.

References

Alvarez, J. (1991) *How the García Girls Lost Their Accents*, Chapel Hill, N.C.: Algonquin Books.

—— (1994b) *In The Time of Butterflies*, Chapel Hill, N.C.: Algonquin Books.

—— (1994a) "Las Mariposas," Interview with Ilan Stavans, *Nation*, November 7, pp. 552–6.

—— (1997) *¡Yo!*, New York: Plume.

Anaya, R. (1972) *Bless Me, Ultima*, Berkeley, Calif.: Quinto Sol Publications.

—— (1992) *Alburquerque*, Albuquerque, N. M.: University of New Mexico Press.

—— (1995) *Zia Summer*, New York: Warner Books.

—— (1996) *Rio Grande fall*, New York: Warner Books.

—— (1999) *Shaman Winter*, New York: Warner Books.

Anzaldúa, G. (1987) *Borderlands/La Frontera: The New Mestiza*, San Francisco, Calif.: Aunt Lute Books.

Cano, D. (1991) *Pepe Ríos*, Houston, Tex.: Arte Público Press.

Castillo, A. (1986) *The Mixquiahuala Letters*, Binghampton, N.Y.: Bilingual Press/Editorial Bilingue.

—— (1990) *Sapogonia*, Houston, Tex.: Bilingual Press/Editorial Bilingue.

—— (1993) *So Far From God*, New York: W. W. Norton.

Chávez, D. (1986) *The Last of the Menu Girls*, Houston, Tex.: Arte Público Press.

—— (1994) *Face of an Angel*, New York: Farrar, Straus & Giroux.

Cisneros, S. (1991) *Woman Hollering Creek*, New York: Random House.

Cofer, J. O. (1993) *The Latin Deli: Prose and Poetry*, Athens, Ga.: The University of Georgia Press.

—— (1995) *An Island Like You*, New York: Orchard Press.

30   *A. Robert Lee*

Díaz, J. (1996) *Drown*, New York: Riverhead.

Fernández, Roberta (1990) *Intaglio: A Novel in Six Stories*, Houston, Tex.: Arte Público Press.

Fernández, Roberto (1988) *Raining Backwards*, Houston, Tex.: Arte Público Press.

—— (1995) *Holy Radishes!*, Houston, Tex.: Arte Público Press.

Firmat, G. P. (1994) *Life on the Hyphen: The Cuban-American Way*, Austin, Tex.: University of Texas Press.

Flores, L. (ed.) (1998) *The Floating Borderlands: Twenty-Five Years of US Hispanic Literature*, Seattle, Wash.: University of Washington Press.

Garcia, C. (1992) *Dreaming in Cuban*, New York: Alfred A. Knopf.

Goldman, F. (1992) *The Long Night of White Chickens*, New York: The Atlantic Monthly Press.

Gómez-Peña, G. (1993) *Warrior for Gringostroika*, St. Paul, Minn.: Graywolf Press.

Hinojosa, R. (1976) *Klail City y sus alrededores*, Havana: Casas de las Americas.

—— (1987) *Klail City*, Houston, Tex.: Arte Público Press.

—— (1998) *Ask a Policeman*, Houston, Tex.: Arte Público Press.

Hijuelos, O. (1989) *The Mambo Kings Play Songs of Love*, New York: Farrar, Straus & Giroux.

—— (1993) *The Fourteen Sisters of Emilio Montez O'Brien*, New York: Farrar, Straus & Giroux.

Islas, A. (1991) *Migrant Souls*, New York: William Morrow.

Martínez, D. (1994) *Mother Tongue*, New York: Random House/Ballantine.

Morales, Alejandro (1992) *The Rag Doll Plagues*, Houston, Tex.: Arte Público Press.

Obejas, A. (1994) *We Came All the Way from Cuba So You Could Dress Like This?* San Francisco, Calif.: Cleis Press.

—— (1996) *Memory Mambo*, San Francisco, Calif.: Cleis Press.

Pérez, L. M. (1999) *Geographies of Home*, New York: Viking.

Rechy, J. (1991) *The Miraculous Day of Amalia Gómez*, New York: Little, Brown & Company.

Rivera, T. ([1971] 1987) *"...y no so se lo tragó la tierra"/And The Earth Did Not Part*, Houston, Tex.: Arte Público Press.

Suarez, V. (1995) *Havana Thursdays*, Houston, Tex.: Arte Público Press.

Vega, E. (1985) *The Comeback*, Houston, Tex.: Arte Público Press.

—— (1991) *Casualty Report*, Houston, Tex.: Arte Público Press.

Viramontes, H. M. (1995) *Under The Feet of Jesus*, New York: Dutton.

3 "Come change your destiny, turn suffering into silver and joy"

Constituting Americans

Nahem Yousaf

In 1986 in *Beyond Ethnicity: Consent and Descent in American Culture*, Werner Sollors argued that the new mythos of America would be the narrative of immigration, replacing the mythologically tenacious settler-frontier story. The archetypal American story had been recognized for what it had always been: a transnational or global phenomenon that refashioned the nation, as well as a narrative of self-fashioning. The form such narratives took in the 1990s is the subject of this essay: Their structural elasticity or restricted scope denoting ethnic enclaves at points of friction; their (a)typical protagonists; and the metaphors through which the nation's continually evolving story engaged with academic "culture wars" over multiculturalism and patriotism. While Edward Said argued that patriotism was an obscure dead language and African American writer John Edgar Wideman professed "race" to be "obsolete, anachronistic, dysfunctional" (Wideman 1994: xii), conservative evocations of a "color blind" Constitution, the Simi Valley verdict on Rodney King's attackers, reactions to O. J. Simpson's trial and reports such as "The Millennium Breach" (1998) emphasized racial tension. Established North American writers—such as E. Annie Proulx and T. Coraghessan Boyle—grappled with ideas of nation at the height of the culture wars, especially with regard to (neo)liberal debates about the evolving notion of "multiculturalism."

Although (neo)conservative commentators battled over the centrality of minority cultures in defining the nation's conscience and complexion, the ideological tussle over the nation was largely a liberal dilemma. While the liberal right were often cultural nationalists who saw the "polarization" of "identity politics" as a struggle over representation that failed to acknowledge national history or a modernist discourse of progress, the cultural left believed that any modern conceptualization of the nation must value ethnic diversity in order that displaced and disaffected groups might benefit in a participatory democracy. Liberal anxieties over tolerating or endorsing the perceived identitarian claims of some racial and ethnic groups were examined by Stuart Clarke in "Fear of a Black Planet" (1991) in which he alleged that "identity politics" was an instrument constructed by the right wing to "blunt progressive social possibilities" and that "race" (and ethnicity) was being constructed as a "sign of social order and decay" (Clarke 1991: 37–59). Such ideas entered studies of fiction, as, for example, when Toni Morrison argued that race had become metaphorical, "a way of referring to and disguising forces, classes and expressions of social decay and economic division far more threatening to the body politic than biological 'race' ever was" (Morrison 1992: 63).

In *The Disuniting of America* ([1991] 1992), Arthur Schlesinger Jr. celebrated *E Pluribus Unum* as the assimilationist credo that would ultimately undo a "cult of ethnicity" that he believed to be factionist and un-American (Schlesinger 1992: 10–14). Robert Hughes's *The Culture of Complaint* (1993) bemoaned the "fraying of America" and the confusion of "multiculturalism" with "political correctness." Hughes argued that America was "a collective work of the imagination whose making never ends," but feared that "once that sense of collectivity and mutual respect is broken, the possibilities of Americaness begin to unravel" (1993: 16). To the left of the spectrum, liberals emphasized a voluntary or symbolic attachment to ethnic identity, but Arif Dirlik warned that "To avoid the question of culture is to avoid questions concerning the ways in which we see the world; it is to remain imprisoned, therefore, in a cultural unconscious" (1996: 395). Both "hard" and "soft" multiculturalists used the distinction between "old," "white ethnic" immigrants (1880–1930) and "new" immigrants (post-1965 Immigration Act) in their commentary. American writers' intervention into such debates often exceeded them in "forensic" inventiveness. It is axiomatic to state that writers imagined the lonely postwar immigrant (Susan Choi's *The Foreign Student* [1998] and Esmeralda Santiago's *America's Dream* [1996]), but they also imagined a cosmopolitanism and acculturation that would loosen the supposedly parochial grip of ethnic identity (Bharati Mukerjee's *Jasmine* [1989] and Shawn Wong's *American Knees* [1995]), and a panoply of characters caught up in a cultural pluralism that returned to the 1960s as a liberal touchstone (Maxine Hong Kingston's *Tripmaster Monkey* [1989] and Gish Jen's *Mona in the Promised Land* [1994]). Jen, writing with comic brio, engaged specifically with contemporary discourse by having Mona look forward to when even her father would be affirming his heritage, "celebrating diversity in this our country the melting pot—no, mosaic—no, salad bowl" (Jen 1995: 129). Writers imagined a national "we" which was broadly encompassing and which situated the immigrant within very traditional narrative formulae (Oscar Hujelos' *Mr. Ives's Christmas* [1996] and David Guterson's *Snow*

Falling on Cedars [1995]). An old-fashioned period drama, *Snow Falling on Cedars* emphasizes well-paced realist observations but includes a shifting instability of generic concerns that might be described as postmodernist: a crime mystery becomes a love story, a historical novel, and, finally, a story of national identity with Japanese Americans at its centre. The action shifts from the past of 1941–2 when Japanese Americans were interned, to a murder trial in 1954, two years after they regained their lost citizenship via the Immigration and Nationality Act. Guterson chooses to tell this story of a community—its conflicts, secrets, loves, and betrayals—in the 1990s when the idea of "community" was a contentious subject in culture wars' debates.

In 1995, Japanese American Francis Fukuyama followed his controversial bestseller *The End of History* (1992) with *Trust*, a conservative critique of the erosion of civil society. Guterson's novel engages with a lack of social trust through a quiet island-community's belief that Kabuo Miyamoto is guilty of murder: "Here was the Jap [the sheriff] had been led to inexorably by every islander he'd spoken with" (Guterson 1995: 236). Kabuo's bravery in World War II is the very factor that may sway the all-white jury against him. Patriotism is an expected norm, but it is also a calculated national battle Kabuo fights on "home" ground, impossible to win unequivocally: "because his face was Japanese. There was something extra that had to be proved" (Guterson 1995: 81). Kabuo becomes an almost willing scapegoat: "He was, they decided, not like them at all" (Guterson 1995: 362). The jury is called upon by the prosecutor to condemn him for his "otherness": "Look into his eyes, consider his face, and ask yourselves what your duty is as citizens of this community" (Guterson 1995: 365). "Citizen" and "community" were loaded terms in the 1990s, and Guterson depicts Amity Harbor's white community as a heterogeneous mix of Scandinavian and German Americans united against the supposed "enemy": as Kabuo recognizes, "They're going to want to see me hang" (Guterson 1995: 344).

By the end of the decade, even bestselling blockbusters had begun to engage with "multicultural" issues. Michael Crichton's *Rising Sun* (1992) controversially explored Japanese and American stereotyping as it affected business culture. John Grisham—who published the No. 1 bestselling novel in each year of the decade and made the Southern legal thriller his own—returned to his childhood to write *A Painted House* (2000), an autobiographical novel of Mexican migrant workers clashing with white "hill people" while harvesting his father's cotton crop in rural Arkansas. Proulx, already the Pulitzer Prize and the National Book Award winner for *The Shipping News* in 1994, in her epic second novel explores America as a nation of immigrants through metaphors distinctive of the decade's struggles with multiculturalism: the kaleidoscope and the mosaic. In *Accordion Crimes* (1996), the most potent signifier of mobility is an object rather than a new "American" subject. The accordion is the only "character" to move across states and between ethnic groups and to suffer no borders or barriers to break its progress. At the novel's close in 1989, stuffed with 1,000-dollar bills hidden since the 1930s, it sits on a Mississippi highway about to be destroyed by the next car, its bounty distributed in the poorest of American states. A symbol of optimism and mobility, it proves more resilient than any immigrant character.

Proulx's characters are products of distinctive historical circumstances. In this way, Sollors' model of communities of primordial descent is privileged over his postmodern model of ethnic identity as consent. Through its kaleidoscopic vision, *Accordion Crimes* explores how the immigrant subject could be defined in a nation, more fabulated than real, when there is no immigrant norm. From the novel's beginning in the 1890s, each immigrant's story is separate, distinct like a tile in a mosaic; characters are often strangers or foreigners rather than citizens. Geographer Yi-Fu Tuan, weighing the local and the global in a discussion of new technologies, bemoaned the "cult of peculiarity and difference" that failed to include "the stranger" within any larger vision of national community (Tuan 1989: 279). Proulx and T. C. Boyle write dilemma texts that focus on the vicissitudes of immigrant life and in which isolated strangers and immigrant families are forced to deal with the ways in which their lives intersect with "Americans"; those they seek to emulate and to become. With the emphasis on alterity, each encounter with the "other" is fraught with the threat of violence. In *The Tortilla Curtain* (1995), illegal immigrants Candido and América Rincon live in at the bottom of a canyon, scrabbling for work and food. The Mossbachers, "liberal humanist" nature writer Delaney (Boyle 1997: 3) and realtor wife Kayta, are Los Angeles yuppies for whom fear of ubiquitous Mexican "wetbacks" camping nearby in the state park overwhelms all sympathy and spirals into corrosive racism. The novel is an inventive working out of California's Proposition 187 intended to prevent illegal immigrants from using public services and is frightening in its exposé of "postethnicity" as a fiction. A ritual cleansing finally takes place during a flood after a forest fire leaves the Mossbachers homeless like the destitute immigrants they fear and despise. Candido and América are "saved" by a national institution when amidst the swirling water they secure a perch on the roof of the US Post Office. Though their baby has drowned in the flood, as the novel closes Candido is saving nemesis Delaney, reaching into the water to pull the white man to safety. Boyle's Los Angeles is heavily dramatized as a battlefield, a border zone, dependent on but resenting of migrant labor. Proulx's New Orleans is similarly represented as "a fetid stink of cesspools" combined with "the smell of burning sugar" (Proulx 1996: 27).[1] Mexican writer Carlos Fuentes has famously described the Mason-Dixon line between the North and the Old South in the USA as the border to Latin America, the emphasis on continent or hemisphere a reminder of a long and bloody history of tense syncretism. In one of Proulx's stories "Tejanas," living in "Hornet," Texas for centuries before Texas existed, though American citizens since 1848, are deported to Mexico, and the "brutal joke" is that Texas Rangers have Mexican blood—on their boots (Proulx 1996: 101). Proulx's "continental" story begins and ends in the South, an ironic nod, perhaps, to the North's traditional association of the South's with "race" and region.

If Proulx and Boyle reterritorialize as they dramatize American places, the "minority" literature of Edwidge Danticat, Junot Diaz and Lan Cao begins to deterritorialize; the latter is reflexive about the poststructuralist decentering of subject and nation, especially with regard to hybrid linguistic forms and to narrative formations. Although Diaz's *Drown* (1996) recalls Piri Thomas' *Down These Mean Streets* (1967), the differences are more significant. Diaz refuses teleology and the burden of representation. Edwidge Danticat, lauded as one of *Granta*'s best young American writers in 1996, had little English when she arrived in New York City in 1981, but by 1994 she had published her Masters thesis, *Breath, Eyes, Memory* (1996), to acclaim. In 1995, she was shortlisted for the National Book Award for her collection of stories *Krik? Krak!*, losing to Philip Roth, and declared by the *New York Times* one of the thirty young artists most likely to change American culture. Diaz was *Newsweek*'s "New Face" on the literary scene in the same year and showcased his stories in the *New Yorker* before they were published as *Drown* in 1996. Together with Cao, who was the first Vietnamese American to publish a novel about the aftermath of the Vietnam War, they ask searching questions about the spiritual, cultural, and linguistic luggage that even the poorest refugee brings to America. While Proulx's focus on color-coded "white" identities exposes how much more assimilable to the category of "American" were European immigrants, "new" immigrant writing in the 1990s exposes the ways in which reterritorialization and deterritorialization provokes an understanding of the tension between the centripetal pressure for cultural unity and the centrifugal force of ethnicity. Fiction often performed the delicate negotiation between assimilation and distinctiveness that social commentators were slower to grasp.

The stories in *Accordion Crimes* seem, at first, to cohere in what might be called an immigration tableau, a consequence of Proulx basing her research on photographs of immigrants. She describes her compassion for those trapped within an assimilationist model:

> You erased everything you had been, everything that meant anything
> to you. ... You gave up the landscape ... Your clothing was not
> accepted (the old photos are indicative of this—Italian peasants,
> German nobles, Jewish refugees, constrained in dark Victorian
> clothes), you had to make yourself into something new.
>
> (Patterson 1997: 11)

There would seem to be nothing new about Proulx's stake in fiction on
immigration; the idea that "the new American leaves behind him all his ancient
prejudices and manners ... for the new mode of life he has embraced"
derives from De Crèvecour's eighteenth-century letters (De Crèvecoeur
1782: 70). However, *Accordion Crimes* also unpacks the normative racial
whiteness according to which American national myths cohered. In 1998,
Manning Marable could still state that: "To be white in the United States
says nothing directly about an individual's culture, ethnic heritage, or biological background ... White culture does not exist. White power, privileges,
and prerogatives within capitalist society do exist" (Marable 1998: 153).
Whiteness studies was evolving, and Proulx make the invisible "visible" by
distinguishing between "white ethnic" immigrants, their geographies of
home, and the biases of whiteness within which they were implicated.

The problems Proulx faces in contriving an American epic reflect the
risks she takes in making each protagonist representative of an ethnic
group. We know that, between 1880 and 1924, 25 million immigrants
came to America, and the nativist discourse within which they were con-
tained is captured in enduring metaphors in Proulx's saga. In the first
section, "The Accordion Maker," the Palermo wharf "boils" with immigrants (Proulx 1996: 24); "Sicily was pouring out as cornmeal from a
ripped sack" (1996: 21); they are "Greenhorns" or "dagos" (1996: 23). In
the second story, set during World War I, anti-German feeling flares and
"German blood is poisoned blood" (Proulx 1996: 79). In a story set in
1988–9, Norwegian immigrant Ivar finds some old copies of *Klansman's
Call* and *White America*, which he sells to the American Civil Liberties
Union library. His material comfort is the result of creative thinking about
the racist past. However, his brother Conrad believes the country is

> sinking under these people—chinks and spicks and pakis and those
> aye-rabs from the Middle of the East. It's not the same thing as when
> our grandparents came over; they were white, they had guts, a good
> work ethic ... These are not white people. They're swarthy; they're
> not mongrels. It's simple the country's filled up, there's not enough
> room, not enough jobs to go around.
>
> (Proulx 1996: 365–6)

Conrad's "new" nativism recalls the Klan newspapers his brother has consigned to historical record, and the words of a Klansman writing in 1928: "What has become of the American? Is he vanishing from the earth? ... America today is not the America of twenty-five years ago, but stands mongrelized, alienized, and demoralized in the eyes of her own citizens. Volumes might be written regarding the pot that failed to melt" (quoted in Winter 1971: 245). Proulx exposes a history of racist discourse posing as civic nationalism, her novel ending amidst the culture wars, with Public Enemy successfully vying with Myron Floren's "Polka Maniacs" for Conrad's daughter's attention, while her parents eat pizza watching the (first) American war in Iraq on television (1996: 373–4).

The nation's flaws—racism, inequity, violence—are brazenly catalogued in *Accordion Crimes* through a series of crimes and disasters, often historical, as in the 1891 lynching of Italian immigrants in New Orleans that informs the first story. America's reputation as a "land of justice" (Proulx 1996: 40) is juxtaposed with lies, criminal murder, and random violence. By the end of the first immigration tableau, the Accordion Maker has been murdered, as has his only friend, an African American, and his son's violent death is anticipated. Proulx's inclusion of Apollo in this story may be read as a pre-emptive strike against those culture warriors who skirted race and racism or denied its significance in the "multicultural" 1990s; Boyle and Proulx each expose optional ethnicity as a fiction when combined with black or Hispanic racial visibility. The crimes begin and with the shift from New Orleans to the Midwest, they continue: Characters are injected with plutonium in secret medical experiments; one is boiled alive visiting a national beauty spot; new technologies presage doom as in the cases of one character crushed by a radio tower and another whose arms are sliced off by flying metal. Domestic environs are as dangerous as city streets or wide-open plains: A farmer reaches up to what he thinks is a balloon, and a bomb explodes. Dolor Gagnier, the most pitiful of Proulx's many characters, exemplifies the fate of immigrants who fail to cope. He suffers a condition of hysterical paralysis, before committing suicide. Dolor and the Sicilian Accordion Maker are equally susceptible to the American Dream to "come change your destiny, turn suffering into silver and joy" (Proulx 1996: 19) and are each victims of that same mythology when suffering overwhelms material gain.

The most important "immigrant act" for an American writer in the 1990s was, according to Lisa Lowe, "breaking the dyadic, vertical determination that situates the subject in relation to the state, building instead horizontal community with and between others who are in different locations subject to and subject of the state" (1996: 36). The local and the global have striking resonance in Junot Diaz's *Drown:* New York City is "Neuva York" and Washington Heights a satellite of the Dominican Republic which by 1997 a city planners' report on "The Newest New Yorkers" specified accounted for one in five new immigrants. Diaz explores American places as transformed by the immigrants who become their constituents. Across his stories, location shifts from the Dominican Republic to the USA, and temporal switches compound the instability. Yunior and Ysrael—boys who grow up near Santo Domingo—are the pivots on which the switches are made. Changes of perspective are one way of ensuring the reader never feels entirely comfortable either with the subject matter or its presentation. In "How to Date," for example, the reader becomes complicit in the ruses Yunior employs to get a girlfriend. In sinuously realist prose marked by a streetwise knowingness, only the government cheese hidden at the beginning of the date and returned to the refrigerator at the end belies Yunior's anxiety about his poverty. There are many such examples in a book that is a series of risks and anxious maneuvers for characters hobbled by ambivalence and fear of failure. The metaphors are drained of warmth; the sun "sliding out of the sky like spit off a wall" (Diaz 1996: 18) and the river "as shiny as an earthworm" (1996: 78). A teacher compares the kids to shuttles: "a few of you are going to make it. These are the orbiters. But the majority of you are just going to burn out. Going nowhere" (Diaz 1996: 83). Yunior feels he is losing what purchase he has on life in America in the troubled period of youth: "I could already see myself losing altitude, fading, the earth spread out beneath me, hard and bright" (Diaz 1996: 84).

On arrival in America, Yunior's father Ramon discovers that the Dominican Republic is just visible in the bottom right-hand corner of his American map. Diaz maps new territory in contemporary American fiction. The US invasion of the Dominican Republic took place when anti-Vietnam War protests were increasing and is frequently overlooked in surveys of the period. In *Drown*, it is embedded in the narrative and could be passed over on first sight. Yunior's mother is scarred from the US rocket attack she survived in 1965, and, although "none of the scars showed when she wore her clothes" (Diaz 1996: 55), Yunior can feel them when he embraces her. Diaz has celebrated Danticat as "the quintessential American writer tackling the new world's hidden history of apocalypse and how one survives it," (Jaggi 2004: 20), and he treads similar ground. As in *Breath, Eyes, Memory*, in which the past is carried "like a hair on your head" (Danticat 1996: 234), Diaz portrays through a damaged female character an "ethnic" past in which American imperialism is implicated. Mami is obsessed by the lack of security in her apartment and with crime in the community, the same drug-related crime that ensures her son makes his living as a pusher. As children in Santo Domingo, Yunior and brother Rafa give themselves American names to signal their "third world" hopes in a "first world" future (Diaz 1996: 61), yet all but the most basic of material hopes disintegrate. Each relationship in *Drown* is fragile, and much of Yunior's anxiety is forged in the crucible of his childhood relationship with his father about whom he writes an essay "My Father the Torturer" and says "I'd never once been out with my family when it hadn't turned to shit" (Diaz 1996: 32). The family teeters on the edge of an abyss into which hopes for security are falling. Ramon's affairs contribute—"the affair was like a hole in our living-room floor" (Diaz 1996: 31)—and, whether in New York or the Dominican Republic, poverty supersedes any rallying of entrepreneurial energy. Nowhere is safe: Lying in his cot as a baby, Ysrael's face is mutilated by a pig that wanders into the house.

An accordion is the basis for a rare instance of crosscultural connection in *Drown* as in *Accordion Crimes*. Ramon hitches a ride, carefully hiding his identity because his visa has run out: "He'd heard plenty of tales about the North American police from other illegals, how they liked to beat you before they turned you over to la migra and how sometimes they just took your money and tossed you out toothless on an abandoned road" (Diaz 1996: 136). His ride is a police car and a man is handcuffed and weeping in the back seat, but Ramon is asked, since he travels, if he is a musician and when he answers that he plays the accordion, "That excited the man in the middle. Shit, my old man played the accordion but he was a Polack like me. I didn't know you spiks played it too" (Diaz 1996: 136). The interrecognition that music creates is a trope in novels in which different Americans are constituted and characters' relationships to the signifier "American" are contingent, displaced and disturbing. Priscilla Wald's *Constituting Americans* (1994) concludes that the "official" story of a nation "invariably lags behind the seismic demographic changes and corresponding untold stories that ultimately compel each revision" (1994: 299). *Drown* is one such revision. The constitution of Dominicans as Americans becomes the modus operandi of a harsh and heavily ironic book. Wald asserts that "A national narrative must make the concept of a 'home' for a 'people' appear intrinsic and natural rather than contingent and ultimately fictive" (1994: 299). Diaz's focuses on what is contingent, and "home" is one of *Drown*'s most tenuous concepts.

Anxiety and fear are structuring principles in *Breath, Eyes, Memory*. While Sophie reconciles herself to her Haitian past and an American future, the violent circumstances of her birth—the result of rape—and the "unspeakable act" of genital mutilation work through their tragic effects on her mother. The women in Sophie's family are embattled and embittered, damaged and diminished, but they are also sustained by each other and by stories in which "the words bring wings to our feet" (Danticat 1996: 123, 234). The daffodil prized because it grows where it should not survive is the signifier of their ability to cling to a place and grow there: "My mother is a daffodil, but in the wind iron strong" (Danticat 1996: 29). As with Diaz's characters, little is expected: "We were going to be the first women doctors from my mother's village ... We were going to be engineers too. Imagine our surprise when we found out we had limits" (Danticat 1996: 43). While her mother fails to free herself by refashioning her existence in New York City, though it is "a place where you can lose yourself easily (Danticat 1996: 103), Sophie learns to adapt rather than elide herself, melding Haitian and Creole ways with the culture of her African American husband, a southerner from New Orleans, through whom she rediscovers her "Africanness" and that her "native" Creole is a language spoken by many other "Americans."

Danticat represents voodoo—or Vodun—as peaceful. It is the religious means by which the souls of dead Haitians are returned to ancestral Guinea, as Tante Atie calls her vision of Heaven in the novel; it is folk wisdom, a resource for the rural poor rather than a frightening picture of zombies as presented in much American fiction and film.[2] The relationship between the USA and Haiti has been conflicted, and, like *Drown*, the novel is structured into sections that alternate national contexts. In the year Danticat published *Breath, Eyes, Memory*, the USA invaded Haiti again (in "Operation Uphold Democracy" when 24,000 troops occupied Haiti ostensibly to restore Jean-Bertrand Aristide, the country's first democratically elected president). Danticat fixes the traumatic relationship between Haitians and America within a discourse in which democracy is withheld rather than upheld. Louise plans to get to America by boat but is warned that "the sharks from here to there, they can eat only Haitian flesh. ... Thousands of people wash up on the shores. They put it on television, in newspapers" (Danticat 1996: 99). The withholding of refugee status from Haitians while their Cuban counterparts were granted asylum in the 1980s and 1990s was often attributed in the liberal press to their Africanness, the same connection that Sophie's husband Joseph identifies as their bond and the global connection that places them at the margins of the nation: "I am not American ... I am African-American ... It means you and I, we are already part of each other" (Danticat 1996: 72).

Large urban centers, such as Los Angeles and New York City, have habitually been the focus of fiction with immigrant protagonists—as represented by Boyle, Danticat and Diaz—but the US South had not been associated with immigrant writing. Like Robert Olen Butler in Pulitzer Prize-winning *A Good Scent from a Strange Mountain* (1995), similarly about Vietnamese Americans, Lan Cao's *Monkey Bridge* (1997) is deeply rooted in a changing South. The 2000 census counted only around 6 percent of Asians in its population, but, in Cao's novel, Vietnamese refugees create a Little Saigon, only thirty minutes from the capital Washington, DC. In 1996, Jefferson Humphries, praising Butler's stories, said "surely this community will be speaking in its own voice shortly and we will need critics who know how to properly hear it" (Humphries 1996: 16). Cao published *Monkey Bridge* a year later. Her novel is sensitive to differences in the Vietnamese-American community—Catholic or Buddhist; from the North or the South; old and young; those who adapt to a new life, those who cannot. Cao tells what Lisa Lowe has called the "erased and evacuated histories of Asian Americans" (Lowe 1996: 34), and her novel extends consideration of ethnicity and religion in what has traditionally been under-read as a biracial but monocultural region.

It is often the case that new immigrants find a place in fiction before they are studied as a social phenomenon. In the year following the novel's publication, a nonprofit research firm released "The State of the South," a report specifying that its changing demography included a 42 percent increase in "Asians" settling in the region, bringing their numbers to 1.7 million between 1990 and 1997. In the 1990s, around 1.6 million adults from other nations moved to the South so that the region experienced "a larger share of total foreign immigration to the United States than at any time in its history." For the first time, Asian and "Hispanic" immigration outnumbered "black and white" migration.[3] While there were general and area studies of Indochinese immigration in the 1980s, only in 1997 would Joseph Wood produce a regional study of the acts of appropriation and accommodation that Vietnamese immigrants had taken to "elaborate" the northern Virginia landscape since 1975 (Wood 1997: 58–72). His conclusion that, "Like other American frontiers in other generations, suburbs are now the geographical spaces in which Americans of all sorts of origins are creating America" (Wood 1997: 70–1) recalls Sollors' thesis that the traditional settler-frontier story would be revised in the 1990s by new immigrants in new places.

The American South had also traditionally been seen as a ghost-ridden culture still grappling with defeat in the Civil War, but the ghosts of the Vietnam War haunt *Monkey Bridge* and fuse with Confederate ghosts. The spot Mai's mother declares "the safest in the world" was the site of the Civil War battles of Fredericksburg and Bull Run that form part of the American history Mai learns (Cao 1997: 31). Cao overlays one war on another to create a reflexive narrative in which Vietnam is reconstituted in the American South. Watching the television when she first arrives, Mai sees Vietnam presented through the "ice-white lens of an American camera"; the place has become synonymous with war, but the image of the war in which a world superpower was defeated by a guerilla army has been corrected as an intervention that failed. Mai realizes that "The Vietnam delivered to America had truly passed beyond reclamation. It was no longer mine to explain" (Cao 1997: 128). Nevertheless, her rage to explain Vietnam is as strong as Faulkner's imperative to tell about the South: "It was not all about rocket fires and body bags" (Cao 1997: 128).

Instead, Mai approaches Vietnam through memories—of a children's festival to celebrate the mid-fall moon, with bakers' trays full of moon cakes; of the smells of the open markets in which her mother shopped; of playing hopscotch on a Saigon street in the evening light, watching her father and his American friend drinking *café au lait* and eating sea swallows' nests, and, finally, through the story of the betel nut her mother tells her. This form of sensual nostalgia retrieval constructs ethnic memory. As Cao's novel struggles against American images of Vietnam which masquerade as sovereign, Vietnam is made visceral. The metaphors are organic, and a changing mother–daughter relationship is a structuring principle (as in novels by Amy Tan and Maxine Hong Kingston), as is a childhood friendship. Bobbie, Mai's white high-school friend, helps to bridge the gap for her Vietnamese "best friend." Another character, Mrs. Bay, mediates the Mekong Delta into the Mekong Grocery, where she sustains Vietnam veterans who feel at "home" only with those who shared their experience. Most importantly, the monkey bridge is the overarching metaphor that works to connect two geographies of the mind, Mai's and her mother's. Mrs. Nguyen worries that Mai is "lost between two worlds," but Cao situates the aporia in the character of the mother, who loses her footing on the bridge and is adrift in America, "caught in a vortex of mystical forces, in a ferocious continental drift—one mass splitting in two, going in opposite directions" (Cao 1997: 71).

As in *Drown*, Cao's encodings of subjectivity bespeak a fascination with shifting and ambivalent meanings and interpretations and with language as not only a locus of difference but also the nexus where generations, cultures and memories meet. Mai is a subject-in-the-making; she seems to absorb America as she absorbs the language: "English revealed itself to me with the ease of a thread unspooled" (Cao 1997: 37). Unlike her mother, she does not hold America at bay but maps her world anew in language in this dense and lyrical novel. But Mai's search for an authoritative present to secure the bridge to her future is finally seen to be untenable without an authorizing past. The stories she inherits from her mother are fictions told to protect her from the past, and she discovers that the myths that immigration offers unlimited possibilities for reinvention are also "fancy euphemisms for half-truths and outright lies" (Cao 1997: 124). Mai, it turns out, has only a partial knowledge of her familial past: her mother's scarred face, supposedly the result of a domestic accident, is the consequence of napalm, and her suicide is a sacrifice for her daughter. Mai has underestimated her cultural inheritance at every turn; her reinvention has involved dismissing her mother's Vietnamese dress as "tropical garb" (Cao 1997: 70), disavowing her beliefs and disrespecting her as "Bob," a code word she uses with her friend that signifies "bag of bones" (1997: 144). Unlike Mrs. Bay, who performs the most successful negotiation of cultural affiliations, Mai has only been passing as a "new" American who can flow wherever life takes her.

Ideas of "home" and nation were embattled in the 1990s, but new immigrant writers were unflinching. Migrants maintain connections with their past—sometimes with their homeland—via stories, rituals, language, as in painful multigenerational sagas such as *Breath, Eyes, Memory* and transnational stories such as *Drown*. In unsentimental, ironic, and lyrical narratives, they told quintessentially American stories, enfolding them into the "national narrative."[4] When Francisco Goldman, Guatemalan-American author of the "cult" fiction *The Long Night of White Chickens* (1992), reviewed *Drown* in 1996, he piled into the closing paragraph all the rhetoric of a bona fide American literature:

> Diaz writes in an authentic and true language of his own, obeying only himself—and ends up speaking for everybody. His characters and settings may be new to our literature, but his themes are universal, and also classically American. Coming of age, broken families, wayward and yearning youth, personal betrayals, the painful and ambiguous journey of immigration. Junot Diaz definitely is a wonderful and unique talent. He is a natural.
>
> (Goldman 1996: 18)

Goldman escorted "inside" the writer, whose status marked him as an outsider.

George W. Bush's inaugural address of January 20, 2001 declared "Every immigrant by embracing American ideals makes our country more not less American." Bush described citizenship as "community over chaos," thereby espousing the traditional assimilationist model to which Proulx's novel returns in exposing the chaos and the crimes of a "national" community. If nationalism continually reinvents nations where they do not naturally exist, Proulx and Boyle question the mutual tolerance that a national allegory implies, *Accordion Crimes* constituting a jeremiad and *Tortilla Curtain* a declensionist tale relieved only superficially by its final image of crosscultural affiliation. In *Breath, Eyes, Memory* and *Drown*, the socially corrosive inequities of racism and poverty give the lie to the democratizing commonality of the imagined community. *Monkey Bridge* returns to the national story of self-fashioning, but the impossibility of an exilic character existing in a state of cultural unconsciousness is made painfully clear.

Notes

1 For a discussion of migrant labour in the South, see Yousaf (2006: 155–65).
2 The USA made attempts to eradicate voodoo when they occupied Haiti from 1915 to 1934. See Dash (1988).
3 See "The State of the South 1998" at www.mdcinc.org/knowledge. See also "Diversity Is Changing the Face of the South Report Finds," *The Daily Progress*, September 6, 1998, pp. A1, A10.
4 Diaz states: "I have multiple traditions like anyone else. I'm part of the mainstream 'American' literary tradition. I'm a part of the Latino literary tradition. I'm a part of the African Diaspora literary tradition as well as the Dominican literary tradition" (2000: 904).

References

Andrews, A. C. (1984) "Indochinese Resettlement in Virginia," *Virginia Social Science Journal*, 19 (2): 72–8.
Boyle, T. C. (1995) *The Tortilla Curtain*, London: Bloomsbury.
Cao, L. (1997) *Monkey Bridge*, New York: Penguin.
Clarke, S. A. (1991) "Fear of a Black Planet," *Socialist Review* 21 (3–4): 37–59.
Danticat, E. (1996) *Breath, Eyes, Memory*, London: Abacus.
Dash, J. M. (1988) *Haiti and the US: National Stereotypes and the Literary Imagination*, London: Macmillan.
De Crèvecoeur, J. Hector St. John (1782) *Letters from an American Farmer*, New York: Penguin.
Diaz, J. (1996) *Drown*, London: Faber and Faber.
—— (2000) "Fiction is the Poor Man's Cinema," *Callaloo*, 23 (3): 892–907.
Dirlik, A. (1996) "Culturalism as Hegemonic Ideology and Liberating Practice," in Wilbur C. Rich (ed.), *The Politics of Minority Coalitions: Race, Ethnicity and Shared Uncertainties*, Portsmouth, N.H.: Praeger.
Goldman, F. (1996) "The Super Barrio Brother," *The Guardian*, November 3, p. 18.
Guterson, D. (1995) *Snow Falling on Cedars*, London: Bloomsbury.
Hollinger, D. A. (2000) *Postethnic America: Beyond Multiculturalism*, New York: Basic Books.

Hughes, R. (1993) *The Culture of Complaint*, London: Harvill.

Humphries, J (1996) "Introduction," in J. Humphries and J. Lowe (eds), *The Future of Southern Letters*, Oxford: Oxford University Press.

Jaggi, M. (2004) "Edwidge Danticat," *The Guardian*, November 20, p. 20.

Jen, G. (1995) *Mona in the Promised Land*, London: Granta.

Jordan, J. (1992) *Technical Difficulties*, London: Virago.

Lowe, L. (1996) *Immigrant Acts*, Durham, N.C.: Duke University Press.

Marable, M. (1998) "The Rhetoric of Racial Harmony," in *Black Leadership*, New York: Columbia University Press, pp. 149–59.

Morrison, T. (1992) *Playing in the Dark: Whiteness and the Literary Imagination*, Cambridge, Mass.: Harvard University Press.

Proulx, E. A. (1996) *Accordion Crimes*, London: Fourth Estate.

Patterson, C. (1997) Review of *Accordion Crimes*, *The Independent*, June 1, p. 11.

Rushdie, S. (1992) *Imaginary Homelands*, London: Granta.

Schlesinger, A. M. ([1991] 1992) *The Disuniting of America: Reflections on a Multicultural Society*, New York: W. W. Norton.

Sollors, W. (1986) *Beyond Ethnicity: Consent and Descent in American Culture*, Oxford: Oxford University Press.

Tuan, Y.-F. (1989) "Cultural Pluralism and Technology," *Geographical Review*, 789: 269–79.

Wald, P. (1994) *Constituting Americans: Cultural Anxiety and Narrative Form*, Durham, N.C.: Duke University Press.

Wideman, J. E. (1994) *Fatheralong: A Meditation on Fathers and Sons, Race and Society*, London: Picador.

Winter, P. M. (1971) "What Price Tolerance?," in David Brion Davis (ed.), *The Fear of Conspiracy: Images of Un-American Subversion from the Revolution to the Present*, Ithaca, N.Y.: Cornell University Press, pp. 240–6.

Wood, J. (1997) "Vietnamese American Place Making in Northern Virginia," *Geographical Review*, 87 (1): 58–72.

Yousaf, N. (2006) "A Sugar Cage: Poverty and Protest in Stephanie Black's H-2 Worker," in Suzanne W. Jones and Mark Newman (eds), *Poverty and Progress in the US South since 1920*. Amsterdam: VU University Press, pp. 155–65.

4 America as diaphor

Cultural translation in Bharati Mukherjee's *The Holder of the World*

Krishna Sen

Bharati Mukherjee's *The Holder of the World* (1993) interrogates the accepted paradigms of "Americanness"—Eurocentrism, exceptionalism, the Puritan heritage, the "melting pot"—as they came to be inflected by new and more assertive waves of non-European immigrants following the 1965 Immigration Act that dramatically increased legal entry into the USA from Asia and Latin America. The 1990s was the decade during which what Patrick J. Buchanan famously dubbed "The Cultural Wars for the Soul of America" in his polemical address of September 14, 1992, were raging in their full fury, and non-white immigration had emerged as one of the major provocations. Neoconservative agendas such as the regulation of sexual preference, the focalizing of Christian values, and the prioritizing of English were coupled with the xenophobia that permeated both Buchanan's abrasive Announcement Speech for the Presidency in 1996 and the acrimonious rhetoric of his 2002 "*New York Times* Best-seller," *The Death of the West: How Dying Populations and Immigrant Invasions Imperil Our Country and Civilization*, which was the prequel to his apocalyptic 2006 title, *State of Emergency: The Third World Invasion and the Conquest of America*. *The Holder of the World* is an intervention in this controversy that problematizes (to quote Mukherjee) "the making of America and American national mythology. That's why I used the two women characters, Hannah the pre-America American, and Beigh, the post-de-Europeanized American, to dramatize the need to redefine what it means to be an 'American' in the 1990s" (Chen and Goudie 1997: 15). In presenting the two white women, one colonial and the other contemporary, as undergoing cultural "translation" and being "transformed" (Mukherjee 1993: 106) through their interface with India, Mukherjee not only destabilizes the normative status of "whiteness" (a central tenet of the cultural wars) as the signifier of American identity but simultaneously clears a space within that identity for the inscaping of the Other. If *Jasmine* (Mukherjee 1989a) demonstrated through its assimilationist perspective that America has the power to induce "unpredictable transformations upon its latest newcomers," *The Holder of the World* is the revisionist counternarrative of "the sometimes painful recognition on the part of America's native sons and daughters that their identity had been changed by these new 'exotic' immigrants" (Mukherjee n.d.: n.p.). Hence, *The Holder of the World* focuses the "deeper rhythms of America" and subverts "an American history that seems, on the surface, to have denied their very existence" (Mukherjee n.d.: n.p.).

Beigh Masters, the narrator of *The Holder of the World* and an asset-hunter tracking the "Emperor's Tear," a legendary diamond owned by the Mughal Emperor Aurangzeb, stumbles upon the trail of her colonial ancestor Hannah when she discovers in an obscure Museum of Maritime Trade "in an old fishing village many branches off a spur of the interstate between Peabody and Salem" (Mukherjee 1993: 5–6) a set of exquisite Mughal miniatures featuring a blonde woman in Oriental attire amid Eastern landscapes. As Beigh delves deeper into this fascinating odyssey, she finds herself more and more enmeshed in "the tangled lines of India and New England" (Mukherjee 1993: 9). For Hannah, born Hannah Easton in 1670 at Salem, the "traditional capital of Puritan restraint" (Mukherjee 1993: 6), and then adopted and renamed Hannah Fitch after her widowed birth-mother Rebecca's scandalous elopement with an Indian Nipmuc lover, was none other than the fabled Salem Bibi, a Puritan woman "undreamed of in Puritan society" (Mukherjee 1993: 60).

Hannah's marriage with the British adventurer Gabriel Legge had led her from Massachusetts to England and then to the clamorous trading enclaves of the East India Company on the Coromandel coast of faraway India: after Gabriel's death, she became the paramor of the Hindu raja Jadav Singh (whence the pseudonym "Salem Bibi" or "the wife from Salem"). Finally, in a bizarre turn of events, Hannah and her faithful attendant Bhagmati were detained by Aurangzeb, who was, however, so impressed with "the luster of [her] spirit" that he christened her "Precious-as-Pearl" (Mukherjee 1993: 279). When, on the death of Jadav Singh, Hannah, the "White Pearl," finally returned from an India opulent with Mughal wealth and European commerce to the cold austerity of Salem along with the child of "*her* Indian lover" (dubbed "Black Pearl" by the disapproving neighbors because of her dusky complexion), thus reprising her mother's lapse and inviting similar censure for miscegenation, the free nation of America had yet to be born. Ironically, though Salem children were warned away from "the House of Enchantment, meaning the place of ultimate debauchery," it was there rather than in the loyal God-fearing Puritan homes that "seditious sentiments were openly aired" against British colonial rule. "'We are Americans to freedom born!' White Pearl and Black Pearl were heard to mutter," and Black Pearl "saw in her old age the birth of this country, an event she had spent a lifetime advocating, and suffering for" (Mukherjee 1993: 293). *The Holder of the World* clearly suggests that free America had had foot soldiers other than those of unblemished European origin.

As for the "Emperor's Tear," Beigh "discovers" that it had been secreted in the lacerated entrails of Bhagmati during a fateful battle between Aurangzeb and Jadav Singh and remains still buried with her: She learns this when she takes a trip through virtual reality into Hannah's past and transitorily *becomes* Bhagmati (Mukherjee 1993: 289) by means of a futuristic software program written by *her* Indian lover, the Asian Indian computer scientist Venn. Beigh's quest for the truth of Hannah's story becomes self-reflexive in that she, too, has stepped "over the border" (Mukherjee 1993: 152) in her relationship with Venn, "who would seem alien to my family" (1993: 30). In this metafictonal interweaving of science fiction and colonial history (Joseph A. Cincotti records that Mukherjee had actually seen a miniature of a Caucasian woman in ornate Mughal costume at a 1989 pre-auction viewing in New York), virtual reality functions as the trope that narrativizes Beigh's "hunger for connectedness" (Mukherjee 1993: 9), dissolving the distinctions between India and America, and between the white and the brown women. As a "searcher-after-origins" (Mukherjee 1993: 8), as she describes her profession, the unusually named Beigh—pronounced "Bay-a" (1993: 8), possibly indicating that hers is the authentic perspective on Massachusetts Bay—recuperates, not some monologic ur-narrative of Puritan virtue triumphing over pagan vice but a multilayered saga of opposed but intersecting cultural universes that constitute a part of the occluded pre-history of modern America.

Mukherjee has ascribed her predilection for the polyvalent to her heritage—"I suppose that's being a Hindu, I mean, this being constantly aware of the existence of many universes"—and has connected this to cutting-edge science—"Current discoveries in astronomy are certainly pointing up the existence of universes other than ours" (Chen and Goudie 1997: 3). Beigh's contention that "everything in history (as Venn keeps telling me) is as tightly woven as a Kashmiri shawl" (Mukherjee 1993: 195) is also Mukherjee's—the epigraph to *Jasmine*, taken from James Gleick's *Chaos*, had already affirmed "the new geometry ... of ... the twisted, tangled and intertwined" (Mukherjee 1989a: n.p.). Bruce Simon notes that the narrator Beigh Masters is an alter ego of Mukherjee in that they share initials and the connotations of their last names (though Simon errs in translating "Mukherjee" as "master of liberation" (Simon 2000: 423): "Mukherjee" is the colonial abbreviation for the upper-caste Bengali Brahmin surname "Mukhopadhyay," meaning "master of Vedic learning," which can perhaps be glossed as a kind of searching after origins and truths). In fact, the two given names are also similar in their implications—like "Bay-a," "Bharati" gestures towards "Bharat," the indigenous name for India. More significant than the conundrum of the names, however, is the commonality of purpose—through *The Holder of the World*, Mukherjee, too, is disinterring forgotten affiliations between the apparently discrete parts of her own identity, India and America. And since "every time-traveler will create a different reality" (Mukherjee 1993: 4), the intercultural America of *The Holder of the World*'s interpenetrated topographies counters the myth of an "eternal, stable and static" (Sollors 1989: xiv) monocultural nation.

The dialectical relationship between the imaginary homeland and what Mukherjee calls the "continuum" of "diasporality" (Chen and Goudie 1997: 12) underscores the archetypal immigrant trajectory from dislocation to relocation, a journey marked by a multiplicity of transforming moments. Shirley Geok-lin Lim has described this contested process of transculturation as spanning three distinct stages of identity-formation—the nationalist or pre-ethnic stage when the call of the old homeland is still stronger than that of the new; the ethnic stage when the expatriate bonds with others from the same background against the bitter experiences of exclusion in the new home, thus fashioning a community of sorts; and the post-ethnic stage when he or she claims legitimacy as an acceptable, albeit hybrid, insider (Lim 1993: 152). These successive psychological locations are inhabited also by the eponymous Jasmine as she transits from "the pride of cultural retention (exile/expatriation)" through "the fear of cultural surrender (immigration)" to assimilation (Mukherjee n.d.: n.p.). In Mukherjee's own experience of migration, this is the passage from "An Invisible Woman" (Mukherjee 1981), which records the tribulations of immigrant life in Canada, to the celebration of her American citizenship in "Immigrant Writing: Give Us Your Maximalists!," that opens with the exuberant declaration—"I am one of you now!" (Mukherjee 1988: 28). This reversal is not as unexpected as it appears. Even while lamenting "the absolute impossibility of ever having a home" in an alien land (Mukherjee and Blaise 1977: 287), Mukherjee had been sensitive to the protean possibilities of immigration as projected through Naipaul's evocations of "unhousing ... and at the same time [being] free" to re-fashion oneself (Mukherjee and Boyers 1981: 4): she then grew to appreciate Rushdie's position that "immigration ... is a net *gain* ... as opposed to Naipaul's loss and mimicry" (Mukherjee 1989b: 12). *The Holder of the World*, however, marks a phase beyond post-ethnic assimilation that might be termed transnational ethnicity—the immigrant now not only negotiates both the old and the new identities with equal facility but sees the new as productively inflected by the old through a complex process of rememoration, refiguration, and cultural translation.

The trace of a transnational ethnicity "provincializing" America, to use Dipesh Chakrabarty's felicitous term (2000), infused Mukherjee's earlier fiction as well, despite criticism of her complicity with the "Western centre" from commentators such as Aijaz Ahmad (1992: 207–8). Panna, in "A Wife's Story," instinctively configures American racism in terms of politically incorrect religious communalism in India (Mukherjee 1988: 26); in both "Wife" and *Jasmine*, Dimple's and Jasmine's transitions from the Indian to the American identity are troped as transmigration and reincarnation; the fluidity of Jasmine's hybrid immigrant self—"How many more shapes are in me, how many more selves ...?" (Mukherjee 1989a: 215)—is repeatedly referenced by Hindu myths of shape-changing and miraculous transformation; and in Dimple's and Jasmine's slaughtering of Amit Sen and Half-Face respectively, New World feminism's victory over Old World patriarchy is transculturated as *shakti* and represented through the iconic image of the Bengal Kali with her upraised scimitar. But the glocalizing of America in *The Holder of the World* in terms of Hannah's journey from America to India (as opposed to the normal flow of modern migration) is more audacious, for here Mukherjee claims America in reverse, as it were, through appropriation rather than acculturation. This agenda had been proposed shortly before *The Holder of the World* in "A Four-Hundred-Year-Old Woman" in which Mukherjee's declared mission was to be "an American writer in the American mainstream, *trying to extend it*" (emphasis added)—the form of this "extension" would be to "redefine the nature of *American* and what makes an American by making the familiar exotic; the exotic familiar" (Mukherjee 1991: 24–5). Clearly, she has no intention merely to emulate the canonical texts: "I'm having to invent a whole new structure for American fiction, a whole new kind of sentence to express non-traditional immigrant emotions and psychic texture" (Chen and Goudie 1997: 12).

The most obvious strategy for appropriating America in *The Holder of the World* is intertextuality, as the author herself indicates—the novel is, on one level, a rearticulation of that archetypal Puritan drama of moral lapse, Nathaniel Hawthorne's *The Scarlet Letter*, "that morbid introspection into guilt and repression that many call our [i.e., America's] greatest work" (Mukherjee 1993: 294). Hawthorne operates as a deliberately intrusive parallel text and not only offers a literary matrix for *The Holder of the World* but contextualizes it historically as well. Weaving fact and fiction together, Mukherjee locates the apocryphal Hannah within a recognizably historical Salem through her adoptive parents' connections with John Hathorne, the "witchcraft judge" (1993: 294) of the Salem witch trials of 1692 (he was, in fact, the inquisitor and not the judge) and an ancestor of Nathaniel's; John Hathorne's son Joseph went to sea, fascinated by Hannah's tales of the fabulous China and India trade—"His great-grandson, Nathaniel Hawthorne, was born in Salem in 1804" (Mukherjee 1993: 294). There are also a myriad echoes, direct and oblique, of *The Scarlet Letter* in *The Holder of the World*. To name only a few: Hannah's mother, Rebecca Easton, with her brood of Nipmuc children has "the shameful *I* boldly sewn in red to her sleeve" to denote "Indian lover" (Mukherjee 1993: 293); Hannah's closest friend in Salem is Hester Manning ("Manning" was Hawthorne's mother's family name), and Hester is also the name Hannah gave to Bhagmati; like Hester Prynne, Hannah, after becoming the concubine of Jadav Singh, "tattooed a pink alphabet of guilt all over her body with the fibrous roots Bhagmati had taught her to use as cleansing agents" (Mukherjee 1993: 237); Hannah seeks solace in her needlework; her daughter, Pearl Singh, recalls the elf-child Pearl, the illegitimate offspring of Hester and Arthur. Both Hawthorne and Mukherjee interrogate the reified Puritan ethic by affirming the "errant" subject positions of their protagonists through the iconoclastic reinscription of theological imagery: Hester Prynne standing before the colonial magistrate with her illegitimate infant in her arms brings to mind, "if only by contrast," "the image of Divine Maternity" (Hawthorne 1986: 53), while Hannah, in whom "the Coromandel had started something as immense as a cyclone deep inside her body and mind" is "a goddess-in-the-making" (Mukherjee 1993: 167).

However, since every re-citing is also a re-siting, the familiar Hawthorne story becomes "strange" in *The Holder of the World*. Mukherjee provocatively argues that Hawthorne did not go far enough in exploring alternate models of American identity due to the moral constraints of his time: "Who can blame Nathaniel Hawthorne for shying away from the real story of the brave Salem mother and her illegitimate daughter?" (Mukherjee 1993: 292). Hester Prynne and Arthur Dimmesdale had only agonized over the possibility of escaping from Salem to Indian territory in the "Western wilderness" (Hawthorne 1986: 54), or even of fleeing "our native land ... [to] vast London,—or, surely in Germany, in France, in pleasant Italy" (1986: 172), as a way of authenticating their relationship. Rebecca Easton actually flees with her Indian brave to the woods around Brookfield, subversively described as "that New World Eden" (Mukherjee 1993: 107) in contradistinction to Hawthorne's dreary forest, while Hannah finds fulfillment in the real India where "she felt her own passionate nature for the first time" (1993: 244). Mukherjee plays here on "Indian" (Native American) and "Indian" (native of India), terms that have been homologous since Columbus' original error. Hawthorne's tale of guilt and punishment is reinvented as a story of possibility: mother and daughter stand as the forerunners of a hybrid multicultural America through their acts of miscegenation. The notion of hybridity as the morally decadent product of miscegenation, "the ultimate unnatural crime of Puritan life" (Mukherjee 1993: 29), had been further complicated in pre-twentieth-century America by suggestions of sexual infertility and cultural impotence (Young 1995: 118–41); and, though critics like Benita Parry have objected to contemporary recuperations of hybridity that occlude the specificity of historical trauma (Parry 1987: 42), Mukherjee has, in fact, refigured it here as inclusive, culturally potent, and therefore redemptive.

The Holder of the World invokes and then transforms into oppositional discourse, not Hawthorne alone but other classic American texts as well. Mary Rowlandson's celebrated narrative of captivity by diabolical Indians (Mukherjee 1993: 52) becomes for Rebecca, though temporarily, a narrative of liberation. Rebecca rephrases the popular psalm from the Bay Psalm Book, "Ask thou of me," in which God is a benevolent master, to "Desire of me," making the Lord a loved companion. The many accounts of the Salem witchcraft trials and Arthur Miller's "Salem" play, *The Crucible*, appear in the references to "sightings" (Mukherjee 1993: 26, 53) and to Hannah's reputation for being formed in the "crucible" of "the devil, the forest, the Indians" (1993: 60). Paradoxically, however, it is Hannah/White Pearl's "Enchanted House" that is the crucible of American revolutionary activity at Salem. Finally, Pynchon's science-fiction classic *V* (Thomas Pynchon's ancestor Solomon Pynchon of Salem enters the novel (Mukherjee 1993: 55) as Hannah's unsuccessful suitor) anticipates the multiple worlds and futuristic time travel of *The Holder of the World*, with Hannah as "another V, ... the encoder of a secret history" (1993: 60)—yet, where *V* projects an entropic universe, *The Holder of the World* communicates hope as well as horror (1993: 295).

The Holder of the World, however, is hybrid also in its intertextual provenance, reflecting the transcultural literary inheritance of a multiethnic America. A major cultural text underpinning *The Holder of the World* is the *Ramayana*. As the devoted wife in the captivity of demons, Sita's story in the *Ramayana* parallels Mary Rowlandson's (Mukherjee 1993: 180–1), while the self-assertive Sita rejecting patriarchy in the final scenes of the epic is the prototype of Rebecca and Hannah (1993: 178). The analogy, says Bruce Simon, "emphasizes cross-cultural continuities between East and West" (2000: 422). Equally significant is the alignment of the Nipmuc brave with Hanuman of the *Ramayana*—allegorically, Hanuman represents the power and divinity of nature, implying here an affirmation of the sacredness of unchartered nature over the cloistered theocentricism of Puritan nurture. Though Hawthorne as "exoticized" by the *Ramayana* provides the framework for the modern story, one should not overlook the British subtexts in *The Holder of the World*, English literature being an integral component of Mukherjee's middle-class inheritance from colonial India.

America as diaphor   53

Beyond the references to Joyce, Dylan Thomas, and, especially, Conrad, stands Keats whose *Ode on a Grecian Urn* provides epigraphs to every section of the novel—and this poem is on one level about the artist's capacity to create meaning by reimagining the subject in a variety of ways. Then there is (inevitably) Kipling, with Hannah a Kim-persona "sick of the Great Game" (Mukherjee 1993: 207). This single reference to Kipling ties up, somewhat cryptically, with one of Mukherjee's concerns in the novel: "I certainly know what I love about the spirit of America, but I've also written at great length about the underside of the American Dream. Hannah, in *The Holder of the World*, is an embodiment of the guts, imagination and assertiveness of that American spirit, and its underside—the will to imperialize" (Chen and Goudie 1997: 12). The hegemonistic negation of the Other is critiqued in *The Holder of the World* through Rebecca/Hannah/Beigh's dialogical capacity for cultural translation.

To a reader located in India, it is this trope of cultural translation that reverberates in *The Holder of the World*, as opposed to Western readings that interpret the novel primarily as a feminist or postcolonial restatement of *The Scarlet Letter*. The site of this translation, India, is the locus of a potentially global identity through which, according to Beigh, "we can deconstruct the barriers of time and geography" (Mukherjee 1993: 9). Strangely, Aurangzeb and his Mughal splendor, the radical obverse of Salem sobriety, is generally dismissed, if touched upon at all in discussions of *The Holder of the World*, as no more than an exotic backdrop to an American woman's seventeenth-century adventure safari. Yet, important as Hannah's odyssey is in articulating many of the key concerns of the novel regarding Eurocentrism and whiteness in America, the titular figure of the novel is not Hannah but Aurangzeb, one of whose honorifics was "Alamgir, the World-Holder" (Mukherjee 1993: 290). His "one stark symbol of power," the jeweled globe suspended above the imperial throne, crested by the Emperor's Tear, and cupped in a pure gold replica of the Emperor's hand (Mukherjee 1993: 271), is crucial to the larger argument of the novel.

In *The Holder of the World*, Mukherjee has not only inserted India into early American history through Hannah's travels—an "alternative history" according to Claire Messud (1993: 23)—but simultaneously interchanged the positions of the boundary and the centre. As in Amitav Ghosh's *The Shadow Lines*, in which a colonized Calcutta looks at colonizing London and finds it wanting in certain respects, Mukherjee swivels the Eurocentric perspective and reverses the Occidental gaze: Hannah "did not hold India up to inspection by the lamp of England, or of Christianity" (1993: 106). What a dramatic change of perspective now occurs: "it is the story of North America turned inside out" (Mukherjee 1993: 164). In those days, the Coromandel Coast and not the American West tempted men with "the frontier dream, ... the immigrant dream" (Mukherjee 1993: 170). Rich in resources coveted by Christians, Muslims, and Hindus alike, India stood in the seventeenth century at the centre of a globalized world of international commerce presided over by Shah Jahan, the "New World Emperor" (Mukherjee 1993: 10), whereas Salem in the new world of America was but a dot on the periphery—"while the Taj Mahal was slowly rising," Beigh's colonial ancestor "was erecting a split-log cabin adjacent to a hog pen" (1993: 10). Even Shah Jahan's son Aurangzeb "was older than America, older than Massachusetts Bay Colony, more experienced in conquering and acquiring than anyone but the kings of Spain, France and England" (Mukherjee 1993: 270). By contrast, hard-scrabble New England was "a reverse of Australia. Puritans to pirates in two generations" (Mukherjee 1993: 8–9), a place where "[the] spoils of the Fabled East [were] hauled Salemward by pock-marked fortune builders" (1993: 7). Yet, the glory of India is shadowed by tragedy; we know from hindsight that Aurangzeb's regime was the last great moment before India succumbed to British colonial rule. Neither is Mukherjee uncritically romantic in her view of India. The practical Gabriel Legge rightly wonders at the flaunting of wealth for its own sake, "ignorant of investment, leading to no greater social good" (Mukherjee 1993: 78). Bruce Simon perceptively comments that in the heterotopic universe of *The Holder of the World* Hawthorne's Hester surfaces again and again as "a floating signifier" (2000: 423), moving from Rebecca/Hannah/Hester Manning/Beigh to Bhagmati/Hester Hedges. But where Simon sees in this only "complicated desires" (2000: 423) because of his prioritization of Hawthorne, what is obviously at play is the Hindu philosophical paradigm of macrocosmic transformation that had once made India the metaphorical holder of the world and has now passed the mantle to America. It is not a defeat or victory but only "a new name for a new incarnation" (Mukherjee 1993: 229). As Beigh says, echoing Venn and deconstructing Western intentionality, "We do things when it is our time to do them. ... It's a question of time, not motive" (Mukherjee 1993: 71).

What this orientation effects in terms of form is to focus on juxtaposition rather than succession, interconnectedness and metamorphosis rather than disjunction and hierarchy. The most potent symbol of this is, of course, Hannah who in "one rainy season" went from Puritan maiden to British wife, to the sari-clad consort of a Hindu king, to the respected hostage of a Muslim Emperor (Mukherjee 1993: 279–80). But there are other metamorphoses that also cross and re-cross ethnic and racial lines: Bindu/Bhagmati/Hester and Beigh/Bhagmati. The narrative strategy is to foreclose historical difference through a metahistorical maneuver that places past and present on a seamless grid of continuity where cultures intertwine, and individual lives reiterate patterns from the past. Fakrul Alam has observed that *The Holder of the World* is a quest narrative in the well-established tradition of the American romance (1996: 124), but if so, then Mukherjee has transfused the linear logic of the quest with the circular time of Oriental cosmology and superimposed alternative epistemologies that project different strategies of world making to that of the romance with its unambiguously dichotomized universes of good and evil. The non-Eurocentric aesthetics of the Mughal miniature that erases linearity, selectivity, and difference has frequently been noted as a framing device in *The Holder of the World*, "an art that knows no limit, no perspective, no vanishing point ... *that temperamentally cannot exclude*" (Mukherjee 1993: 17–18; emphasis added). Earlier, in *Days and Nights in Calcutta*, Mukherjee had cited the nonperspectival technique of Hindu temple architecture as her formal inspiration (Mukherjee and Blaise 1977: 171). But Mukherjee has drawn from the Indian folk aesthetic of orality as much as from the "high" aesthetic of the temple art and the miniature: In *The Holder of the World*, Beigh says, "Orality, as they say these days, *is a complex narrative tradition*. Reciters of Sita's story indulge themselves with closures that suit the mood of their times and their regions" (Mukherjee 1993: 181; emphasis in the original). In creating a story of cultural crosspollination, Mukherjee has reaccentuated, to use Bakhtin's term (Bakhtin 1981: 421), Hawthorne and Pynchon, the captivity narrative and the romance, in ways that suit the exploration of American identity and its borders in her own time and place.

The most common criticism of *The Holder of the World* is that, despite Beigh's weighty pontifications to the contrary, Mukherjee has fallen plumb into the trap of exoticizing and Orientalizing India and, especially, Bhagmati, in ways that cater after all to the American insistence on othering and difference; the charges have been levelled most strongly by Susan Koshy (1994), Uma Parameswaran (1994), and Bruce Simon (2000). The fact remains that aristocratic Mughal India, to which the purview of *The Holder of the World* is limited, was incredibly opulent, as Mughal pictorial art, architecture, and material artifacts prove without question, while Bhagmati's early history as the twice-betrayed Bindu is certainly no Orientalist romance but poignantly reminiscent of Saratchandra Chattopadhyay's classic Bengali novels about the plight of rural women in colonial times. Then again, Simon unfavorably compares *The Holder of the World*'s socially privileged world with Maryse Condé's sensitive representation of the pain of the disenfranchised in *I, Tituba*, another reinscription of *The Scarlet Letter* from the perspective of the African-American slave (Simon 2000: 428). But, as Susan Koshy demonstrates in her analysis of Asian immigration into America, the class profile of the Asian-Indian immigrant has always been relatively privileged, registering none of the brutal marginalization meted out to the Chinese and Japanese diasporas

(Koshy 2001)—or, for that matter, to the African-American community. Indeed, Mukherjee has been quite caustic about stereotypical expectations that the India-born American writer should speak only of poverty and victimization when "the majority of South Asians granted visas are urban, educated professionals" (Chen and Goudie 1997: 8). The problem in *The Holder of the World* seems to stem, rather, from the strategy of placing the onus of connecting cultures solely on the flimsy device of the virtual-reality machine and the quasi-mythical Salem Bibi—these fail to carry the weight of linking America's past with India's. Mukherjee could well have located that interface on a more historically verifiable foundation.

For Massachusetts Bay Colony and India did, in fact, share a long history. On June 23, 1672, the first colonial American, Boston-born Elihu Yale (later to give his money and name to the great university) arrived on the Coromandel Coast as a clerk of the British East India Company and soon built a fortune in spices. Within a century, the Salem spice trade (mainly pepper), led by the Carne and Peele families and centered on the arc from Madras to Sumatra, was making as much as 700 percent profit and, before its eclipse due to piracy in the early nineteenth century, was contributing through import duties approximately 5 percent of the expenses of the entire US government. But there were other commercial connections as well between Salem and India, most of them crystallizing by the eighteenth century. Two of the earliest Salem families to trade almost exclusively with Calcutta were the Derbys and the Crowninshields—Elias H. Derby (1739–99) is said to have been America's first millionaire, while Jacob Crowninshield imported from India the first elephant ever seen in the USA. The extent of this trade can be gauged from the many extant catalogues of "Calcutta Goods," including fine fabrics and foodstuffs and running to over thirty items each. The next great builder of Salem fortunes was ice. In 1833, Frederick Tudor pioneered the insulated ships that carried ice from Salem and Boston to Calcutta, and there are many accounts of Calcutta's British gentry consuming frozen drinks made with American ice at Peleti's on fashionable Chowringhee boulevard. Indeed, so lucrative was the Calcutta trade that an American consul was appointed there by President George Washington as early as 1792 (Caterini 1992: 8–25 *passim*). A greater emphasis on fact might have provided a more solid basis for colonial India-America connections than fantasy and virtual reality that fail to bridge the gap effectively between modern America and the India of yore.

In marking out *The Holder of the World*'s variety of transnational ethnicity as her riposte to the cultural wars of the 1990s, Mukherjee in no way approximates what Said called "adversarial internationalism in an age of continued imperial structures" in his essay "Third World Intellectuals and

Metropolitan Culture" (quoted in Ahmad 1992: 207). America remains the destination, though it is now a striated rather than a smooth and uncontested space. But, in a reversal of Buchanan's xenophobia, the novel identifies "diasporality" and "interculturality" as the privileged sites of a specially insightful narrative of the nation, since "diasporic communities occupy the border zones of the nation where the most vibrant kinds of interaction take place" and where "domination and territoriality [are] not the preconditions of nationhood" (Mishra 1996: 67). Indeed, Mukherjee's succeeding novels continue to prioritize the synoptic vision and the syncretic identity formations of *The Holder of the World* rather than the assimilationist mantra of *Jasmine*. The adopted child Debbie/Devi of *Leave It to Me* struggles to synthesize "American wants with Asian needs" (Mukherjee 1997: 34), while for the triad of Calcutta sisters in *Desirable Daughters* immigration is no "one-way procession" (Mukherjee 2002: 3) but the synergy of memory and rememory. In the most recent novel, *The Tree Bride*, the double persona of Beigh/Hannah is repeated in the identification of the contemporary immigrant Tara with her ancestor Tara Lata from a remote village in East Bengal (now Bangladesh). Tara Lata was alienated from her own identity under the pressure of British colonial rule and then had to reclaim herself, just as the modern Tara has to in America—"everything and everyone had always been there" (Mukherjee 2004: 28)—and it is contingent upon the immigrant to search out these obscured selves and to integrate them within the diasporic identity. Thus, in *The Holder of the World* and the novels that follow, America is not a metaphor in which two related but different entities, the immigrant's native and diasporic selves, merge or melt into one another to create a new assimilated whole. It is, rather, a diaphor in which the constituent parts are mutually inflected so as to evolve a new yet composite substance, where the focus is as much on the process as on the product. James Machor has defined the diaphoric trope as the combining of "two seemingly disparate ideas, so that the linking itself becomes the vehicle for the creation of new meaning by juxtaposition and synthesis" (1980: 133). Alex Houen defines diaphor as "the transference of the singular through an infinite field of relations. This we could call the diaphor from the Greek 'diaphora.' ... An image of the sum of discontinuities" (2000: 186). In *The Holder of the World*, indigeneity, invention, and identity merge through cultural translation in the diaphoric space of the transnational homeland.

References

Ahmad, A. (1992) *In Theory: Classes, Nations, Literatures*, London: Verso.
Alam, F. (1996) *Bharati Mukherjee*, New York: Twayne.

Bakhtin, M. M. (1981) *The Dialogical Imagination*, trans. Caryl Emerson and Michael Holquist, Austin, Tex.: University of Texas Press.

Buchanan, P. J. (2002) *The Death of the West: How Dying Populations and Immigrant Invasions Imperil Our Country and Civilization*, New York: St. Martin's Press.

—— (2006) *State of Emergency: The Third World Invasion and the Conquest of America*, New York: St. Martin's Press.

Caterini, D. (ed.) (1992) *Calcutta's 200-Year Link with America*, Calcutta: United States Information Service.

Chakrabarty, D. (2000) *Provincializing Europe: Postcolonial Thought and Historical Difference*, Princeton, NJ: Princeton University Press.

Chen, T. and S. X. Goudie (1997) "Holders of the Word: An Interview with Bharati Mukherjee," *Jouvert*, 1 (1): 1–18.

Cincotti, J. A. (1993) "Same Trip. Opposite Direction," *New York Times Book Review*, October 10, p. 7.

Hawthorne, N. (1986) *The Scarlet Letter*, Harmondsworth: Penguin.

Houen, A. (2000) "Various Infinitudes: Narration, Embodiment and Ontology in Beckett's *How It Is* and Spinoza's *Ethics*," in Martin McQuillan (ed.), *Post-Theory*, Edinburgh: Edinburgh University Press, pp. 176–87.

Koshy, S. (1994) Review of *The Holder of the World*, by Bharati Mukherjee, *Amerasia Journal*, 20 (1): 188–90.

—— (2001) "Morphing Race into Ethnicity: Asian Americans and Critical Transformations of Whiteness," *Boundary 2*, 28 (1): 153–94.

Lim, S. G.-L. (1993) "Assaying the Gold; or, Contesting the Ground of Asian-American Literature," *New Literary History* 24: 147–69.

Machor, J. L. (1980) "Emily Dickinson and the Feminine Rhetoric," *Arizona Quarterly* 36: 131–46.

Messud, C. (1993) Review of *The Holder of the World*, *Times Literary Supplement*, 12 November, p. 23.

Mishra, V. (1996) "New Lamps for Old: Diasporas, Migrancy, Border(s)," in Harish Trivedi and Meenakshi Mukherjee (eds), *Interrogating Post-Colonialism: Theory, Text and Context*, Shimla: Indian Institute of Advanced Study, pp. 67–86.

Mukherjee, B. (n.d.) "On Being an American Writer," in *Writers on America: 15 Reflections*. US Department of State. Online. Available at http://usinfo.state.gov/products/pubs/writers (accessed February 2, 2006).

—— (1981) "An Invisible Woman" *Saturday Night*, 96 (March): 36–40.

—— (1988) "Immigrant Writing: Give Us Your Maximalists!" *New York Times Book Review* 1, August 28, pp. 28–9.

—— (1989a) *Jasmine*, New York: Viking/Penguin.

—— (1989b) "Prophet and Loss: Salman Rushdie's Migration of Souls," *Voice Literary Supplement*, (March): 9–12.

—— (1991) "A Four-Hundred-Year-Old Woman," in Janet Steinburg (ed.) *The Writer in Her Work*, Vol. II, New York: W. W. Norton, pp. 33–8.

—— (1993) *The Holder of the World*, Toronto: Harper Perennial.

—— (1997) *Leave It to Me*, New York: Knopf.

—— (2002) *Desirable Daughters*, New York: Hyperion.

—— (2004) *The Tree Bride*, New York: Hyperion.

Mukherjee, B. and Blaise, C. (1977) *Days and Nights in Calcutta*, New York: Doubleday.

Mukherjee, B. and Boyers, R. (1981) "A Conversation with V.S. Naipaul," *Salmagundi* 54 (Fall): 4–22.

Parameswaran, U. (1994) Review of *The Holder of the World*, by Bharati Mukherjee, *World Literature Today* 68 (3): 636–7.

Parry, B. (1987) "Problems in Current Theories of Colonial Discourse," *Oxford Literary Review* 9 (1–2): 27–57.

Simon, B. (2000) "Hybridity in the Americas: Reading Condé, Mukherjee and Hawthorne," in Amritjit Singh and Peter Schmidt (eds), *Postcolonial Theory and the United States: Race, Ethnicity and Literature*, Jackson, Miss.: University Press of Mississippi, pp. 412–43.

Sollors, Werner (ed.) (1989) *The Invention of Ethnicity*, New York and Oxford: Oxford University Press.

Young, Robert J. C. (1995) *Colonial Desire: Hybridity in Theory, Culture and Race*, London and New York: Routledge.

Part II
Race cathexes

5 Red, white and black

Racial exchanges in fiction by Sherman Alexie

Andrew Dix

How do people navigate the repressive alternatives of universalism and separatism?

(Clifford 1997: 11)

How should we think about American Indian identity and its intersections with other racial identities? What assumptions should inform our debates and policies on and off the reservation?

(Garroutte 2003: 4)

The three races

Near the end of the first volume of his definitive social survey, *Democracy in America* (1835), Alexis de Tocqueville offers a hopeful fable of future relations between "the three races that inhabit the territory of the United States": white, African American, Native American. While anxious about current forms of coexistence between these "naturally distinct, one might almost say hostile, races," he is encouraged by recalling a time in Alabama when he came across an Indian woman "holding by the hand a little girl of five or six who was of the white race and who, I supposed, must be the pioneer's daughter" (Tocqueville 1994: 317, 320). The potential already here for encounter across historically formidable boundaries is enhanced as these two are joined beside a spring by a "Negro woman." Tocqueville looks on as the two women, undeterred by the lack of familial or racial or cultural connection to the child, lavish "fond caresses" upon her (1994: 320). Taking place in a barely cultivated forest, the scene seems to contain within itself, in condensed form, an optimistic narrative of movement from American wilderness to multiracial polity.

However, by way of anticipating this chapter's exploration of often troubling exchanges between red, white, and black in 1990s fiction by the

Native-American writer Sherman Alexie, I want to suggest that even this apparently Utopian episode in Tocqueville negates as much as it affirms the sense of American multiculturalism. To begin with, white privilege is hardly relinquished here in the interests of a more equal racial settlement: Despite "her weakness and her age," the young girl exhibits "by her slightest movements a sense of superiority" (Tocqueville 1994: 320). And, just as whiteness stays aloof from other ethnicities in this passage, so, too, there is no convincing rapprochement of red and black. Though both women are tender towards the child, their ways of expressing this confirm a sense of distance between themselves and their respective cultures rather than movement towards what Paul Gilroy celebrates as "outer-national, transcultural reconceptualisation" (1993: 17). If the African-American woman seems "equally divided between almost maternal affection and servile fear," the Native American, even in attending to the child, looks "free, proud, and almost fierce" (Tocqueville 1994: 320).

In thinking about the implications of this episode for the mapping of race relations in later American culture—including Alexie's fiction—we can turn for a moment to the concept of "triangular desire" (Girard 1965: 1–52). Following Girard's model, the white girl described here may, positively, be understood as mediating a desire for political and social connection between representatives of the other two races who have historically been detached from each other within the USA. Yet, for Girard, this sort of triangulated situation is also liable to warp from a figure of desire to one of competition: Instead of mutually supportive contact between two previously separated parties, there may be savage struggle for the mediator's favor. This appears to be the case in Tocqueville: The interposition of white America as represented by the little girl divides black and red races again rather than facilitating their alliance. And, as these two women from the first half of the nineteenth century communicate most intimately, not with each other, but with the dominant racial force in the USA, they exhibit a type of consciousness that bell hooks, writing in the mid-1990s, identifies as still a risk for America's minority populations: "Such jockeying for white approval and reward obscures the way allegiance to the existing social structure undermines the social welfare of all people of color" (1996: 199).

There are cogent historical reasons for tension and difference between red and black in the USA. Writing elsewhere about the relationship of these two ethnicities, hooks projects "a vision of cross-cultural contact where reciprocity and recognition of the primacy of community are affirmed" (1992: 81). Yet, this statement may be premature in its universalizing aspiration: hooks understates the complicity of representatives of red and black in the other race's subjugation by white power in

America. While some Native Americans shared the fate of slavery with African Americans, other Indian nations—Cherokee, Chickasaw, Choctaw and Creek among them—were themselves, at times, slaveholders (Kolchin 1995: 7–8, 99). Recollection of red/black military cooperation against white armies during the three Seminole Wars (1817–58) has to be offset by reference to the "buffalo soldiers," those black troops deployed in the suppression of Native-American resistance on the Great Plains in the 1870s and 1880s (Marable 1984: 37–8). Nonmilitarily, racial divisions were also exacerbated during the nineteenth century by what Michael Elliott calls a federal "strategy of triangulation" (1999: 625). "Triangulation" here is of the competitive rather than connective sort and refers to white authority's policy of playing off one subordinate race against the other (for example, by offering Indians US citizenship on certain conditions, yet withholding this privilege from African Americans).

We should not expect to find, then, in Alexie's mapping of exchanges between red and black, an idealization of contact between the races. Nor does his work relinquish a sense of the particularity of the Native-American situation; all of his writing endorses one social scientist's belief that although Indian struggle "has complex continuities with, and linkages to, the situations of other oppressed peoples in America," it is not identical with or reducible to these (Biolsi 2001: 175). Nevertheless, Alexie's fiction emerges in the wake of a period of increased, youth-led Indian militancy that witnessed the productive exchange of ideas, strategies, and political languages between African and Native Americans. The "Black Power" movement in the 1960s nourished the formulation of "Red Power" by, among others, the Standing Rock Sioux activist, Vine Deloria, Jr. In another political exchange across racial lines, the American Indian Movement (AIM), founded in Minneapolis-St. Paul in 1968, echoed the Black Panther Party in Oakland by selecting as its first target racist urban policing. Indeed, by repositioning Indian nationalism within a general critique of racism and inequality in the USA and by drawing upon both native resistance leaders of the nineteenth century and the African American-centered work of Malcolm X and Martin Luther King, AIM seems exemplary of new kinds of coalition between red and black.

In what follows, I aim to assess the prospects for red and black hybridity—also, at times, red, black, and white hybridity—in three texts by Alexie: the novels *Reservation Blues* ([1995] 1996) and *Indian Killer* ([1996] 1998), and the short story collection *The Lone Ranger and Tonto Fistfight in Heaven* ([1993] 1997). The chapter investigates, in particular, the politics of racial and cultural hybridization. Here it both borrows from and wishes to contest Paul Gilroy's influential work on race. His critique of all notions of racial purity and cultural self-sufficiency, his investment instead in "the flows, exchanges, and in-between elements that call the very desire to be centred into question" (1993: 190) are axiomatic for the following discussion. Yet, in considering Alexie's fiction, I want also to guard against a tendency—sometimes visible in Gilroy—to absolutize hybridization as the only desirable model of culture and politics. Such thinking risks obscuring the strategic uses that, in certain circumstances, might still be made of concepts of home, cultural separatism, even—perhaps—ethnic purity. We can usefully follow James Clifford's injunction to practice detailed conjunctural analysis when assessing different positions on race; the political consequences of hybridity, as of "universalism" and "separatism," cannot be assumed in advance but have to be newly tallied in each specific case:

> [T]here is no reason to assume that crossover practices are always liberatory or that articulating an autonomous identity or a national culture is always reactionary. The politics of hybridity is conjunctural and cannot be deduced from theoretical principles. In most situations, what matters politically is who deploys nationality or transnationality, authenticity or hybridity, against whom, with what relative power and ability to sustain a hegemony.
>
> (Clifford 1997: 10)

The problems of cosmopolitanism

For Arnold Krupat, there are, broadly speaking, three contemporary Native American perspectives (2002: 1–23). The first two of these—which he calls nationalism and indigenism, respectively—tend to separate out Indian experience from other communities and traditions in the USA. Drawing upon centuries of negotiating treaties with white settlers as one sovereign power to another, Native-American nationalism emphasizes an autonomy—territorial, political, psychic—that is not subject to moderation or revision by external forces. "Indigenism" grounds Indian identity in the secure transmission over generations of a body of ancestral lore. In much of Alexie's fiction, however, both positions are in a state of crisis. Any assertion of Indian sovereignty, for example, has to resort to counterfactual, wish-fulfilling forms in view of the multiple evidences provided in his work of white rule (from nineteenth-century cavalry generals to meddling contemporary emissaries of the Bureau of Indian Affairs). And, while the indigenist voice is certainly heard in Alexie—the novels and short stories are studded with traditional storytelling—it tends to be qualified, italicized, vulnerable to parody. This is the note struck when the narrator of an early story states that a visionary experience to be sought near a lake will be "very fucking Indian. Spiritual shit, you know" (Alexie 1997: 14).

Alexie's fiction thus seems likely to be aligned instead with the third, more outward-looking Indian perspective identified by Krupat: namely, cosmopolitanism, which is based upon a sense of continuous, productive encounter with cultures beyond Native America. Such a position is decentered, pluralist, impure, conscious of the socially health-giving "antitoxins that can be discovered and celebrated in crossing cultures" (Gilroy 2001: 93). It provides some conceptual underpinning for Alexie's work from the beginning. While *The Lone Ranger and Tonto Fistfight in Heaven*, his first full-length collection of stories, is largely reservation-set and has an almost exclusively Native-American cast of characters, it is still recognizably the product of a cosmopolitan imaginary. An Indian father here finds valuable resources for understanding his own situation in the varied musics of the white Hank Williams and black Jimi Hendrix (Alexie 1997: 30). Although a Native American woman's distinctive ability to dance both "Indian and white" (Alexie 1997: 200) is more ambiguous—the two kinds of dancing remain "mutually exclusive" rather than generating a hybridized third style—it, too, has at least the potential for a liberatory crossing of borders. More urgently political border crossing also occurs in these stories. When Thomas Builds-the-Fire, the Spokane tribe's indefatigable storyteller, is on his way to prison, he shares a bus with inmates whose ethnic diversity goes beyond Tocqueville's enumeration of the races composing the USA: "four African men, one Chicano, and a white man from the smallest town in the state" (Alexie 1997: 103). Prompted by this spectacle of multicultural America, Thomas conceives of prison as "a new kind of reservation, barrio, ghetto, logging-town tin shack" (Alexie 1997: 103), and thereby achieves a sense of common cause with other ethnicities and cultures that would be less available to nationalist or indigenist ways of being Indian. During *The Lone Ranger and Tonto Fistfight in Heaven*, this transnational imperative, on occasion, extends beyond the territory of the USA to galvanize a more global antiracist project. Note the Native American combatants in the Vietnam War who recognize themselves more in the enemy than in the state for which they are ostensibly fighting: "Seymour said every single gook he killed looked exactly like someone he knew on the reservation" (Alexie 1997: 121).

The cosmopolitan perspective is also very apparent in Alexie's first novel, *Reservation Blues*. Indeed, from its title onwards, the text appears to make the fusion of cultural traditions not only its central thematic concern but also its chief compositional method. Mindful of the fact that the cultural "combinations and entanglements" Alexie maps here are "fraught with tension," Douglas Ford nevertheless argues forcefully for the reach and value of the novel's hybridities (2002: 211). *Reservation Blues* "rejects oversimplified heritages" and leads us "directly into the complexities of mixed heritages, both in people and in expressive forms" (Ford 2002: 202); its insistence on "miscegenation" at every level from narrative to discourse makes it a riposte not only to white and black nationalisms in the USA but also to "the kind of nationalism or tribalism we might see in other Native American writers" (2002: 210). Certainly, the text has a powerful cosmo-politan strain that goes some way to justifying Ford's argument. Its action, in the first place, is generated, not by a gesture of Indian nationalism, but rather by the arrival on the Spokane reservation of the legendary black musician Robert Johnson. For a time, at least, prospects for cross-cultural contact seem good and extend even to whites. A Native-American dreamcatcher presented to the Catholic priest Father Arnold is decorated with rosary beads, hinting at the emergence of a syncretic white/red faith rather than the preservation of two opposing and static forms of belief (Alexie 1996: 250). Consider also the coyote which is referenced by the novel's Native-American musicians in the name of their rock and blues band: Coyote Springs. While this choice of name would seem to express a Native-American indigenism because of the coyote's central place in tribal myth, Thomas Builds-the-Fire also notes in his journal that the cry of the coyote has been compared to the voices of two great American blues singers: the black Sippie Wallace and white Janis Joplin (Alexie 1996: 48). A motif previously associated with only one community is thus loosened and becomes the means of connecting with other ethnic and aesthetic traditions of the USA. In similarly expansive spirit, a list of the American dead in *Reservation Blues* includes not only the Indian victims of massacres at Sand Creek (1864) and Wounded Knee (1890), but also the non-Indians Malcolm X, Martin Luther King, Jimi Hendrix (fondly remembered again), John and Robert Kennedy, and even Marilyn Monroe. Only The Doors' Jim Morrison—a recurrent hate-figure in the novel, his music said to appeal only to "White guys"—is refused a place in this multiracial commemoration (Alexie 1996: 117).

As Ford and other critics have noted, multiculturalism in *Reservation Blues* is communicated not only by narrative investigation but also by textual performance. Alexie frequently declines here a mythic or folkloric Native-American discourse in favor of a pop-postmodern idiom that takes its references and rhythms from many cultures across the USA and beyond. The novel's more magical narratives may owe as much to recent anti-colonial Latin-American fiction as to traditional Indian storytelling. Nevertheless, it is with this strain of magical narrative that we can begin to assess the strength of Alexie's cosmopolitanism. Take, to begin with, the representation in *Reservation Blues* of red/black contacts. Certainly, the

presence of Robert Johnson's guitar on the reservation opens up a potentially discrete Indian nationalism to knowledge of cognate sufferings of
African Americans: "The smell of sweat, blood, and cotton filled the room.
Cotton, cotton" (Alexie 1996: 175). hooks points out that the construction
of reservations away from major centers of black population has tended
historically to isolate Native-American and African-American liberation
struggles from one another (1996: 197). Thus, the bonds between black
and red in the novel seem wish-fulfilling rather than an extrapolation from
tendencies in actually existing American politics. Fantasy here consists less
in the relatively banal fact of Johnson's survival after his recorded death in
1938 than in this degree of exchange across boundaries of race and culture.

Reservation Blues also raises questions of red/white relations that Alexie
will explore in more ominous, vengeful mode in his subsequent novel, the
crime thriller *Indian Killer*. Even in the earlier text, occasional gestures
towards incorporating whites in a remodeled racial dispensation in the
USA are neither sustained nor programmatic. A type of vision entirely
distinct from the dominant culture's optic is allegorized near the end when
Johnson's sight is said to have improved "tremendously" during his time on
the reservation: whereas "White spots clouded one eye" in his youth in racist
Mississippi, now he sees clearly (Alexie 1996: 261). Elsewhere in *Reservation
Blues*, white modalities of response to Native Americans range from mas-
sacring them in the nineteenth century to impoverishing and exploiting
them in the twentieth. The fact that "Sheridan" and "Wright" here name
both cavalry generals in the Indian Wars and present-day record producers out to fleece Coyote Springs suggests that white oppression of Native
America has not so much fallen into abeyance as been subtly retooled.

For both *Reservation Blues* and *Indian Killer*, and even for some of the
stories in *The Lone Ranger and Tonto Fistfight in Heaven*, the issue is whether, in
the presently unequal society of the USA, there can be *any* white relationship to or mediation of red which is not marked by power. To adopt
Clifford's terms from above, white "deploy[ment]" of "hybridity" and
"transnationality" in Alexie's fiction is more often hegemonic and oppor-
tunist than it is liberatory. There is no clearer example than the white
record producers' attempt in *Reservation Blues* to preserve a Native-
American band—"People want to hear Indians" (Alexie 1996: 269)—even
after its original, ethnically appropriate members have left. Sheridan
announces that Betty and Veronica, two white "Wannabe Indians," are
viable replacements. Admittedly, some cosmetic adjustment will be necessary—"Get them into the tanning booth. Darken them up a bit ... Dye
their hair black"—but this is a mere formality, since the women "really
understand what it means to be Indian" (Alexie 1996: 269). The producers' behavior is egregious, of course, but usefully discloses how border

crossing is politically undecidable rather than uniformly progressive. As commentators from a nonliterary field have recently argued, there are two, opposing cosmopolitanisms: the first "adversarial" and directed against dubious nationalisms and oppressive power blocs; the second "corporatist" and pursued—as here in *Reservation Blues*—for reasons of economic and political advantage (Hess and Zimmermann 2006: 99).

Alexie has spoken in interview about his own facility in cultural border crossing. Because of structural inequalities in the USA, the performance or mimicry of another culture's signs is a regular occurrence for him: "I live in the white world ... I have to be white every day" (Fraser 2000–1: 61). Yet, the tone here is downbeat: What might be seen from a cosmopolitan perspective as a liberating movement across cultural lines is recast as an act of ethnic alienation or betrayal. Given this sentiment, it is unsurprising that in both fiction and extra-fictional pronouncements Alexie should have cast doubt upon the prospects for a politically radical crossing-over from white to red culture. During the same interview with Joelle Fraser he asserts that well-regarded texts about Indian communities by such non-Indians as Larry McMurtry and Barbara Kingsolver are actually "outsider books" or, worse, "colonial literature," since their authors do not have the guarantee of authenticity that comes from "liv[ing] in the Indian world" (Fraser 2000–1: 61). What hooks calls "the authority of experience" (1990: 130) is sometimes supplemented in Alexie, as an underpinning of Indian identity, by the authority of genetics itself. When an apparently white boy in *Reservation Blues* demonstrates sensitivity and skill in native fancydancing, this is attributed not to sensitive engagement with another's culture but to the Indian component of his previously unidentified mixed parentage (Alexie 1996: 82–3).

Alexie's critique of cosmopolitanism intensifies in *Indian Killer*, the disturbing successor to the textually more playful and dishevelled *Reservation Blues*. Despite work by Garroutte and other social scientists on present-day diverse and contested grounds for Native-American identity, the novel is suspicious of culturalist argument that "Indianness" may be affirmed in performance of traditional customs rather than by membership of a tribal roll or possession of an adequate blood quantum. A key figure here is Clarence Mather, the novel's white lecturer in Native-American literature. Mather's reading list includes several texts that display knowledge of Indian lore, but, as his Indian student Marie Polatkin points out, were actually "co-written by white men": *Black Elk Speaks, Lame Deer: Seeker of Visions* and *Lakota Woman* (Alexie 1998: 58). Though damaged by his personal mannerisms, the case Mather makes for the hybridized, double-voiced nature of much Native-American writing—its inscription of both red and white—is still a cogent one. His critique of essentialist thinking about Native-American writing and identity is persuasive (not least to the anxious, non-Indian writer of this article). Yet, rhetorically, it is overpowered by the nativist ideology of Marie, who functions almost as "the voice of the text," given that her views are subjected to significant dialogism neither by other characters nor by the impersonal narrator. Marie wants to replace Mather's canon of hybridized Native-American writings by "real Indian books" (Alexie 1998: 67); she also appeals to Indian blood as the prerequisite for those who profess to teach this community's literature (1998: 312). Elsewhere, too, *Indian Killer* seems to substitute for a model of cultural exchanges and movements what Gilroy deplores as "the sedentary poetics of either soil or blood" (2001: 111). It is to the politics of this position that we now turn.

Red fascism

In texts including *The Black Atlantic* and *Between Camps*, Gilroy has not exempted victimized peoples from his critique of ethnicities that seek to base themselves upon authentic bloodline: proponents of black—and, for our purposes, red—nationalism are included in his strictures against "cultural absolutists of various phenotypical hues" (1993: 223). As a moment on the way towards a fully postracial future in which the pigmentation of skin will cease to signify, he projects a vision of "polychromatic and multiethnic utopias" (Gilroy 2001: 51). Demographically, Native Americans seem already headed for such polychromaticity: in 1990, the latest US Census to be compiled before Alexie wrote the fiction discussed here showed that while only 1 percent of married white Americans and 2 percent of black had partners from another race, the comparable figure for married Native Americans was higher than 50 percent (Wilson 1998: 424). Not all commentators welcome this social development: In a nation where state and federal aid to tribes is dependent upon accurate population survey, some kind of defense of Indian blood—or "strategic essentialism"—may be one of the community's political options (Biolsi 2001: 176).

However, social-scientific hesitations on the subject of multiethnicity are discreet when compared with the animus directed against it in much of Alexie's writing. Racial hybridity figures here as dangerous, even politically suicidal for Native Americans. In *The Lone Ranger and Tonto Fistfight in Heaven*, it is true, there is a "child born of white mother and red father," and "Both sides of this baby are beautiful" (Alexie 1997: 148). Typical of the novels that come after, however, is a genetically based proposition of Indian identity. Ford's essay on hybridity in *Reservation Blues* is a little too relaxed about the rhetorical verve summoned up against miscegenation by such figures as Chess. And what are only sporadic instances of biological thinking in the earlier novel become a key part of the narrative logic itself of *Indian Killer*. Krupat argues that the text's "type of 'racism' … is not based on 'racial' assumptions about biology or blood" (2002: 115); yet this seems too kind an assessment of its racial discourse. Note the novel's failure to include any fulfilled character of mixed race: Biological impurity as much as inappropriate cultural conditioning seems to be to blame for the fact that, compared with full-blooded Marie's strong sense of Indian identity, part-white characters like her cousin Reggie Polatkin endure a rootless, alienated existence.

Might the ideological position of *Indian Killer* properly be described as one of "red fascism"? In raising the question, I draw again on Gilroy, who has identified "black fascists" as responsible for certain formulations of African-American identity (2001: 231–7). This racial variant of fascism is, like its parent ideology, to be regarded as "both a minor political option and a major cultural reference point" (Gilroy 2001: 149). For Gilroy, it is characterized not only by "biopolitics" but also dissolution of individual will in the collective; performance of an often theatricalized violence; and commitment to a state of "permanent emergency" in which "anything is possible" (2001: 84). All of these markers of fascism can be traced in *Indian Killer*. Violence is enacted in the novel against a range of white victims who are frequently figured, in fascist style, as social trash (from the "Wannabe Indian" thriller writer Jack Wilson to the businessman who dies after visiting a pornographic bookstore). Marie points out that scalping is itself a cross-cultural practice, adopted by Native Americans from French colonists (Alexie 1998: 57); yet, the novel's descriptions of scalping and distribution of owl feathers hint at the revival of Indian identity in alien Seattle through a ritualized violence. The variations which Alexie plays upon thriller conventions also advance a sense of Native-American collectivity. Rather than identifying the killer according to generic norms— thereby making him less of an incarnation of communal will—the text gives clues to multiple suspects, including Reggie and Marie Polatkin as well as John Smith. Although suspicion also falls upon a white murderer who may be acting out racist stereotypes of Native-American cruelty, this option is the least likely and does not alter the way in which the unsolved crimes permit fantasies of collective Indian vengeance against the white oppressor. Alexie's reworking of the crime genre to emphasize a near-fantastical, unremitting violence carried out in the name of his community thus has echoes of that marginalized, sublime variant of historiography which Hayden White notes is "charged with avenging the people" and refuses "to recognize that 'the war is over'" (White 1987: 81).

Put this way, the politics of Alexie's novel may seem irredeemably reactionary. One reviewer calls *Indian Killer* "nasty" and "ugly," and objects to the way in which racial hostility here is "structural" rather than merely a subject matter (Gorra 1998: 22). This type of ideological critique is indispensable: Krupat, too, in a generally positive response to the novel, acknowledges its "fairly straightforward, if rather sinister politics" (2002: 116). Nevertheless, I want to sketch a more progressive reading of *Indian Killer* to run alongside such a negative hermeneutic. Here we might follow Fredric Jameson's suggestion in the closing pages of *The Political Unconscious* that a "functional" or "instrumental" analysis of cultural artifacts should always be combined with an interpretative method that is "anticipatory" or "collective-associational" (1981: 296). From this perspective, nationalistic or fascistic elements of *Indian Killer* are not only morbid political symptoms but also traces of longing for Utopia; indeed, this degree of fantasy is disclosed precisely by those uglier textual instances. While the unleashing of purgative violence against whites described here is disquieting, it encodes, too, a dream of communal restoration at a time when Native Americans still face racism, poverty, and injustice at the hands of white-dominated authority in the USA. In insisting upon the primary claim made by his people, Alexie also avoids any premature or naïve appeal to universality; as he has said in interview: "I don't want to be universal" (Fraser 2000–1: 68).

Indian Killer ends by dreaming of return to a monochromatic America. The novel's final sequence, "A Creation Story," traces a reverse movement from that with which we began in Tocqueville: instead of projecting transracial connections, this ending describes a single race gathered ritually together in a setting free of the marks of American modernity such as miscegenation, urbanization, even money. Although the reservation cemetery and the "two bloody scalps" (Alexie 1998: 419) the killer carries are signifiers still of an antagonistic white presence, the episode also includes the revival of a politically charged communal dance (compare the reference to the militantly anti-white Ghost Dance in the seemingly more cosmopolitan *The Lone Ranger and Tonto Fistfight in Heaven* [Alexie 1997: 17]). Here, finally, by a great effort of counterfactual thinking, is "Red Power." Writing in the mid-1990s, Alexie thereby reoccupies that Native-American ideological terrain of the 1960s and 1970s most strikingly explored by Vine Deloria, Jr. Despite the movement's analogies with African-American struggle, Deloria suggests that "Red Power" is valuable not for building coalitions across the oppressed of several races but for sharpening theorization of Indian separatism. Red relationship not only with white but with black, too, is annulled, or at least depleted, as Deloria argues that "we must all create social isolates" (1969: 194). Affinities between land and blood are so primal that only a given territory's "original" inhabitants may successfully occupy it. "So will America return to the red man" (Deloria

1969: 178), Deloria prophesizes—a position that effectively repatriates not only whites but also African Americans (to say nothing of Latinos and those other ethnic groupings that have arrived in the USA subsequent to Tocqueville's relatively simple racial configuration).

It is precisely this mythic reclaiming of America as essentially Indian which seems attempted at the end of *Indian Killer*. I want to finish, however, by suggesting that, ultimately, the text cannot manufacture enough purist antibodies to ward off invasion from other, non-Indian cultures: A novel at least partly given over to the thesis of national, even racial self-sufficiency is actually constituted in large measure by acts of cross-cultural borrowing. Compared with *Reservation Blues*, *Indian Killer* indeed goes a long way towards erasing hybridities not only between red and white but also between red and black. "Black music was rare" (Alexie 1998: 275)—and black presence at the level of plot is similarly attenuated. Yet, despite these narrative omissions, African-American culture is always already present in *Indian Killer*. For what is this novel but a contemporary Indian reworking of the black novelist Richard Wright's *Native Son* (1940)? Ultimately, mobilizing a discourse of class that has only faint echoes in *Indian Killer*, *Native Son* projects coalitions across racial lines: Black and white are mediated by the different red of Communism. Nevertheless, pre-empting Alexie, Wright adopts for potentially nationalist purposes popular genres such as Gothic and the thriller; his text, too, is ambiguous in how it evaluates a wrathful violence unleashed against white power. While Krupat notes this particular literary debt, he fails to consider how it undermines *Indian Killer*'s separatist politics. And, besides this borrowing from Wright, Alexie's novel is further "African-Americanized" where it draws tacitly upon the oratory and autobiography of Malcolm X for its shorthand anathematizing of whites as "blue eyes." Even as Alexie's work speaks officially of communal autonomy, then, it continues in its deepest structures to bear witness to complex, inescapable exchange across races and cultures.[1]

Notes

1 Alexie's evolving racial imaginary may be traced in two post-1990s short story collections. From *The Toughest Indian in the World* (2000), see, for instance, "The Sin Eaters," "Indian Country," "Dear John Wayne" and the title story; from *Ten Little Indians* (2003), see, for instance, "The Search Engine" and the African-American-centred "Lawyer's League."

References

Alexie, S. ([1995] 1996) *Reservation Blues*, London: Minerva.
—— ([1993] 1997) *The Lone Ranger and Tonto Fistfight in Heaven*, London: Vintage.

—— ([1996] 1998) *Indian Killer*, London: Vintage.

Biolsi, T. (2001) "Contemporary Native American Struggles," in I. Susser and T. C. Patterson (eds), *Cultural Diversity in America: A Critical Reader*, Malden, Mass.: Blackwell.

Clifford, J. (1997) *Routes: Travel and Translation in the Late Twentieth Century*, Cambridge, Mass.: Harvard University Press.

Deloria, Jr., V. (1969) *Custer Died for Your Sins: An Indian Manifesto*, New York: Avon.

Elliott, M. (1999) "Telling the Difference: Nineteenth-Century Legal Narratives of Racial Taxonomy," *Law and Social Inquiry*, 24: 611–36.

Ford, D. (2002) "Sherman Alexie's Indigenous Blues," *MELUS*, 27 (3): 197–215.

Fraser, J. (2000–1) "An Interview with Sherman Alexie," *Iowa Review*, 30 (3): 59–70.

Garroutte, E. M. (2003) *Real Indians: Identity and the Survival of Native America*, Berkeley, Calif.: University of California Press.

Gilroy, P. (1993) *The Black Atlantic: Modernity and Double Consciousness*, London and New York: Verso.

—— (2001) *Between Camps: Nations, Cultures and the Allure of Race*, Harmondsworth: Penguin.

Girard, R. (1965) *Deceit, Desire, and the Novel*, trans. Y. Freccero, Baltimore, Md.: Johns Hopkins University Press.

Gorra, M. (1998) "Hopeless Warriors," *London Review of Books* 20 (5): 21–2.

Hess, J. and Zimmermann, P. R. (2006) "Transnational Documentaries: A Manifesto," in E. Ezra and T. Rowden (eds), *Transnational Cinema: The Film Reader*, London and New York: Routledge.

hooks, b. (1990) *Yearning: Race, Gender, and Cultural Politics*, Boston, Mass.: South End Press.

—— (1992) *Black Looks: Race and Representation*, Boston, Mass.: South End Press.

—— (1996) *Killing Rage: Ending Racism*, Harmondsworth: Penguin.

Jameson, F. (1981) *The Political Unconscious: Narrative as a Socially Symbolic Act*, London: Methuen.

Kolchin, P. (1995) *American Slavery 1619–1877*, Harmondsworth: Penguin.

Krupat, A. (2002), *Red Matters: Native American Studies*, Philadelphia, Pa.: University of Pennsylvania Press.

Marable, M. (1984) *Race, Reform and Rebellion: The Second Reconstruction in Black America, 1945–82*, Basingstoke: Macmillan.

Tocqueville, A. de (1994) *Democracy in America*, trans. G. Lawrence, ed. J. P. Mayer, London: Fontana.

White, H. (1987) *The Content of the Form: Narrative Discourse and Historical Representation*, Baltimore, Md.: Johns Hopkins University Press.

Wilson, J. (1998) *The Earth Shall Weep: A History of Native America*, London: Picador.

6 In the shadow of the gun

African-American fiction and the anxieties of nostalgia

Andrew Warnes

In a certain white Chicago neighborhood in 1966, hatred did not bother to wear a mask. It felt little shame; only dismay at the Civil Rights campaigners invading the white streets, marching to protest unofficial segregation practices in the city as they had the official racism long upheld across the South. Nor was this hatred camera shy. It looked television audiences in the eye, chanting "White Power!" while hurling rocks and spit into the faces of those on the ground (Ling 2002: 220). No strangers to racial extremism, even Martin Luther King Jr. and other veterans of the old Civil Rights struggle to secure Southern voting rights were shocked by what they saw in suburban Chicago. But strategists close to King were also quick to grasp that, like 1957 footage of white mobs screaming at Little Rock Central High School's new black entrants, newsreel of thugs tearing into the first American to receive a Nobel Peace Prize would prove a godsend to the movement. Evidence of who is and is not on the side of civilization rarely comes clearer than images captured on tape that summer, in which King, walking through a city he called the richest in the world, talks to journalists with customary patience and beauty while all around him bigots yell out in voices made strange by brute and savage hate (King 1968: 113).

After Chicago and news events like it, American racial discourse changed. From then on, it became harder to defend the blistering and unmasked display of racial hatred while remaining part of polite society. Opponents of black equality began to find that they could ill afford to say so publicly, being better advised to play on fears of crime, talk about state rights, or otherwise intimate racist attitudes without mentioning them outright. King's assassination in 1968 and the wave of national remorse that followed it forced overt racism further underground. From the 1980s onward, as few openly racist politicians clung to office, and as the national media reveled in rap and other black cultural products, it even became possible to depict racism as a thing of the past. As George Bush Jr.'s Press

Secretary Tony Snow put it in October 2003, the "unmentionable secret" is that "racism isn't that big a deal any more. No sensible person supports it. Nobody of importance preaches it. It's rapidly becoming an ugly memory."[1] Today, a wealth of evidence appears to support this belief. Reports of the rising numbers of black millionaires, the unprecedented visibility of black faces in national politics, and the establishment of African-American studies throughout the country's university system persuade conservatives both black and white that the days of widespread racist hatred are over. Equality, in their eyes, has become a matter of binding up the wounds of the past. It will be reached the moment African Americans "get over" their bad memories, seizing opportunities now before them.

Throughout the 1990s, black political and cultural commentators spent much time grappling with this growing conservative feeling. Even those keen to shut out white interference and concentrate on their black constituencies felt duty bound to explain why, if racism belonged to the past, so many African Americans were still languishing in jail and dying before their time. The Million Man March on Washington, DC of October 1995 was the most prominent response to this troubling chasm between rhetoric extolling the new "postracist" consensus and the harsh realities of ghetto life. Organized by Nation of Islam figureheads Louis Farrakhan and Benjamin Franklin Chavis and designed to echo the famous Civil Rights March on Washington of 1963, the protest set out a position that, while loudly insisting that white racism was alive and well, was louder still in its demand that black men stand on their own two feet. Rightwing propagandists like Rush Limbaugh were too busy fulminating against the Nation of Islam to notice that this "extremist" movement was espousing classic American values, championing family life, self-reliance, and other principles of which Chavis's namesake would have approved.

Nor were Chavis and Farrakhan the only black leaders who seemed to concede ground to conservatism. Importantly, Stephen Steinberg accused Cornel West of a loss of nerve, arguing that, while the Christian philosopher's seminal *Race Matters* (1993) asks all the right questions, insisting that attempts to combat ghetto "nihilism" cannot just offer "a vulgar rendition of Horatio Alger in blackface," the answers that it goes on to give are inadequate, abandoning any demand for government intervention in favor of a new "love ethic": an initiative Steinberg dismisses as a conveniently "inexpensive ... crusade against nihilism to be waged from within the black community." Whereas King demanded decisive government leadership, arguing that "a society that had done something special *against* the Negro for hundreds of years must now do something special *for* him" (1968: 106), West "explicitly divorces nihilism from the political economy, thus implying that moral redemption is to be achieved through ... [an]

utterly inconsequential 'politics of conversion'" (1998: 38). Still the sense remains that Steinberg's is the anger of disappointment. West, he still seems to feel, strikes at the heart of things when he comments:

> The genius of our black foremothers and forefathers was to create powerful buffers to ward off the nihilistic threat, to equip black folk with cultural armor to beat back the demons of hopelessness, mean-inglessness, and lovelessness ... In fact, until the early seventies black Americans had the lowest suicide rate in the United States. But now young black people lead the nation in suicides.
>
> What has changed? What went wrong? The bitter irony of inte-gration? The cumulative effects of a genocidal conspiracy? The virtual collapse of rising expectations after the optimistic sixties?
>
> (West 1993: 15–16)

Contemporary black fiction offered other responses to these dispiriting questions. Throughout the 1990s, as arguments over ghetto nihilism raged, many novelists sought shelter in history, seeing the century out by return-ing to key episodes from the past. Toni Morrison's *Beloved* (1987) did much to bring about this historical turn, its powerful vision of slavery and even of the slave trade from a black point of view persuading other writers to approach the novel as a form that could give voice to people marginalized or altogether missing from the historical record. Numerous artists rallied behind Morrison's demand that fiction fill in the gaps of American history. John Edgar Wideman's shuttling between the slave past and the post-1980 present in *The Cattle Killing* (1996) and other novels, Walter Mosley's per-sistent return to postwar Los Angeles in his Easy Rawlins fiction, and Ernest Gaines's evocation of 1940s Florida in *A Lesson Before Dying* (1993) all confirmed that, during the 1990s, the African-American novel was remaking itself into a quintessentially historical form. Certainly these wri-ters all seem to regard theirs as a historical vocation. Literature appears itself to them a chance to imagine ordeals suffered and resistance under-taken by forebears ostracized from recorded, mainstream American nar-rative. Novels challenge the legacy of Eurocentrism, recovering black voices lost to the past.

This retreat into history can suggest a sense of ambivalence about the complex tragedies besieging 1990s America. It can suggest a desire to escape into history, to vanish into the past to escape the ugly present. The least we should say is that 1990s black fiction is marked by generational difference, its historical turn being an unsurprising move by writers who reached adulthood in the radical and sometimes optimistic 1960s and who now looked on aghast at the rise of ghetto and gangsta style. At the same time, however, 1990s black novels by no means evade the tough questions being asked by Cornel West. Even those who seem engulfed by nostalgia, whose narratives seem determined to remain at all times in the past, critique the present insofar as they place the living moment of literary creation into an unspoken but urgent comparison with a history that West was not alone in considering inspirational. Fictional memories of the complex heroism of yesterday, such as Gaines's *A Lesson Before Dying*, speak powerfully to the complex tragedies of today, obliquely appealing "for a renewal of belief in black community" across a contemporary black world torn asunder by drugs and gang violence (Byerman 2005: 53). John Edgar Wideman's postmodern habit of breaking narrative apart in order to juxtapose history and the present only brings to the surface a widespread impulse to place ghetto nihilism onto a long timeline and thence to contrast it with the astonishing forbearance of the past.

It is a process brought to perfection in *Jazz* (1992). Here, in Toni Morrison's sixth novel, we witness a kind of master class in the production of African-American literary narrative. Hallmarks of the tradition, from its use of improvisation to the celebration of black orality that Henry Louis Gates Jr. has called "the speakerly" (2004: xxxviii), achieve a new aesthetic brilliance over the course of this dazzling novel. The sheer audacity of Morrison's one-word title alone announces that she is fully aware that it rightfully belongs at the heart of the American canon.

At length, however, and without ever quite forgetting its landmark status, *Jazz* reveals that it is otherwise a conventional work of 1990s black fiction—a work every bit as eager to avoid directly confronting ghetto nihilism as *A Lesson Before Dying*, Albert French's *Holly* (1994) or Alice Walker's *Possessing the Secret of Joy* (1992). Nor is this retreat from the present only apparent in the fact that, like these bestselling novels, *Jazz* takes place in the period before King's Civil Rights achievements. Morrison had long since staked her reputation on the production of historical fiction. All of her novels, from her 1970 debut *The Bluest Eye* onward, proceed from the premise that "there once was a *there* there and now it is gone," as Barbara Johnson has put it (1998: 76–7). And, even as these works anticipate the historical turn of 1990s black fiction, *Song of Solomon* (1977) especially looks ahead to the political crises of that decade, all but prophesying West's concerns with the growing nihilism among black youth. So it becomes hard not to notice that, compared to *Song of Solomon*'s National Suicide Day, nothing of obvious relevance to such nihilism appears in *Jazz*. Talk of gangsterism or drugs fades from this novel as, throughout, Morrison steers clear of naked allegory, concentrating instead on the development of a truly jazzlike prose that can do justice to all things beautiful in black life.

I'm crazy about this City.

Daylight slants like a razor cutting the buildings in half ... A city like this one makes me dream tall and feel in on things. Hep. ... When I look over strips of green grass lining the river, at church steeples and into the cream-and-copper halls of apartment buildings, I'm strong. Alone, yes, but top-notch and indestructible—like the City in 1926 when all the wars are over and there will never be another one. The people down there in the shadow are happy about that. At last, at last, everything's ahead. ... Here comes the new. Look out. There goes the sad stuff. The bad stuff. The things-nobody-could-help stuff. The way everybody was then and there. Forget that. History is over, you all, and everything's ahead at last. ... The A & P hires a colored clerk. ... Nobody wants to be an emergency at Harlem Hospital but if the Negro surgeon is visiting, pride cuts down the pain.

(Morrison 1992: 7–8)

Even if we remove its cataloguing of social progress, deeper structures in this prose ensure that it would remain readable as a testimony to as well as an enactment of black liberation. *Jazz*'s rather cinematic play with light and shade in Manhattan, for example, perfectly complements its desire to tell the untold history of those who "train-danced" to the city as refugees from Jim Crow segregation (Morrison 1992: 36). The feel of the New York sun on the face of Morrison's narrator arguably constitutes a larger freedom than the recruitment of a few "colored clerks" to sell groceries or a single "Negro surgeon" to tend the Harlem sick. While these latter suggest social change is in fact happening slowly and in piecemeal fashion, New York's ability to "do an unbelievable sky," a sky more "like the ocean than the ocean itself," reveals that its greater and far less quantifiable freedoms stem from its sheer scale and ability to let people live life untroubled by outside scrutiny (Morrison 1992: 35). *Jazz*'s insistence that the sun shines brighter in New York than in the subtropical South suggests that black life in this tough and amazing city need no longer lurk in shadow and corner, need no longer hide behind the curtains that keep the races apart on Joe and Violet's northbound train, and can at last proceed in the open and full light of day. Discrimination might persist in Manhattan. Fifth Avenue might remain a hive of "freezing faces." Even such racism, however, seems blunted by the fact that those who endure it can travel back north of 110th Street and to a city within a city where they are anything but victims (Morrison 1992: 54).

No less than Ella Fitzgerald's "Take the 'A' Train" (1944) and its celebration that the city's subway had finally reached Harlem, *Jazz*'s brilliant prose thus seems alive with pleasure at black culture's entry into the city's public domain. Sedimented in this voice, augmenting its breathtaking

swings from story to song, is a desire to pay full tribute to "low" as well as
"high" cultural milestones achieved by black artists of the so-called Jazz
Age. Not only Jean Toomer's experiments towards a new blues literature
but also the performances of Bessie Smith among other blueswomen
return to life as *Jazz* moves from snatches of scat ("Hep") to address the
imagined black community ("you all"). From its use of alliteration and
rhyme and half-rhyme to the syllable-perfect A-A-B-A song structure that
it weaves around the word *stuff*, Morrison's prose courts comparisons with
the blues. The tricks and turns in this prose could even indicate that it is
trying to reach beyond the "speakerly," laying claim to a radically new
prose aesthetic euphonious enough to be called "singerly."

This convergence of literature and black music style, however, by no
means manifests itself as an unequivocally positive force. Ambivalence
enshrouds it. Over the course of this passage, the blurring of a blues into a
literary climax seems at last to produce a too-potent effect that propels the
narrator into what we can only call a deliberate naivety: *History is over, you
all, and everything's ahead at last.* The holler repays careful consideration. At
first glance, it captures the actual hopes that followed Armistice, nicely
conveying the optimism of those who had survived the killing fields of
northern Europe, fled the Jim Crow laws and lynchings of the South, and
now felt themselves at long last free: at long last able to become what
Alain Locke, chief publicist of the Harlem Renaissance, called full actors
"in American civilization" (1992: 15). As with the brief but vicious
description of the slaying of Dorcas's father, however, a second glance at
this holler allows us to apprehend its wider resonance—allows us to
apprehend that this image that seems so faithful to *Jazz*'s historical setting
has in fact begun to flirt with the crises of the present, allowing a displaced
and recondite consideration of 1990s America to creep back into the narrative. And it is as though *Jazz* needs this emotional distance before it can
deal with the uncomfortable violence of the present. It is as though, kick-
ing him to death, leaving his "entrails" lying on the street (Morrison 1992:
57), the white St. Louis mob who murder Dorcas's father must remain
solid and historic, aloof from naked allegory, if they are to haunt the present, if the sound of their sickening blows is to endure in camcorder footage of the police assault on Rodney King, in drive-by shootings, in the
mail and other bombings that by 1990 had become the preferred means of
white supremacist violence in America. It is as though Morrison's holler
must remain likewise loyal to its place, likewise aloof, if it can call to mind
Francis Fukuyama's "end of history" thesis—another news story hard to
avoid in 1991—and conjure from it a Joycean warning that these supposed liberations from history are so many illusions, conjured in the course
of a cruel and ongoing American nightmare.

Jazz unequivocally affirms the Great Migration. Morrison's novel accepts that this was an emancipatory movement, escorting the likes of Joe and Violet from the claustrophobic violence and spurious evictions of the South to deliver them into an altogether "sunnier," metropolitan realm. At the same time, however, Morrison clearly insists that such freedom is being imperiled by the persistence of violence in urban life and by its infiltration of the black community in particular. *Jazz* conveys this position through form as much as through content. Violet's unsuccessful attempt to desecrate Dorcas's body merely consummates omens stitched into the very fabric of Morrison's prose. Even the beautiful New York light that warms her narrator's face resembles "a razor cutting the buildings in half." Such images forever rest on the surface of *Jazz's* prose, their sharpness forever waiting to cut into its beautiful skin.

> She had been looking for that knife for a month ... But *that* Violet knew and went right to it. Knew too where the funeral was going on. ... And the ushers, young men the same age as the deceased ... gathered. ... They were the ones *that* Violet had to push aside, elbow her way into. ... The ushers saw the knife before she did. Before she knew what was going on, the boy ushers' hard hands ... were reaching toward the blade she had not seen for a month at least and was surprised to see now aimed at the girl's haughty, secret face.
> It bounced off, making a little dent under her earlobe, like a fold in the skin that was hardly a disfigurement at all.
>
> (Morrison 1992: 90–2)

Jazz's preoccupation with blades both real and metaphoric exemplifies the historical turn away from and subconscious reengagement of ghetto nihilism that I am suggesting is seminal to 1990s black fiction. Knives are like guns. Knives are not like guns. And, as the weapon of choice in rougher parts of 1920s Harlem, knives can even inspire an uncanny nostalgia: an anxious nostalgia for a time when, as addicts still drank or smoked opiates rather than crack, so violence was still penned into the tawdrier or more passionate quarters of the ghetto, the innocent having little fear of its crossfire. In its narration of events leading to Violet's schizophrenic disembodiment, *Jazz* in fact comes close to affirming these weapons, reveling dangerously in the intimacy of their violence, in their ability to draw skin against skin. You can "smile at the knife when it misses and when it doesn't," we are told (Morrison 1992: 11). Joe's mother Wild is described as a "used-to-be-long-ago-crazy girl whose neck cane cutters liked to imagine under the blade" (Morrison 1992: 167). This image is particularly ambiguous, the fantasy of misogynistic violence remaining disconcertingly tender, as though, back in the Old South, you could confuse stabs with caresses, murder with love. No such confusion effects Joe's shooting of Dorcas. He "handle[s. .. the] fat baby gun that would be as loud as a cannon," laughing as he does so (Morrison 1992: 181). "He isn't going to aim," we learn: "Not at that insulted skin" (Morrison 1992: 181). Apparently closing his eyes before firing, Joe's is less a crime of passion than a crime to *end* passion—a crime portentous and disengaging, suggestive of the nihilism that bulks large in the ghetto's impendent future.

For it is a crime whose consequences go beyond Joe, eventually echoing in the social fabric of Harlem itself. Like Sethe's decision to kill her daughter Beloved rather than send her into slavery, Joe's violence produces profound epistemological change. But if Sethe's soul is gathered back up, piece by piece, in that earlier book, Joe's shooting heralds wholesale ghettoization. Dorcas's shot and "insulted" skin is thickened by his bullet, even in death repulsing Violet's blade; knives now seem antique, as anachronistic as the fingers that did the work of "hot comb[s]" back in Virginia (Morrison 1992: 14). And, as these materials fade from the new urban landscape of African-American life, so human touch, the feel of skin against skin, grows scarce. People other than the white-gloved ushers begin to seem "hard-handed." Fingers seem to cease to "unwind" hair (Morrison 1992: 225). And knives no longer violate, no longer gain terrible knowledge of skin and the flesh behind it. Guns, *Jazz* makes us see, cause greater slaughter for more than mechanical reasons—cause greater slaughter because they make violence too easy, too remote, allowing killers to kill without even touching their victims. This, then, is how *Jazz* greets the black exodus from Jim Crow: without doubt that it spells progress, but without illusion that touching bonds of brotherhood and sisterhood first forged in the South will survive urbanization intact. Certainly it seems that, after Joe's gunshot and all that it portends, "black foremothers and forefathers" will find it hard to keep a hold of their children, harder still to "equip" them with what Cornel West called the "cultural armor" with which to ward off the "nihilistic threat."

Everything changed in Chicago. At least since World War II, Civil Rights activists had concentrated on two goals in particular: the desegregation of public facilities and the enfranchisement of black Southerners. Reports of the terrible conditions of black life in Chicago, however, ended any hope that this assault on Jim Crow could lead the country straight to complete racial harmony. No segregation laws existed on the statute books of this vast metropolis. No one of influence was going about disenfranchising black citizens. Still, however, racial inequalities were flourishing. Still, de-facto discrimination trapped black families in specific quarters of the city, forcing them to pay exorbitant rents for the limited housing stock that they found there. Still, school spending in such districts lagged far behind levels found in wealthier white neighborhoods. Dismal healthcare, job discrimination, nonexistent police attendance, and endemic police brutality all reinforced the feeling that slum life required a new, more radical agenda. Experiencing such conditions firsthand in a Lawndale apartment, Martin Luther King Jr. straightaway saw how sullen his children grew in these cramped and unclean lodgings. Soon other transformations would make him see "anew the conditions which make of the ghetto an emotional pressure cooker" (King 1968: 133), again convincing him of the need to broaden his Civil Rights ideology and to link his old and continuing concern with racism with the new issues of economic inequality and poverty. Explaining why "Molotov cocktails and rifles would not solve" ghettoization (King 1991: 389), risking accusations of Marxism, demanding governmental action against racial inequality: These were the measures that, King now saw, he needed to take if he was to offer positive change to the city's disaffected youth. Only exceptional and determined intervention stood a chance of overturning this masked American racism. As he would put it in his last and most important book, *Where Do We Go from Here: Chaos or Community?* ([1967] 1968):

> Being a Negro in America means listening to suburban policemen talk eloquently against open housing while arguing in the same breath that they are not racist. It means being harried by day and haunted by night by a nagging sense of nobodyness and constantly fighting to be saved from the poison of bitterness. ... It means the pain of watching your children grow up with the clouds of inferiority in their mental skies. ...
>   After 348 years racial injustice is still the Negro's burden and America's shame. Yet for his own inner health and outer functioning, the Negro is called upon to be as resourceful ... as those who have not known such oppression[.]
>
> (King 1968: 141–2)

Charles Johnson's *Dreamer* ([1998] 2000a), a wonderful fictionalization of King's last years, marked a fitting climax to a decade in which black novelists had repeatedly turned to the past and sought in its recreation both shelter from and a means of coming to terms with the vexatious and dispiriting present. Beginning with a vision of King and his family's life in their "wretched" and roach-infested "dump" in Lawndale (Johnson 2000a: 19), *Dreamer* soon reveals itself as a lamentation, blaming 1990s ghetto nihilism on America's failure to implement the special measures urged by this man Johnson has called the country's "preeminent moral philosopher"

(2000b: 6). America's failure to offer full reparation for slavery and racism stands behind *Dreamer* as gun crime stands behind *Jazz*. Both novels interrogate the past to comprehend the present, seeking in it the roots of the nihilism now besetting black communities nationwide.

Rudolph P. Byrd has shown that allusions grace every page of *Dreamer*, a novel almost as rich and complex as Johnson's masterpiece *Middle Passage* (1990). Both by exploring *Dreamer*'s doppelganger plot and by noticing that King's "less fortunate double" Chaym Smith lives at the same address as Bigger Thomas, the nihilistic protagonist of Richard Wright's *Native Son* (1940), Byrd demonstrates that *Dreamer* is a fluid, multilayered novel, its enquiries into violence and identity remaining forever open and unfinished (2005: 192). Having established *Dreamer*'s fluidity, however, Byrd tends to fix on the more explicit allusions of the novel: on its contemplation of the Cain and Abel story, on its doubling of King and Smith, and on its enquiry into whether "it was possible to end social evil through actions which did not then engender a greater, more devastating evil" (Johnson 2000a: 113–14). Byrd's interest in Johnson's depiction of "characters who embody the human potential" (2005: 9) leads him to view King's doppelganger Smith as a figure in whom arise new possibilities of "sacrifice, subversiveness, and improvization, [and] for advancing progressive social change" (2005: 192). Because these doubles grow more alike as the narrative progresses, because Smith lacks King's advantages yet comes to share his commitment to human love, and because both ultimately "choose to affirm life even when confronted with death," *Dreamer*, in Byrd's reading, turns out to be an affirmative work. It reveals that the:

> question of how to end evil without engendering evil is a question with which we must be continually engaged, a question for which there is no single answer … Certainly Johnson leaves us with an example in Smith and King that points the way toward the achievement of the beloved community. … *Dreamer*, Johnson's own bright book, … is, finally, … a book, like a palimpsest, that reveals and conceals its meanings.
>
> (Byrd 2005: 192)

I want to conclude by arguing that this is a bland conclusion to take from *Dreamer*. *Dreamer*, I want to suggest, is better seen as a cry of despair, a jeremiad against vulgarization and violence, against the treacherous decisions that the American leadership and people took in the years after King's early career. That is, Smith's taking of a "bullet intended for King" towards this novel's conclusion strikes Byrd as proof that these doubles overcome their mutual antipathy, overcome the Cain and Abel analogy that stalks their every encounter, to forge an inspirational fraternal bond that can light a path ahead for the fractured black society (Johnson 2000a: 209). Recollecting Dorcas's fate in *Jazz*, however, it becomes evident that this is altogether too optimistic, a reading that pays too much attention to *Dreamer's* explicit biblical allegory and too little to the eschatological and apocalyptic images through which it more generally dramatizes its increasingly violent 1960s American context. It becomes evident that Byrd is neglecting the fact that King and Smith achieve brotherly understanding at the point of annihilation. Violence certainly engulfs *Dreamer's* setting:

> The minister was now on the West Side, preaching brotherhood and peaceful revolution on streets that ran slick with blood. Black blood. ... I feared the fires might burn forever. ... Looters spilled from the building, hauling away portable Motorola televisions, shotguns, bolt-action rifles. ...
>
> When the boy slipped on broken glass from the store's shattered window the cops fell upon him, cracking his bones with a flurry of blows I felt echo through my own body. My stomach clenched. Spotting another looter, the cops took off, leaving the boy bleeding on the sidewalk. As in a dream, I watched myself running toward the spot where the boy lay. ... "Don't move," I said. "Let me help you, brother." I reached down, holding out my right hand so the boy could rise. Without warning, he kicked straight up at my knees, bringing me crashing to the sidewalk.
>
> (Johnson 2000a: 52)

Parallels exist between Violet's attempted desecration of Dorcas's corpse and this episode, in which *Dreamer's* narrator Matthew Bishop fails to reenact the Parable of the Good Samaritan. Both characters' attempts to reach out and touch another are preceded by strange feelings of disembodiment. Both find that their efforts are not spurned so much as they encounter a forcefield of some kind. Violet finds her knife repulsed by skin that seems toughened by its experience of gunshot. And Bishop, it seems, cannot cut through the glass and blood that envelops the young boy. Strange moral burdens are upon both characters. *Jazz* seems almost to admire Violet's violence, almost approving her efforts to cling to an emotional intimacy menaced by industrial modernity. *Dreamer*, too, seemingly hopes Bishop here will carry King's spirit into the ghetto's heart. It forces this narrator into "a dream," endowing him with something like King's capacity for empathy until each blow "echo[s]", until he cannot but step forward and reenact Christ's parable.

Dreamer deceives as it does so, convincing us and Bishop that the young boy will welcome his offer of help. Shards of smashed glass suggest the melting of ghetto ice, references to dreams indicate we are far from reality, and so we forget that the injured boy is unlikely to look upon this stranger's offer of help without fear or suspicion. Only with his first kick do we remember that a new and masked American racism has left him with what King called "a nagging sense of nobodyness." Only then, as we remember that the sight of a gun would shock him less than Bishop's outstretched hand, do we recognize his inability to believe another human being could neither loathe nor ignore him. Though their brotherhood inspires Byrd's optimism, King and Smith here fail the young boy. King is absent, present in the scene only as an old inspiration made moribund by ghetto hate. Smith, arriving on the scene and forcing the boy off Bishop, only insists that such "people can't be helped," hoping a car will ferry him out of this disintegrating terrain he once called home (Johnson 2000a: 55). Whatever bonds these old men manage to forge are alien, irrelevant, as anachronistic as the knives forever resting on *Jazz*'s skin. *Dreamer* blames the ghetto's collapse on America's failure to heed King's insistence that it tackle a white supremacist heritage older than the Constitution itself. Today's secret racism—the racism that dare not speak its name, the racism that stands back and watches as ghettos crumble and hurricanes wreak havoc—stands unmasked by Johnson's brilliant novel. It stands exposed for exacting a price still more terrible than the spitting and hectoring thugs of Cicero. And so *Dreamer* suffers its subject's fate, falling under the shadow of the gun, nervously eyeing every rooftop, every passing car, for the bullet to herald a nightmare to come.

Notes

1 White House Press Secretary Tony Snow made these comments on the October 6, 2003 edition of *Fox News Sunday*.

References

Byerman, K. (2005) *Remembering the Past in Contemporary African American Fiction*, Chapel Hill, N.C.: University of North Carolina Press.

Byrd, R. P. (2005) *Charles Johnson's Novels: Writing the American Palimpsest*, Bloomington, Ind.: Indiana University Press.

Fukuyama, F. (1992) *The End of History and the Last Man*, London: Penguin.

Gates, H. L. Jr. (2004) "Introduction," in H. L. Gates Jr. and N. Y. McKay (eds), *The Norton Anthology of African American Literature*, New York: Norton, pp. xxxvii–xlvii.

Johnson, B. (1998) *The Feminist Difference: Literature, Psychoanalysis, Race, and Gender*, Cambridge, Mass.: Harvard University Press.

Johnson, C. ([1998] 2000a) *Dreamer*, Edinburgh: Payback.

—— (2000b) "Introduction" in B. Adelman and C. Johnson (eds), *King: A Photobiography of Martin Luther King, Jr*, New York: Viking Studios, pp. 2–8.

King, M. L. Jr. ([1967] 1968) *Where Do We Go from Here: Chaos or Community?* Bantam: New York.

—— (1991) "A Time to Break Silence," in C. Carson, D. J. Garrow, G. Gill, V. Harding, D. C. Hine (eds), *Eyes on the Prize: Documents, Speeches, and Firsthand Accounts from the Black Freedom Struggle*, Harmondsworth: Penguin, pp. 387–93.

Ling, P. (2002) *Martin Luther King, Jr*, London: Routledge.

Locke, A. (1992) "The New Negro," in A. Locke (ed.), *The New Negro*, New York: Touchstone, pp. 3–16.

Morrison, T. (1992) *Jazz*, London: Chatto & Windus.

Steinberg, S. (1998) "The Liberal Retreat from Race During the Post-Civil Rights Era" in Wahneema Lubiano (ed.), *The House that Race Built*, New York: Vintage, pp. 13–47.

West, C. (1993) *Race Matters*, Boston, Mass.: Beacon.

7 Tragic no more?

The reappearance of the racially mixed character

Suzanne W. Jones

At the end of Danzy Senna's *Caucasia*, a black anthropology professor is reunited with his biracial daughter who has been passing as white while living in hiding with her white mother. Deck Lee attempts to theorize Birdie's emotional agony away: "But baby, there's no such thing as passing. We're all just pretending. Race is a complete illusion, make-believe" (Senna 1998a: 391). To make her feel better, Deck shows Birdie his chart, complete with photographs of famous biracial people and their sad "fates" but ending with a happy childhood photo of Birdie and her sister Cole. Declaring that like canaries in coal mines, "mulattos had historically been the gauge of how poisonous American race relations were," Deck hypothesizes that "you're the first generation of canaries to survive, a little injured, perhaps, but alive." Birdie questions his abstract conclusions: "Fuck the canaries in the fucking coal mines. You left me. You left me with mom, knowing she was going to disappear. Why did you only take Cole? Why didn't you take me? If race is so make-believe, why did I go with Mum? You gave me to Mum 'cause I looked white. You don't think that's real? Those are the facts" (Senna 1998a: 393).

During the nineteenth century and early in the twentieth, the tragic mulatto/a figured prominently in American fiction, only to recede after the Harlem Renaissance when African-American writers called for "race pride" and racial solidarity and to disappear entirely in the late 1960s after the Black Power movement ushered in racially conscious concepts such as "Black Is Beautiful." Since 1990, however, the mixed black–white character has made a significant comeback in American fiction. Contemporary representations suggest that choosing one's racial identity is only slightly less difficult than it used to be because of American society's conflation of skin color and identity. Senna's Birdie looks white but identifies as black, Rosellen Brown's Ronnee looks black but wants to explore her "white side" (Brown 2000: 249), and John Gregory Brown's

Meredith looks and identifies white but fears revealing her biracial ancestry. For a while, each young woman lets her body speak for her, accepting socially ascribed definitions of her racial identity, but each is eventually called on to negotiate the conflicting racial realities of her life. Senna, who is biracial, Rosellen Brown, who is white and Jewish, and John Gregory Brown, who is white, all poignantly illustrate that "a racialized subjectivity has everything and nothing to do with the body" (Boudreau 2002: 59).

This fact reflects the legacy of slavery and de-jure and de-facto segregation in the USA, which resulted in myths about white racial purity and rigid social definitions about black and white identity. In many ways, contemporary American popular culture's preoccupation with racial authenticity continues to promote racial stereotypes and to perpetuate the "one-drop" rule, which rendered black anyone with any known African ancestry. At the same time, the 1960s biracial baby boomlet, which began after the 1967 *Loving* v. *Virginia* US Supreme Court decision struck down miscegenation laws, has slowly but steadily grown as American society has become more tolerant of interracial marriages, although less so of black–white marriages. The maturation of biracial children born in the late 1960s and 1970s, the recent upsurge in immigration to the USA, new theories about the social construction of identity and the value of multiculturalism, as well as an intense debate during the 1990s about changing the instructions on the 2000 Census, which for the first time allowed respondents to check more than one racial or ethnic category, have all contributed to the reappearance of the racially mixed figure in the contemporary American imagination.

Senna's *Caucasia* and Rosellen Brown's *Half a Heart* focus on biracial protagonists with white mothers and black fathers who met and fell in love during the 1960s but whose relationships collapse under the weight of society's racial divisions. The novels explore how the biracial daughters of these liaisons come to understand and assert their own identities and move beyond socially ascribed definitions. Psychologist Charmaine Wijeyesinghe argues that there are several factors that determine which racial or ethnic group an individual identifies with: racial ancestry, early socialization, physical appearance, cultural attachment, social and historical context, political awareness, and spirituality. She explains that "[w]hen there is a congruence between these factors, few if any intrapersonal or interpersonal conflicts may emerge" but that "[g]reater possibilities for internal conflict may exist when there are wide discrepancies between the factors underlying choice of racial identity, and possibly external perceptions or forces" (Wijeyesinghe 2001: 144).

Passing as white

In *Caucasia*, Birdie feels no internal racial conflict as a young child because she and her sister Cole are home-schooled. In "the little world" they have created, race as American society has defined it is not an issue (Senna 1998a: 6). They speak their own private language, Elemeno, named after their favorite letters in the alphabet, and they play "make-believe," which foregrounds questions about racial identity and performance, individual and group identity that occupy Senna throughout the novel. Eleven-year-old Cole says Elemenos are "a shifting people constantly changing their form, color, pattern, in a quest for invisibility. ... less a game of make-believe than a fight for the survival of their species." Eight-year-old Birdie questions, "What was the point of surviving if you had to disappear?" (Senna 1998a: 7–8). The two sisters eventually struggle with this question differently based on their skin color. The young Birdie, who has straight hair and olive skin, does not even realize that her racial phenotype differs from her sister's because she sees her "reflection" in Cole, who is cinnamon-skinned, curly-haired (Senna 1998a: 15)—that is until Deck decides to enroll his daughters in Nkrumah, a Black Power school. This decision strains his marriage to Sandy, a Boston blueblood turned hippie activist, and reveals that both Deck and Sandy have fallen into their society's trap of ascribing race to color. Deck, worrying that Birdie could pass for white, wants her to be socialized as black. Although Sandy recognizes that her biracial daughters will be deemed black in 1970s America, subconsciously she does not see Birdie as black, saying she looks Sicilian. Hearing their parents fight shatters "the little world" the sisters have created. For the first time, Cole sees Birdie as different; for the first time, Birdie feels different.

The novel is structured in such a way as to prove both Deck's theory that race is "make believe" and Birdie's experience of race as a painful reality, birthed out of twin human desires to belong and to create a sense of community by classifying self and others. *Caucasia* offers up proof of contemporary theories that race is socially constructed and correction to notions that acceptance of such abstract facts will erase the concrete reality of how race is experienced. This paradox informs the comparative structure Senna created for her novel, which is divided into three books. In "Negritude," Senna focuses on colorism and the performance of blackness among African Americans. At Nkrumah the black girls accept cinnamon-skinned Cole but marginalize beige Birdie, identifying her as "white," labeling her "ugly" and "stuck up" as a result (Senna 1998a: 45–6). The experience makes Birdie feel shy and fearful. Although Cole comes to Birdie's rescue, "She's black. Just like me" (Senna 1998a: 48), not until Birdie learns the cultural markers of blackness is she accepted. Senna presents Birdie's transformation as a performance. She wears her hair in a braid "to mask" its texture, copies their outfits (gold hoops, Sergio Valente jeans, a pink vest, a jean jacket with sparkles, Nikes), and mimics their language, "practicing how to say 'nigger' … dropping the 'er' so that it became not a slur, but a term of endearment: *nigga*." Birdie's motivation is not only to "blend in" but also to maintain her relationship with her beloved sister, who has already "changed" (Senna 1998a: 62–3). The quality of Birdie's performance is validated by her acceptance: "Now that I had been knighted black by Maria, and pretty by Ali, the rest of the school saw me in a new light." Yet Birdie has a sense that she is acting a part: "But I never lost the anxiety, a gnawing in my bowels, a fear that at any moment I would be told it was all a big joke" (Senna 1998a: 64). The way strangers react to Birdie's skin color makes her self-conscious about the black identity she has embraced. In the park with her father, they are interrogated by a policeman who thinks Deck is a child molester. On meeting Carmen, Birdie gets the cold shoulder—her light skin a reminder to Deck's new lover that he married a white woman. On such occasions, Birdie retreats to Elemeno, seeking in her biracial sister the sense of community that does not come easily to her when she is with some black people. Cole resorts to the same behavior in parallel scenes, such as a visit to her white grandmother's house, where she is ignored because her skin is dark and where Birdie is favored because she looks, as her grandmother says, "French or Italian." Birdie's wish to find a physical similarity with Deck suggests the need for tangible evidence of a genetic connection to verify her racial identity. She takes comfort in her asthma and her eczema, "invisible proof" that she is his daughter (Senna 1998a: 113). Early in the novel, Senna uses the mysterious biracial character Redbone, who is fascinated by Birdie, to cause readers to doubt Birdie's paternity, putting us in the position of those characters who expect race to be written on the body.

The second book of the novel, "From Caucasia, with Love," allows Senna to similarly reveal the performativity of whiteness, to explode the myth of whiteness as a monolithic identity, and to explore various manifestations of white racism. When Deck and Sandy break up, they split the family by racial phenotype, and Sandy disappears into rural New Hampshire with her "white" daughter, in an attempt to elude the FBI. There, taunted by the working-class white girls for her tomboy clothes and twin braids as a "freakazoid" (Senna 1998a: 220), Birdie feels "a yearning to belong that surprised" her (1998a: 219). Much like at Nkrumah, she transforms herself in order to be accepted: "I talked the talk, walked the walk, swayed my hips to the sound of heavy metal, learned to wear blue eyeliner and frosted lipstick and snap my gum" (Senna 1998a: 233).

However, there is an important difference. In performing blackness as Nkrumah girls defined it, Birdie hopes to make visible a chosen racial identity that is not evident from her skin color. In performing whiteness in New Hampshire, Birdie hides her blackness, which she thinks of as "her real self," when she is in the presence of white people (Senna 1998a: 233). Adopting the persona of Jesse Goldman, Birdie passes as white in order to protect her mother's alias and mark time in the hope that her family will be reunited. Sandy attempts to tamp down any guilt Birdie might feel in hiding her racial ancestry by reminding her that she "wasn't really passing because Jews weren't really white, more like an off-white": "She said they were the closest I was going to get to black and still stay white. 'Tragic history, kinky hair, good politics'" (Senna 1998a: 140).

Senna sets up several crucial scenes which suggest that Birdie's socialization, cultural attachments, family dynamics, and performance of blackness have shaped her racial identity as black. Fooling around with her landlord's son Nicholas in his bedroom, they smoke marijuana and flip through his *Tintin in the Congo* comic book. Thinking the pictures of the Congolese "hideous caricatures," Birdie, free of inhibitions, exclaims without thinking, "They've made us look like animals" (Senna 1998a: 204). Because Nicholas has constructed Birdie's racial identity otherwise, this remark does not blow her cover but sends him into reels of laughter and racist jokes. Such racist remarks, whether from upper-class Nicholas or the lower-class white girl Mona, undermine any affinity with whiteness that she had experienced as a young child when she was especially close to her mother. In contrast, similar biased remarks about white people by her father or her black friends at Nkrumah do not cause the same emotional sting because Birdie, in performing blackness, is trying to become black. In New Hampshire ("Caucasia") she performs whiteness as a disguise, and thus often experiences the sensation of being outside of herself, of "floating, looking down" at her friends (Senna 1998a: 248). And yet, Senna does not allow readers to assume that identity can be fixed because when Birdie is back in Boston, no longer willing to pass as a white girl, she feels out of place and wonders if she had "actually become Jesse. ... if whiteness were contagious" (1998a: 329).

Several significant events propel Birdie back to Boston where she can at least openly embrace a black identity. Incidents of prejudice in New Hampshire begin to take a toll on Birdie's willingness to pass as a white Jewish girl. After a white boy calls her a "Fuckin' kike," she lets it be known that because her mother is not Jewish that she is not technically Jewish and she removes her Star of David necklace, the only visible marker of her "Jewishness." Interestingly, the incident makes her feel a "pang of loyalty toward this imaginary father" (Senna 1998a: 246) and immediately catapults her into a memory of her real father's measured reaction to white racism. She knows that because of his skin color, he and her sister Cole can never escape prejudice as she does. Previously, she had made peace with her false position by thinking of herself as "a spy in enemy territory" (Senna 1998a: 259), but gradually she finds this rationalization difficult to sustain. Her best friend Mona greets the arrival of their first black male classmate with speculation about the size of his penis and calls Samantha, the only openly biracial girl in their school, a "hooker" (Senna 1998a: 251) when she transforms herself into a sexual object in an attempt to assert a more appealing identity. On the one hand, Birdie feels guilty about passively listening to her classmates' racist remarks, knowing that she is "protecting" herself from the racism that Samantha experiences every day (Senna 1998a: 259). On the other hand, Birdie does not want to be black in New Hampshire if she will have "to be black like Samantha. A doomed, tragic shade of black" (Senna 1998a: 321), Senna's reference to her own rewriting of the old literary figure. Senna marks the emotional strain on Birdie with asthma attacks that occur when she finds herself in ideologically compromising situations.

A weekend trip to New York with Mona, her mother, and her mother's lover Jim allows Birdie to reconnect with black people and black culture and ultimately with a suppressed part of her identity. Strangers' faces unearth a part of her "that had been buried so long" (Senna 1998a: 258), and a new kind of "talking music" (1998a: 261) played by black and Puerto Rican teenagers has instant appeal. Mona's fears and Jim's stereotypes ("Jesus, it's like some ancient African instinct that gets these kids dancing" [Senna 1998a: 261]) make her fantasize that she does not know these white people. When black teenagers throw a rock at their car, Birdie disavows any connection with whiteness. This incident suggests that Birdie's desire to identify as black is so strong that she has forgotten she looks white. By waving at the black teenagers, she may have unwittingly provoked the rock throwing. Back home in New Hampshire, an encounter with Samantha at a party, in which Birdie at first mistakes her for Cole, provokes Birdie to run away. When Samantha inaudibly answers Birdie's question, "What color are you?" with what Birdie thinks is, "I'm black. Like you" (Senna 1998a: 286), Birdie leaves rather than follow in Samantha's tragic footsteps.

Birdie hopes she is running to another future as a mixed black girl. But in Boston she finds that time and the race relations of the 1970s have not stood still. Nkrumah has folded and the schools are integrated. She turns to her Aunt Dot for refuge and a connection with the black side of her family. But Dot who has had a child with a mystic in India has returned with a more spiritual and less American way of thinking about color.

When Birdie asks Dot, "What color am I?" Dot answers, "a deep dark red" (Senna 1998a: 321–22). Much like Senna, Birdie finds that her early political socialization regarding race makes this apolitical answer unacceptable (Senna 1998b). She no longer wants to be politically silent as she had been when passing as Jesse, "somebody who had no voice or color or conviction" (Senna 1998a: 408). Thinking she will find her lost self in Cole, Birdie spurns her mother's attempt at a reunion and goes to California in search of her sister and her father. While Cole's enthusiastic welcome is more comforting than Deck's theoretical musings, Birdie discovers that she will have to choose her own path, but at least there will be company in California. Cole tells her, "If you ever thought you were the only one, get ready. We're a dime a dozen out here" (Senna 1998a: 412). The last scene of the novel parallels an earlier moment in New Hampshire when Birdie first sees Samantha on a school bus. Then Birdie identifies the unknown girl as "black like me—half that is" (Senna 1998a: 223). At this point, Birdie is still uncertain of how black she really is. In the final scene when she sees a biracial girl on a school bus in California, she terms her "black like me—a mixed girl" (Senna 1998a: 413). This subtle difference in phrasing suggests that Birdie has chosen her cultural identity, "black," without rejecting her genetic identity, "mixed."

Passing as black

In Ronnee Reece, Rosellen Brown creates a biracial protagonist, who lives with her black father in New York and identifies as black, but who, when she gets accepted at Stanford, seeks financial help from her absent white mother, Miriam Vener. Ronnee's renewed relationship with her mother sets her on a course to forge what Lise Funderburg calls "a self-concept that is deliberately biracial" (1994: 15). In *Half a Heart*, Brown registers a complaint about the identity constraints of the one-drop rule, but she does not ignore the racist beliefs that generated the practice or the current social pressures and racism that perpetuate it.

In Miriam, Brown creates a white Jewish Southerner who is passing in a way—hiding her racial politics and her interracial sexual history. By pairing Miriam with Ronnee as dual protagonists and focalizers, Brown nudges readers to consider Ronnee as passing also. Through a flashback to Ronnee's adolescent experiences, Brown suggests why America's insistence on monoracial identity can pose problems for the biracial child. Despite the fact that Eljay has raised Ronnee to identify as black, her light-brown skin elicits a different story, which changes depending on whether her interlocutor is black or white. In the New York public school Ronnee attends, the black students label her "a snob and a house nigger," terms that reflect color-coded class hierarchy within the black community, a cruel byproduct of slavery's many evils. They call her "white" because of her studiousness and her desire to please her teachers (Brown 2000: 76), a paradoxical attempt by black teenagers to control how race is defined in the very schools that have failed them by defining them as incapable. Brown forces readers to consider how many notions about racial identity are really based on what Paul Gilroy calls "oppositional identities" that are created by racist stereotypes (Gilroy 2000: 12).

Ronnee takes matters in her own hands by winning a scholarship to a very selective, but predominantly white, private school—only to be viewed by her father as abandoning her "people" and going over to the "enemies". The insensitivity of his remark is measured by the pain of Ronnee's rejoinder, "half of me is those enemies" (Brown 2000: 79). Adrian Piper explains the persistence of such polarized thinking by arguing that the history of race relations has created a dynamic in which "blacks and whites alike seem to be unable to accord worth to others outside their in-group affiliations without feeling that they are taking it away from themselves" (Piper 1996: 255). Ronnee has come to think of her genes as "born fighting" (Brown 2000: 91), an image that reverberates with the emotional toll taken on Ronnee's health. Like Senna, Brown figures the social construction of race as stressful—whether it is expressed as black appeals to racial authenticity or white presumption of differences that do not exist or white blindness to the causes of differences that do. Stress from black students' accusations that she is not black enough produces the physical sensation of "drowning" (Brown 2000: 77) and actually increases her asthma attacks, while the polite wariness she encounters in the predominately white school creates a social uneasiness, that makes her feel "sick," as if she had "a chronic low-grade illness" (2000: 76). Being forced to disown part of her racial identity no matter whom she is with, Ronnee's search for self becomes far more painful than normal adolescent angst. For her, all dating is interracial. In casting her as a budding actress, Brown refigures the life of the biracial figure as doubly complex because both blacks and whites require Ronnee to play different and often conflicting roles.

Brown's plot enacts the pitfalls that occur, as Diana Fuss has argued, when racial identity is theorized as a strict opposition between essentialism and social construction (Fuss 1989: 73–96). Knowing that Ronnee will be seen as black in the late 1960s, Eljay convinces Miriam when Ronnee is an infant that she will be better off with him because he can best teach her not only about black culture but also about white racism. Ironically, Eljay's lessons about black self-worth essentialize blackness and result in Ronnee judging herself "slightly incomplete in her blackness, flawed" (Brown 2000: 84). His lessons about whiteness—that it is a socially constructed category of oppression—reduce whiteness to "a nothing, an absence, a ghostliness" (Brown 2000: 84).

In order to position Ronnee outside of this American context so that she will be forced to see that her racial identity is constructed, Brown creates an encounter for her with an African student, Nkoma. He fancies Ronnee and she him, but he will not date her because his parents expect him to marry a pure-blooded black woman. Nkoma's definition of race exactly reverses America's one-drop rule, equating blackness with purity and a drop of whiteness with hybridity. While Ronnee views black identity as "culture" and thinks of herself as black, Nkoma views black identity as "blood" and sees her as white (Brown 2000: 82). Rather than label Ronnee "tainted," as she labels herself, Nkoma terms her "ineligible" as a potential mate. Nkoma's perspective causes Ronnee to see that whiteness does have a "presence" in her identity after all. His flattery in comparing her beauty to that of a "hybrid flower" and his patronizing "foreign" gestures meant to bolster her spirits make Ronnee aware of an aspect of her identity she has not considered, her Americanness (Brown 2000: 83–4).

From this point on, Ronnee revises her thinking about "all" black people, just as later when surrounded by white people, she attempts not to generalize about them. Throughout the novel, Brown plays with pronouns because both Miriam and Ronnee must rethink who is "we" and who is "they." Brown's use of this device culminates in Ronnee's remark near the end of the novel when she watches the Jewish children at her half-sister Evie's summer camp, "*They* are *me.* Would she always have to remind herself?" (Brown 2000: 384). Wondering if she could ever understand the Hebrew service these children are conducting, her answer combines the hope of connection, for she sees "the other" as part of herself; the habit of separation, for she has not known of the relationship for eighteen years; and the cultural variations on whiteness.

Being at her mother's house in Houston allows Ronnie to contemplate who she would have been if she had grown up in a white suburb, "Would she, Veronica Whoever, have been white, then?" (Brown 2000: 217). Drawing on her memory of a class discussion about "essence" and "existence" and "which came first," initially Ronnee thinks her "existence" would not have been that different, apart from having more money. Given her mother's liberal values, Ronnee knows Miriam would have exposed her to black history and culture and sent her to the same type of safe, slightly integrated school she chose for herself in New York. Thus, she thinks her mother "would have kept her black. Neatly, exactly half black. As much as she could." But Ronnee finally realizes that because her mother is white and Jewish, she would have acquired a different perspective on the world, which would have made her "existence" very different.

While fully focused on building a relationship with her mother that will produce the much-needed money for her tuition at Stanford, Ronnee works part-time on trying to determine her own "essence," the "nub of her" that lay like a "small jewel somewhere" obscured beneath her racial "existence" (Brown 2000: 217–18).

Brown suggests that Ronnee catches sight of her "essence" in physical similarities to her mother that remind her of their genetic connections— shared mannerisms and hair texture, a similarity which surprises Ronnee because she does not think of "white" women as having "bad hair" (Brown 2000: 269). Miriam's black friend Jewel notices a similarity in temperament—each seems to think she "deserves rejection" (Brown 2000: 275). It is in their biological relationship that Brown figures the "presence" of Ronnee's whiteness; "blood" and "genes" are words that both Ronnee and Miriam keep returning to in their thinking. But only the work of developing an ongoing mother–daughter relationship will sustain this presence. Ronnee's initial repulsion at her mother's desperation to have a relationship with her mellows into pride at Miriam's decision to host a party in her honor and to defy her husband's sense of propriety by doing so.

Brown constructs the plot so that Ronnee must live with her mother for a while, in order to see her as a "real" person (2000: 378) with complex emotions and deep feelings, instead of a "seditty white lady" (2000: 90). By the time Eljay lets Miriam know that Ronnee wanted to meet her solely for financial reasons, Ronnee has been with her mother long enough to sense the bond that she longed for as a child but that as a teenager she had begun to think she no longer needed. As Ronnee ponders the possibility of losing her mother's love when Miriam knows of her ulterior motives, Ronnee thinks that "her mother was the only one, in the end, who didn't see her color first, and she would miss that" (Brown 2000: 394). She compares her mother's and father's comments about skin color: Miriam's yearning for her physical body, her "little brown shoulders," after her father stole her away contrast with Eljay's ideological exhortations, "Black Girl! Bearer of our racial destiny. Counter in the struggle" (394). Ronnee leaps to the conclusion that her mother has understood her "essence," while her father has been preoccupied with "existence." Her second thought more nearly hits the mark Brown seems to be aiming for in this novel: "Essence and existence, *she'd* have said they were indivisible" (2000: 394).

The lengthy telephone conversation between Ronnee's parents near the end of the novel parallels the only other conversation they had about their daughter's identity when existence seemed to win out over essence in the 1960s. Eighteen years later, they reach a different conclusion, one that echoes the debate about how the 2000 US Census categorized identity.

Miriam asks Eljay, "are you willing to let 'your girl' be what she is?" (Brown 2000: 368). Genetically, Ronnee is not simply black, although her father has raised her as a black woman. And Ronnee's ability to negotiate the minefield of prejudice in Houston testifies to Eljay's talent in equipping her with the self-esteem and social skills she needs to live in a world still racially polarized. But Eljay's promise to allow Ronnee ultimately to choose her own racial identity is predicated on the enjoinder that Miriam not force Ronnee into a lawsuit against the Houston police for their racism and neglect of Ronnee's asthma. In other words, Eljay is willing to allow Ronnee to be "half white," if Miriam will not force her into political acti-vism simply because she is "half black." He reminds Miriam that Ronnee is also a teenager—self-absorbed and self-conscious—who would be more hurt than helped by a lawsuit.

When Ronnee learns that Eljay has revealed her mercenary motives, she assumes Miriam will not want anything more to do with her. In a move that seems weakly motivated, although thematically necessary, Ronnee goes to California so that she can at least meet her halfsister Evie before departing the Vener family for ever. In this final scene, which takes place at Evie's Jewish summer camp, the family relationship between Ronnee and Evie supersedes racial identity—evidence perhaps of a liberal white desire to think beyond the one-drop rule, but a desire Brown attri-butes to Ronnee as well. Miriam has scaled back her 1960s thoughts of Ronnee as a "gift" to the world (Brown 2000: 141) and now thinks of Ronnee as a "gift" to Evie (2000: 267), who has always wanted a sister. Miriam hopes that Ronnee and Evie's relationship will be "untainted" with the tensions and misunderstandings that have characterized her own relationship with Ronnee. But to keep the relationship untainted, Brown must fall back on ten-year-old Evie's youthful innocence and her excite-ment about having a sister. Aware of her brothers' fear of black people but uncertain of the reason, Evie dispenses with any scary connotations by viewing Ronnee's skin color literally—"you aren't black at all, really. You're sort of—coppery" (Brown 2000: 389). Stripping skin color of society's ideological constructs recalls her mother's view of the infant's "little brown shoulders." But Evie's explanation makes Ronnee realize that she has much to teach her sister about race relations and demonstrates that Brown resists making her biracial character into an idealistic symbol of improved race relations, even as she positions her within the white half of her family as well as the black.

The novel concludes with a telephone call, in which Miriam expresses worry about Ronnee's disappearance, and Ronnee responds with the one word that Miriam has been longing to hear, "Mom?" (Brown 2000: 402). That Ronnee delivers this word as a question implies that she wants

Miriam to be much more than the "cash cow" she first envisioned but also that she wonders if Miriam is still interested in their blood tie. Readers do not know for sure whether Miriam and Ronnee will continue their relationship. What we do know is how riddled with mixed motives and misunderstandings their relationship has been so far. Although Ronnee has identified herself as "half" black to Evie, we also know that Ronnee will not be trying out her new biracial identity at a Southern university but at Stanford on the more cosmopolitan west coast.

In her new thinking about racial identity, Ronnee, much like Birdie, finds herself looking for a guide. At Evie's camp, she spots "a boy darker than she was with telltale hair, his warm-brown neck lovely against his white Izod shirt. What, she wished she knew, was his story, and how did he like it?" (Brown 2000: 385). Ronnee's desire to know the "story" of this mixed-race child parallels the growing desire for stories about biracial identity, which is evident in the attention reviewers gave not just novels like this one, but the many memoirs and racially revised family histories published in the 1990s as well. Throughout *Half a Heart*, Brown gives Ronnee and Miriam an awareness of the difficulty of writing a new "script" for their relationship (2000: 57, 89), which may be a self-conscious nod toward Brown's own endeavor. In imagining an interracial story about mother–daughter love regained, Rosellen Brown is writing beyond the ending of the tragic mulatta, whose story concluded with romantic or familial love lost. In *Half a Heart*, Jordan auditions Ronnee for that old part by telling her that his mother cried when she learned they were dating, "Like she's already seeing her little grandchildren and they're, what, octaroons? No, wait. Quadroons." But Ronnee refuses the role, "Jesus, those words! That's right out of the Reconstruction or something. What are we, in New Orleans, and I'm the Tragic Fucking Mulatto?" (Brown 2000: 291). With this exchange, Rosellen Brown seems to be calling for an end to stories about the tragic mulatto.

Passing as racially pure

It is easier for Danzy Senna and Rosellen Brown to jettison this old character type than it is for John Gregory Brown, who creates a biracial protagonist who looks and identifies as white and, as a result, finds herself in the same position as earlier literary figures who grew up white, learned of their African ancestry, and led tragic lives. In *Decorations in a Ruined Cemetery* (1994), set in 1960s New Orleans but framed in the present, John Gregory Brown dismantles Southern myths of white racial purity, even as he resurrects the tragic mulatta figure that Rosellen Brown makes such sport of. Significantly, he uses the passing plot to question white racial purity rather

than simply to advocate racial equality as his nineteenth-century predecessors did or to embrace blackness as Senna does. The central problem
in any novel of passing is "whether or not the passer can achieve a healthy
identity," and the fictional prescription for happiness has been for the
passer who has African ancestry to embrace a black identity (Berzon 1978:
149). In *Decorations*, Meredith Eagen never takes this step nor does she
come to terms with her mixed ancestry. At age twelve she learns that her
father's deceased mother was a light-skinned African American, named
Molly, whom her Irish immigrant grandfather married in New York and
brought south to the more complicated racial politics of New Orleans.
Even after Meredith learns of her genetic makeup, she never questions her
cultural identity because she has been raised to think of herself as white,
much as Birdie as a child was socialized to think of herself as black.

But the legacy of the "one-drop" rule means that Meredith becomes
increasingly preoccupied with her racial ancestry. Socially liberal, she
experiences paralyzing guilt for keeping her mixed ancestry secret. The
narrative of *Decorations* is Meredith's attempt as an adult to piece together
the story of her mixed origins. Unlike *Caucasia* and *Half a Heart*, *Decorations*
is less about the travails of mixed identity in the present, which provides
the novel's frame, than about race relations in the past. Meredith's father's
death frees her to research her family history and record her findings in
her journal, but she does not publicly reveal the truth of her mixed
ancestry. Meredith predicts that she will not be able to tell a future husband and child of her discoveries, fearing that if she divulges her secret to
a white man who has grown to love her that he will leave her. This is the
cautionary tale she has gleaned from the breakup of her father's second
marriage. As a result, Meredith lives in retreat from the world, unable to
begin a meaningful relationship with anyone. Brown concludes the novel
by explaining that Meredith hopes to find peace in writing about the past.
This seems doubtful, for as Funderburg has pointed out, "a paradox of the
one-drop rule is that it is never a two-way street": "one can be black and
have 'white blood' (even to the point of having a white parent ...), but one
cannot be white *and* have 'black blood'" (Funderburg 1994: 13).

Adrian Piper, who is racially mixed but light enough to be mistaken as
white, contends that

> among politically committed and enlightened whites the inability to
> acknowledge their probable African ancestry is the last outpost of
> racism. It is the litmus test that separates those who have the courage
> of their convictions from those who merely subscribe to them and that
> measures the depth of our dependence on a presumed superiority.
>
> (Piper 1996: 254)

In *Decorations*, Meredith seems not so much doomed by her desire to feel superior to black people as daunted by the racism of her society—fearful of a loss of "social regard and respect" that Piper describes from personal experience as "practically unbearable" (1996: 256). The result though is the same. Meredith cannot simultaneously reveal her mixed ancestry and assert a self-identity of whiteness. The old one-drop rule still holds in her case, and, although Meredith is not hopelessly split by her dual racial heritage as tragic mulattas had once been depicted, she is paralyzed by guilt because she is passing as racially pure.

Unlike John Gregory Brown, Danzy Senna and Rosellen Brown give their biracial protagonists opportunities that Meredith and biracial characters in earlier American literature do not have: the ability to assert their own racial identity and the chance to have relationships with both white and black family members. If Deck's theory at the end of *Caucasia* is correct, that the mulatto's fate manifests "the symptoms that will eventually infect the rest of the nation" regarding race relations (Senna 1998a: 393), Birdie's and Ronnee's conflicts and Meredith's paralysis suggest that existential angst, if not tragedy, will continue to plague racially mixed people as long as society's demand to define them clashes with their attempts to define themselves, whether that demand originates in the legacy of white racism or the politics of racial authenticity. If the USA is moving toward new ways of thinking about race in the twenty-first century, both Senna and Rosellen Brown figure the west coast as more congenial than the eastern seaboard in contemplating new definitions of race and identity. And all three novelists turn the question, "What are you?" that their biracial protagonists are confronted with back on their readers by dramatizing situations that ask, "What are you that you need to ask?"

Author's note

This essay draws in part on my book, *Race Mixing: Southern Fiction since the Sixties* (Baltimore, Md.: Johns Hopkins University Press, 2004).

References

Berzon, J. R. (1978) *Neither White Nor Black: The Mulatto Character in American Fiction*, New York: New York University Press.

Boudreau, B. (2002) "Letting the Body Speak: 'Becoming' White in *Caucasia*," *Modern Language Studies*, 32 (1): 59–70.

Brown, R. (2000) *Half a Heart*, New York: Farrar, Straus & Giroux.

Brown, J. G. (1994) *Decorations in a Ruined Cemetery*, New York: Houghton Mifflin.

Funderburg, L. (1994) *Black, White, Other: Biracial Americans Talk about Race and Identity*, New York: William Morrow.

Fuss, D. (1989) *Essentially Speaking: Feminism, Nature, and Difference*, New York: Routledge.

Gilroy, P. (2000) *Against Race: Imagining Political Culture beyond the Color Line*, Cambridge, Mass.: Belknap Press of Harvard University Press.

Piper, A. (1996) "Passing for White, Passing for Black" in E. K. Ginsberg (ed.), *Passing and the Fictions of Identity*, Durham, N.C.: Duke University Press, pp. 234–60.

Senna, D. (1998a) *Caucasia*, New York: Riverhead Books.

—— (1998b) "The Mulatto Millennium," in Claudien Chiawei O'Hearn (ed.), *Half and Half: Writers on Growing Up Biracial, and Bicultural*, New York: Pantheon Books, pp. 12–27.

Wijeyesinghe, C. (2001) "Racial Identity in Multiracial People: An Alternative Paradigm," in C. Wijeyesinghe and B. W. Jackson III (eds), *New Perspectives on Racial Identity Development*, New York: New York University Press, pp. 129–52.

Part III
Historical narratives

8   The way we were(n't)

Origins and empire in Thomas Pynchon's *Mason & Dixon*

Stacey Olster[1]

Thomas Pynchon's *Mason & Dixon* ends with the death of Charles Mason in 1786 and the decision of his two eldest children to stay in Philadelphia and "be Americans" (1997: 772). As to just what constitutes that nationality, however, Pynchon remains silent. J. Hector St. John de Crèvecoeur, in contrast, had no such reticence. Addressing the question of "What is an American?" in those *Letters from an American Farmer* published four years before Mason's death, Crèvecoeur defined America with respect to a litany of terms destructive of the past: "new laws, a new mode of living, a new social system," yielding "a new race of men" (1957: 38, 39). And yet, for all the emphasis on "newness" that his paean to American exceptionalism displayed, Crèvecoeur remained acutely aware of the existence of a historical past: His views of America in "embryo" follow those of Italy in exhaustion (1957: 6); frontiersmen free of past constraints live side-by-side with Indians whose past is seen as vanishing. In this understanding, Crèvecoeur was not alone. Colonists in the seventeenth and eighteenth centuries often made a great point of the bond they retained to their British heritage. The Massachusetts Bay Puritans described their immigration as "a *Local Secession*, yet not a *Separation*" (Higginson 1697: 69–70). Virginia's colonists professed "*sentiments of duty and affection*" as late as 1774 (quoted in Bailyn 1967: 142). Viewed with respect to such earlier testimony, one then may assume, as does Mason, that, far from being a nation distinct unto itself, America is but "a Patch of England, at a three-thousand-Mile Off-set" (Pynchon 1997: 248). If such is the case, and the New World is indistinguishable from the Old, its history of empire may simply confirm the view of history implied by the Indian lore of forestry in which, as Pynchon writes, "ev'ryone comes 'round in a Circle sooner or later" until "[o]ne day, your foot comes down in your own shit" (1997: 677).

I use the term "empire" deliberately here, for the critique of American exceptionalism that prompts Pynchon's return to the late-eighteenth-century period during which the modern nation-state was conceived reflects the late-twentieth-century period in which the end of the Cold War and emergence of a globalized economy have led critics to proclaim the entire era of the nation-state as over. Recreating the eighteenth century in fiction as an "Era of fluid Identity" therefore concerns more than postmodern notions of individual selfhood (Pynchon 1997: 469). In terms of national identity, it concerns the relevance of individual nationhood within a world in which a shift from imperialist to imperial sovereignty has resulted in the decentered and deterritorialized apparatus that Michael Hardt and Antonio Negri call "Empire." As even Mason, more at home with stars than stocks, cannot help but notice, "Charter'd Companies may indeed be the form the World has now increasingly begun to take" (Pynchon 1997: 252). Establishing what is an American and, by extension, what is America under these circumstances thus becomes an act of representation, not simply a "making present again" as the word's etymological origins indicate, but "the making present *in some sense* of something which is nevertheless *not* present literally or in fact" (Pitkin 1967: 8–9). Because that act is performative rather than mimetic, representing America in Pynchon's novel will turn out to be less a question of politics, as the colonists demanded, and more a question of aesthetics, as the mapping in which Pynchon's eponymous characters engage illustrates.

Separation, consolidation, and East India Company administration

The modern nation-state, most scholars agree, could not have emerged without the legacies of the American and French Revolutions, whose movements rapidly were turned into models and blueprints. As scholars also acknowledge, the political grounds upon which nations were first proposed had to be supplemented, in the absence of historical rootedness, by a cultural terrain on which nations were created discursively. That Pynchon presents his investigation of America's origins through the vehicle of the novel is, then, historically appropriate given that the novel was the art form most associated with the rise of the modern nation-state since its inception, dependent on the print-language deemed crucial to the creation of national consciousness, fostering community among the bourgeoisie separated by space but connected by similar reading experiences, and developing a brand of social realism that embraced the whole of society in which the masses were beginning to play an increasingly significant role. That Pynchon presents his critique of American exceptionalism through the vehicle of the novel is also appropriate since its subversive "uncrowning" of the epic, as Mikhail Bakhtin recognized, enabled the novel to emerge as the literary form with the greatest potential to provide "parody and travesty of all high genres and of all lofty models embodied in national myth" (1981: 23, 21). In other words, if the modern nation-state emerged from a relativizing of ethnic/class differences and a maximizing of those differences that characterized foreign others, *Mason & Dixon* destabilizes the nation-state by stressing the similarities that bind Americans to foreign others while showing the differences that prevent the provinces from truly merging in any way to become a United States.

Charles Mason and Jeremiah Dixon suspect this to be the case even before they set sail from England in 1763. They wonder whether, given the rumors they have heard, they will be stepping down in a land that is any different from those to which the Royal Society has previously sent them: "Another Slave-Colony," the melancholic Mason notes (Pynchon 1997: 248). Unfortunately, Mason's remark comes in response to Dixon's observation that it is the colonists themselves who are said to keep slaves, "as did our late Hosts" in Cape Town, that "they are likewise inclin'd to kill the People already living where they wish to settle" (Pynchon 1997: 248). And so they do, as is repeatedly confirmed by events either recalled for or witnessed at first-hand by the Englishmen: the massacre of Indians at Conestoga; the murder of twenty-six more men, women, and children taking refuge in Lancaster's jail; the whipping of Africans in chains by a slave-driver in Baltimore.

As readers of Pynchon's fiction are well aware, this is hardly the first time that Pynchon has portrayed America as a land in which the subjugation of others is fundamental—it is, after all, in Columbus, Ohio, that DL Chastain's efforts to start anew in *Vineland* are interrupted by kidnapping and subsequent white slavery. Nor is this to suggest that Pynchon is preaching an equivalency among the various forms of bondage—whether denoted in terms of hirelings, indented servants, contractual agents, or slaves—that the novel depicts. Mason, caught in the hold of a meat ship while returning to his Royal Society employers, does not experience the horrors of the Middle Passage however many hundreds of lamb carcasses "slither'd lethally 'round him" (Pynchon 1997: 736)—sailors rescue him from an entrapment that does not last even one night. But to portray America as *another* slave colony in a novel in which its origins are specifically explored is to expose the vexing contradiction at the heart of revolutionary rhetoric: the fact that those who viewed being taxed without consent as turning them from subjects into slaves were attempting to protect from British interference a trade that had as its economic basis the enslavement of other human beings. Even more important, it reduces to nil any differences by which the country coming into being can claim distinction. Edward Braddock shoots at American Indians, "treacherous Natives, disrespectful, rebellious, waiting in Ambuscado, behind ev'ry stone wall" (Pynchon 1997: 501), in the same spirit that James Wolfe shoots at British weavers, "Red Indians, spying upon them from the Woodlands they thought were theirs" (1997: 313). Sterloop rifles abuse Africans in the Cape of Good Hope just as Sterloops effect "the Catastrophick Resolution of Inter-Populational Cross-Purposes" in Pennsylvania (Pynchon 1997: 343)—making moot all questions of whether the provenance of the gun is Dutch, as Mason insists, or American, as Dixon claims, or whether Americans are any more British than the Cape Dutch are Dutch.

Given these Old World connections, it is not surprising that the anthem to independence sung by voices that are "unmistakably, American" (Pynchon 1997: 571) is listened to by colonists still identified by way of regional origins—"New-Yorkers in Georgia, Pennsylvanians in the Carolinas, Virginians ev'rywhere" (1997: 570)—hardly an imagined community, to borrow Benedict Anderson's term, much less "Americans All," as the song proclaims. Nor is it surprising that the cultural hybridity by which individual colonists are characterized—the Virginian George Washington displaying an old pitman's lilt to the British Dixon and also sounding like an African to Pennsylvanians, his servant Gershom an African American and also a yarmulke-wearing Jew—collapses national distinctions. For, as scholars of the American Enlightenment have argued, colonists prior to the American Revolution had a very limited sense of national identity; it was only after 1764 that the word "Americans" replaced "Englishmen" as the preferred term of self-reference in newspapers (Ferguson 1994: 436). And with no institutions around which to consolidate themselves prior to that time, politics in the colonies remained "piecemeal," "constituted more in the relations of individual provinces with the metropolis than in terms of British America" (Shields 1990: 223). Because it also was the metropolis, or sovereign center, that produced the more valued manufactured goods that were exchanged for raw materials in outposts and colonies, it was in its best interests to keep the provinces separate, restricting them—in this case, through parliamentary Acts upon Trade and Navigation from 1651 onwards—from engaging in free trade and from developing manufacturing economies of their own.

In Pynchon's Maryland and Pennsylvania, as it turns out, there is no need for any sovereign center to prevent the provinces from uniting. The people living near the border are doing that all by themselves, as seen in the experiences of Thomas Cresap (Pynchon 1997: 638–41), who, with fourteen accomplices, defends his residence as being in Maryland while surrounding his house with fifty-five more men. By bringing astronomical tools to resolve formally that eighty-two-year-old disputed boundary (1681–1763), Mason and Dixon only formalize that separation. Therefore, for all Mason's assumption that astronomy removes him from politics, his application of astronomy in the colonies is very much a political activity, promoting as it does the interests of British colonial hegemony. Dixon admits as much about their efforts when earlier distinguishing the practice of British astronomy from that of other nations: "'Tis the British Way, to take the extra step that may one day give us an Edge when we need one, probably against the French. Small Investment, large Reward. I regard myself as a practitioner of British Science now" (Pynchon 1997: 121).

Yet, in a novel in which an earlier world of cores and peripheries is being replaced by "the world that is to come, [in which] all boundaries shall be eras'd" (Pynchon 1997: 406), the surveyors' work to prevent colonial consolidation is as compromised as the colonists' attempts to promote exceptionalist separation. This is not for lack of trying. As a glance at the historical Mason's *Journal* indicates, Mason practiced the fastidious extra steps his partner in fiction is shown to preach. A discrepancy emerges between a mark in one field and a mark by a road leading from Philadelphia to Nottingham, and the two return to the field to begin again. Chain carriers measure 22.51 chains between a point of intersection on the surveyors' Line and the tangent point in a circle around Newcastle, and Mason remeasures it himself to make sure that they have not made any errors. Yet, as the *Journal* also shows, the exactitude of Mason's yearnings is repeatedly frustrated by the inexactitude of his findings, situations whose calculations are most often appended by the adjective "dubious": "By the Pole Star's transiting the Meridian we placed a mark in the Meridian northward, but it was rendered a little dubious on account of flying clouds"; "the 1st Satellite of Jupiter Immerged, very dubious by its near approach to Jupiters Limb" (Mason 1969: 45, 158).

Pynchon traces such uncertainty back to a number of earlier sources. One is the overlapping nature of the original land grants, "Geometrickally Impossible territory" parceled out by Charles II and James II, "as if in playful refusal to admit that America, in any way, may be serious" (1997: 336, 337). Another is the shape of the earth itself, a planet "not known to be exactly a Spheroid, nor whether it is everywhere of equal Density" (Mason 1969: 194), about which all determinations must remain approximate at best and arbitrary at worst. Together they make the surveyors' task to establish a definitive Maryland and Pennsylvania a venture that is doomed from the start:

there exists no "Maryland" beyond an Abstraction, a Frame of right lines drawn to enclose and square off the great Bay in its unimagin'd Fecundity, its shoreline tending to Infinite Length, ultimately unmappable,— no more, to be fair, than there exists any "Pennsylvania" but a chronicle of Frauds committed serially against the Indians dwelling there, check'd only by the Ambitions of other Colonies to north and east.

(Pynchon 1997: 354)

In the case of Maryland, in fact, there is not even very much land to circumscribe, since when "Maryland" is finally "reveal'd" by the surveyors, its area is found to consist mostly of water (Pynchon 1997: 616).

Were the matter left here, Pynchon could be viewed as simply rewriting John Barth's *The Sot-Weed Factor*, whose portrait of a tidewater province's uncertain topography and geography *Mason & Dixon* obviously calls to mind. Yet Pynchon, unlike Barth, repeatedly breaks his novel's early American temporal frame with anachronistic allusions—to coffee bars, split ends, and no-smoking taverns, to name but a few—that suggest that the desire that most informs his historical novel is what Georg Lukács called "bringing the past to life as the prehistory of the present" (1963: 53). This affects the presentations of space that each writer offers in two crucial ways. First, Pynchon attributes geography a moral component that Barth, more concerned with Heraclitean flux and the fears that living on the edge (both literally and figuratively), does not. Heretical in mimicking the first boundary line by which God divided firmament from water, the Visto that Mason and Dixon carve out is presented as eventuating in an eighty-mile shopping mall, "lin'd with Inns and Shops, Stables, Games of Skill, Theatrickals, Pleasure-Gardens ... a Promenade" (Pynchon 1997: 701). The Delaware Triangle, or "Wedge," on whose latitude they later work as "an Atonement" (Pynchon 1997: 701), reflects "an emerging moral Geometry" (1997: 323) in being an area perhaps exempt from slavery. Second, spatial indeterminacy for Barth remains a transhistorical phenomenon, its apocalyptic reverberations as relevant to colonial as contemporary times, whereas spatial indeterminacy for Pynchon, as that envisioned shopping mall implies, reflects the particularities of late capitalism in which globalization has shifted power from nation-states to huge conglomerates.

The most powerful of such conglomerates in *Mason & Dixon*, of course, is the East India Company, located "ev'rywhere, and [in] Ev'rything" (Pynchon 1997: 69), with individual outposts that all perform "the Doings of Global Trade in miniature" (1997: 159). Dixon repeatedly suspects it is the Company, and not the British government, that is the sovereign power from which the surveyors' mission to separate Maryland and Pennsylvania emanates, and the connections between the Company and their Royal Society employers, portrayed in terms of marriages no less dynastic than those between royal families, corroborate his suspicions. Susannah Peach, daughter of a silk merchant who is "a growing Power within the East India Company" (Pynchon 1997: 169), marries astronomer James Bradley, and his observations buy her father a Directorship in the Company. Margaret Maskelyne marries Robert Clive, and her brother Nevil is made Astronomer Royal upon Bradley's death.

As those dynastic connections also imply, this deterritorialized organization possessed few of the more benign qualities by which scholars sometimes distinguish economic from political dealings as noncoercive. Quite the contrary. In *Mason & Dixon*, Pynchon attributes to the East India Company every abuse of power that he formerly had ascribed to the state. The V.O.C. (Vereenigde Oostindische Compagnie) "Searches in the middle of the Night, [and] property impounded" that force farmers in Cape Town to move north (1997: 154) are no different from the D.O.J. (Department of Justice) "search-and-destroy missions" that force pot growers in *Vineland* to move in that same direction (1990: 334); the Company that "desire[s] total Control over ev'ry moment of ev'ry Life" (1997: 154) is no different from the zero-tolerance state that seeks to police "anything that could remotely please any of your senses, because they need to control all that" (1990: 313). Only in *Mason & Dixon*, such intrusions into civil liberties can no longer be dismissed as the product of individual fantasy or an author's long-standing distrust of corporate villainy. The "stately Finger" in *Gravity's Rainbow* that points to a "city of the future where every soul is known, and there is noplace to hide" may prefigure a world in which IG Farben is "*the very model of nations*" or reflect the paranoia of characters who think that Providence is always giving them the finger (Pynchon 1973: 566). The "Invisible Hand," in Pynchon's appropriation of Adam Smith, with whose workings one dare not interfere in *Mason & Dixon*, is indubitably "a superior Power,— not, in this case, God, but rather, Business" (1997: 411).

And, in *Mason & Dixon*, that superior power has the military power to enforce its will, for, by the time that Mason and Dixon make their expedition to America, the East India Company had shifted from a trading to an armed power, mirroring the British Empire's shift from the pacifist trade policies of Robert Walpole to the militaristic ones of William Pitt. Pynchon hints at this shift early in the novel when Mason stumbles into the Jenkin's [*sic*] Ear Museum (1997: 175–80), honoring the captain whose 1738 brandishing to Parliament of mummified ear, severed by the cutlass of a Spanish *guarda costa*, led to war with Spain in Spanish America over the empire of the seas trade (1739–48). Even more important, he suggests the forcible interventions that followed when Mason and Maskelyne trace the doings of "the wealthy-without-limit Clive of India" (1997: 131), whose career embodied that of the Company in miniature:

rising to fame after switching from its civil to military service; leading troops that recaptured Calcutta after the 1756 Black Hole outrage and defeating the forces of the Nawab who had perpetrated it; and, finally, giving the Company, with the post of *diwan* accorded it in 1765, authority over all territorial revenues in the imperial provinces of Bengal, Bihar, and Orissa (Lawson 1993: 85–106).

When Maskelyne, then, describes for Mason the imperial power he holds accountable for their lot in St. Helena, the "Invisible Power" of which he finds them both "Subjects" is characterized by way of global pillage, not governmental policies:

Something richer than many a nation, yet with no Boundaries,— which, tho' never part of any Coalition, yet maintains its own great Army and Navy,— able to pay for the last War, as the next, with no more bother than finding the Key to a certain iron Box,— yet which allows the Brittannick Governance that gave it Charter, to sink beneath oceanick Waves of Ink incarnadine.

(Pynchon 1997: 140)

No wonder Dixon feels discomfort with interstitial spaces in such an "all-business world" (Pynchon 1997: 164), in which Lord Pennycomequick reigns as "global-Communications Nabob" (1997: 721). Conceptually unable, in Fredric Jameson's terms, "to map the great global multinational and decentered communicational network" in which he feels himself ensnared (1991: 44), Dixon cannot locate himself, either perceptually or cognitively, in a mappable external world. The only question that remains is whether the "overhead view" of that world that Dixon must produce as part of his employment, the "Map entirely within his mind" that he begins to contrive before he even gets to America, will represent an alternative "World he could escape to, if he had to" (Pynchon 1997: 242), or remain a miniaturized version of the one in which he finds himself already embedded.

Representation and mapping

Jameson proposes an aesthetic of "cognitive mapping" as a response to these conditions, which, in practical terms, takes the form of a "reconquest of a sense of place and the construction or reconstruction of an articulated ensemble which can be retained in memory and which the individual subject can map or remap along the moments of mobile, alternative trajectories" (1991: 51). Dixon's tutor, Emerson, advances a similar proposal in recommending maps as "*Aides-mémoires* of flight" (Pynchon 1997: 504), and early in their partnership the surveyors gain experience in following his prescription. Sumatra they turn into a game called "Sumatra," "their Board a sort of *spoken Map* of the island they have been kept from and will never see" (Pynchon 1997: 57), St. Helena "a Plantation sent out years since by its metropolitan Planet, which will remain invisible for years indeterminate before revealing itself and acquiring a Name, this place till then serving as an *Aide-Mémoire*, a Representation of Home" (1997: 133). By the time the surveyors get to America, this idea of representation will be particularly important, not only because of the impossibility of establishing with any fixity the actuality of America, but also because one of the ways in which nationhood is constructed is through linguistic identification with kinship or home.

Mason's brother-in-law, in fact, warns him of the importance that representation will have when Mason arrives in the New World. Broaching the future apprenticeship of Mason's sons to their grandfather in exchange for financial assistance in caring for them during Mason's absence, another trade of bodies for booty, Elroy informs Mason that he represents the elder Mason, although not a lawyer himself, because "ev'ryone needs Representation, from time to time. If you go to America, you'll be hearing all about that, I expect" (Pynchon 1997: 202). And so Mason does. But in America, Mason also learns that there are different forms that representation can take. Politically, he discovers this most clearly while listening to Captain Volcanoe's Sons of Liberty ferociously debate whether or not "America has long been perfectly and entirely represented in the House of Commons, thro' the principle of Virtual Representation" (Pynchon 1997: 404). England, of course, contended America was, having defined Parliament as a deliberative assembly of one nation, dedicated to the interests of the whole. The colonies, not surprisingly, alleged they were not, having defined representation, much like Mason's brother-in-law, more in terms of medieval attorneyship in which elected local men, acting on behalf of their constituents, were enabled to seek redress from the royal court of Parliament.

The members of Volcanoe's crew quickly put an end to any British notion that virtual representation has any credence: "Suggest you, Sir, even in Play, that this giggling Rout of poxy half-wits, *embody* us? Embody *us?* America but some fairy Emanation, without substance, that hath pass'd, by Miracle, into *them*?" (Pynchon 1997: 404). Yet, in exposing the futility of Mason encountering his dead wife Rebekah in women whose resemblances constitute a *"Point-for-Point Representation"* (1997: 536), Pynchon also exposes the folly of Volcanoe's crew presuming its notion of proportional representation will "extend beyond simple Agentry [...] unto at least Mr. Garrick, who in 'representing' a rôle, becomes the character, as by some transfer of Soul," and thereby yield "something styling itself

'America'" (1997: 405). Accuracy of depiction does not define any kind of representation. Mason's wife learns this lesson the hard way: Having assumed "*some* Honesty" from those who give her a sketch of the man she is told she must marry, and found "Picture and Man *quite* as different as they prov'd to be," she is told, in explanation, "'Twas but a Representation" (Pynchon 1997: 186). A disappointment. And to found proportional political representation on "the recurrent ideal of the perfect replica" is to assume an unchanging notion of what politically relevant features are meant to be represented (Pitkin 1967: 86–7). A danger.

The artistry that Garrick employs as an actor nonetheless does bear fruit in the form that *Mason & Dixon* finally presents America as being revealed: Dixon's "Pen-and-Paper Representation" (Pynchon 1997: 687), a method of artistic composition Dixon spends years studying, "grinding and mixing his own Inks," much like any painter working with easel and canvas, "[l]evigating, elutriating, mixing the gum-water, pouncing and rosining the Paper to prevent soak-through" (1997: 242), resulting in a picture that he appends by his signature *fleur-de-lis* hallmark. The text of America that emerges from his endeavors is, finally, the Text that the Kabbalists who gather in the Rabbi of Prague tavern have anticipated all along: "Forms of the Land, the flow of water, the occurrence of what us'd to be call'd Miracles, all are Text,— to be attended to, manipulated, read, remember'd" (Pynchon 1997: 487).

In emphasizing the pictorial nature of Dixon's endeavors in this way, Pynchon invokes the elements of craftsmanship that had been a part of cartography since its inception. Medieval cartographers referred to a map as *orbis imago* (representation of the world), or *pictura* (picture), and this view survived well after the close of the Middle Ages. Geographer Philipp Clüver, for instance, characterized a map as a picture "*qua situs terrae vel eius partes in plano artificiosè describitur*" [in which a place on earth or its parts on a flat surface is by art described] at the end of the seventeenth century (Bagrow 1951: 215), the degree of artifice employed extending from the mere use of color (the Red Sea almost invariably appearing as red) to the wholesale contrivance of people and places. The late-thirteenth-century circular world map known as the Hereford map populated Africa with headless men and four-eyed Ethiopians consorting with mermaids, unicorns, and dragons. The 1492 terrestrial globe constructed by Martin Behaim situated the mythical island of "Antilla" or "Isle of the Seven Cities" beyond the already-charted Azores (Wilford 1981: 46–7, 60–1).

Perhaps more important, in emphasizing the textual nature of Dixon's endeavors, Pynchon suggests how much a land's being "attended to, manipulated, read, [and] remember'd" depended upon its having been rendered as recorded document in order to be reached again. Leif

Eriksson may have reached the western hemisphere nearly 500 years before Christopher Columbus, but credit for discovering a fourth continent was accorded Columbus because the Norse produced no maps that had an impact upon the European consciousness, and authenticity of the 1440s map whose inscription attributed discovery of the large "Vinlanda Insula" west of Greenland to Eriksson and Bjarni Herjolfsson continues to be contested. And Columbus may have reached that continent seven years before Amerigo Vespucci, but the maps derived from his voyages continued to refer to the land he discovered as "Asia." So it was the successor whose published letters proclaimed discovery of a New World who had his name immortalized in that of the continent after a German mapmaker, Martin Waldeseemüller, prepared a 1507 woodcut print and scrawled over the region of Brazil the word "America" in Vespucci's honor.

One can argue, of course, that, having earlier been delineated in the utopian tracts of writers such as Thomas More and Francis Bacon, America as a geographical entity had been a text all along. But America as a nation could not be revealed until its colonists had composed texts of their own with which to construct it, since, as Benedict Anderson has argued, in a hemisphere in which "an almost perfect isomorphism" existed between "the stretch of the various empires and that of their vernaculars," it was print-language that enabled colonists to envision a community of thousands like themselves (1983: 75). In one sense, then, it is a relatively minor character, the masquerading fop Philip Dimdown, who does more to advance the cause of nationhood in Pynchon's book than any political pundit, since he is arrested while operating a clandestine printing press whose broadsides proclaim the word "LIBERTY" in large letters (1997: 390). In another sense, however, it is Dixon himself who assumes this role, since appreciation of the text of America that he composes in pictures, no more accurate than any two-dimensional rendering of a three-dimensional reality can be, is not restricted in any way by its audience's degree of literacy.

In assessing this seminal role that Pynchon portrays Dixon as, intentionally or not, enacting, it is worth remembering how many of those who later became known as Founding Fathers—George Washington, Benjamin Franklin, Thomas Jefferson—acted as surveyors over the course of their careers, leaving behind them maps that exist today. These imaginative efforts notwithstanding, the nation that they collectively helped to draft is presented by Pynchon as, ultimately, a tenuous and fragile creation, apt to deconstruct or even self-destruct with very little provocation. The "War" may be "settl'd" in Christmas of 1786, but "the Nation [is] bickering itself into Fragments" (1997: 6), and the historicist perspective from which Pynchon writes allows him to trace the measures that, over time, have been used to rebind it to its very inception. Indeed, in the same year that the nation was being brought into political being, John Adams was proposing a representative delegation of power in his 1776 *Thoughts on Government* as a substitute for Thomas Paine's idea of single democratic assembly. Neither an aberration nor an anomaly, such a reaction was but an inevitable stage in the creation of what Anderson terms "official nationalism," in which "even the most determinedly radical revolutionaries always, to some degree, inherit the state from the fallen regime," and, much like the electrical system in any large mansion that the owner has abandoned, "the state awaits the new owner's hand at the switch to be very much its old brilliant self again" (1983: 145).

We forget how much the mapping of the Mason-Dixon line contributed to this last gasp at traditional empire, so much do we think of it as a dividing line between North and South, between free and slave states, that was made irrelevant after the Civil War. We forget that the Land Ordinance of 1785 that was meant to survey and auction off public lands in order to pay the national debt took as its starting point the Mason-Dixon line, which already had been extended to the southwest corner of Pennsylvania by David Rittenhouse and Andrew Ellicott, and would be extended still farther by Thomas Hutchins as the geographer in charge appointed by Congress. In other words, we forget how fundamental to westward expansion the Mason-Dixon line was, even though the evidence of all those right-angled boundaries that are superimposed upon the landscape today—framing Colorado, Wyoming, Utah, Arizona, and New Mexico—reminds us of how lasting the legacy of that eighteenth-century line is.

With that point in mind, I would like to close with reference to another representation of American right angles, composed exactly 200 years after the colonies first declared their intent to unite in federation, a world map exhibiting all the artistry of the earlier *pictura*, which situates its focal checkerboard in the context of other territories that surround it. On this map, China, Russia, and Japan appear as faint slivers on the horizon, and Mexico and Canada as small triangles off to the sides. On this map, Los Angeles is denoted by a small (somewhat misplaced) butte and Las Vegas by an even smaller cactus. On this map, in other words, there is no question about where the impulse to empire is located—it resides in that urban grid delineated by Ninth and Tenth Avenues, whose looming buildings take up four-fifths of Saul Steinberg's western hemisphere and two-thirds of his entire world's space.

Some might say that this map, which first appeared as the March 29, 1976 cover of the *New Yorker*, is an exaggerated if not, after 9/11, outdated rendering. Others might say it reflects the privileged, but not preeminent, place that the USA still occupies within the global affairs of contemporary

Empire. People like me just view it as an expression of our die-hard residency. New York rules, an unwritten caption might proclaim, and for those of us who continue to live there, that's exactly the way things should be.

Notes

1 An earlier version of this chapter appeared as Stacey Olster (2004) "A 'Patch of England, at a three-thousand-Mile Off-set'? Representing America in *Mason & Dixon*," *Modern Fiction Studies*, 50 (2): 283–302. © Purdue Research Foundation. Reprinted with permission of The Johns Hopkins University Press.

References

Anderson, B. (1983) *Imagined Communities: Reflections on the Origin and Spread of Nationalism*, London: Verso.

Bagrow, L. (1951) *History of Cartography*, trans. D. L. Paisley, rev. R. A. Skelton (1966), Cambridge, Mass.: Harvard University Press.

Bailyn, B. (1967) *The Ideological Origins of the American Revolution*, Cambridge, Mass.: Harvard University Press.

Bakhtin, M. M. (1981) *The Dialogic Imagination*, trans. Caryl Emerson and Michael Holquist, Austin, Tex.: University of Texas Press.

Crèvecoeur, J. H. (1957) *Letters from an American Farmer*, New York: Everyman.

Ferguson, R. A. (1994) "The American Enlightenment, 1750–1820," in S. Bercovitch (ed.), *The Cambridge History of American Literature, Vol. I: 1590–1820*, Cambridge: Cambridge University Press, pp. 345–537.

Hardt, M. and Negri, A. (2000) *Empire*, Cambridge, Mass.: Harvard University Press.

Higginson, J. (1697) "Attestation," in C. Mather (1702) *Magnalia Christi Americana: Books I and II*, ed. Kenneth B. Murdock and Elizabeth W. Miller (1977), Cambridge, Mass.: Harvard University Press, pp. 63–73.

Jameson, F. (1991) *Postmodernism, or, the Cultural Logic of Late Capitalism*, Durham, N.C.: Duke University Press.

Lawson, P. (1993) *The East India Company: A History*, London: Longman.

Lukács, G. (1963) *The Historical Novel*, trans. Hannah and Stanley Mitchell, Boston, Mass.: Beacon.

Mason, C. (1969) *The Journal of Charles Mason and Jeremiah Dixon, 1763–1768*, Philadelphia, Penn.: American Philosophical Society.

Pitkin, H. F. (1967) *The Concept of Representation*, Berkeley, Calif.: University of California Press.

Pynchon, T. (1973) *Gravity's Rainbow*, New York: Viking.

——(1990) *Vineland*, Boston, Mass.: Little, Brown.

——(1997) *Mason & Dixon*, New York: Henry Holt.

Shields, D. S. (1990) *Oracles of Empire: Poetry, Politics, and Commerce in British America, 1690–1750*, Chicago, Ill.: University of Chicago Press.

Wilford, J. N. (1981) *The Mapmakers*, New York: Vintage.

9 Contesting the historical pastoral in Philip Roth's American Trilogy

Derek Parker Royal

In the 1990s, Philip Roth did something few of his readers would have expected: He shifted his narrative gaze from the games of self-reflexivity to the American historical landscape. What is more, he did so by bringing back his perennial artist hero, Nathan Zuckerman. Through a series of three novels, Roth revisited key historical moments of post-World War II America. Each book reads as a fascinating case study of the ways in which an individual must negotiate his (it's usually males in Roth's fiction) life in the face of historical forces beyond his control, or, as Roth has put it, the processes by which an individual becomes "history's hostage" (Roth 2003). The American Trilogy stands as one of Roth's most ambitious achievements and marks what is now being seen by many as the high point in his career.

The emphasis on history, especially recent American history, is nothing new in Roth's fiction. America—America as an idea, America as a promised land, America as a refuge—has always been within Roth's narrative vision. However, his novels of the later 1990s concern themselves more significantly with the dynamics underlying historical identity. What makes the American Trilogy so intriguing are the ways in which history reveals the fiction behind the American dream. In all three novels he writes the individual subject into the fabric of history, and by doing so he illustrates that identity is not only a product, but also at the mercy, of the many social, political, and cultural forces that surround it. Zuckerman in the American Trilogy functions as an interpreter of others' narratives or, rather, a conduit for their histories. Through the process of reimagining events, or "enhancing" the facts that surround him, Zuckerman presents his information in ways that emphasize the links between the fiction of storytelling and the "fiction" of history.

The American Trilogy is not only an account of the individual "held hostage" by the forces surrounding them but also of how those forces are informed by the historical pastoral. By "pastoral," I mean not only praise of the rural or rustic life but also notions of an idealized America, innocent and uncomplicated by contradictions or ambiguities. These could take the form of references to a simple agrarian society, ahistorial readings of race, and, of course, the "American dream" in all of its manifestations. The pastoral becomes historicized when it serves as a *raison d'être* for the national project, a belief in American purity that finds expression in such notions as John Winthrop's "city upon a hill," Manifest Destiny, and American exceptionalism. In the American Trilogy, Roth foregrounds the constructed nature of historiography in order to reveal the fictions that make up our national identity. Read in this manner, the novels form both a sweeping epic of late-twentieth-century America and, perhaps more importantly, a sobering look at the very myths that have sustained it.

The American Trilogy encompasses, at least for Roth, three of the most significant periods in post-World War II America: the Red-baiting heydays in the 1950s of Joseph McCarthy and the House Un-American Activities Committee (the focus of *I Married a Communist* [1998]), the aftermath of the Kennedy assassination and the cultural turmoil of the 1960s (the subject of *American Pastoral* [1997]), and the political witch-hunt surrounding President Bill Clinton's impeachment in the 1990s (the springboard for *The Human Stain* [2000]). Perhaps more significantly, all three novels show how individual identity embodies *national* identity and how the forces of history threaten to overtake personal freedom and individual agency. The first novel of the trilogy, *American Pastoral*, revolves around high-school athletic idol, Swede Levov, his attempts to assimilate into the melting pot of WASP society, and how his daughter's involvement with radical anti-Vietnam politics destroyed this pursuit of the "American dream." *I Married a Communist* recounts the life of Ira Ringold and how his political ties to leftist causes in the 1940s lead to his political persecution in the 1950s. In the third novel, *The Human Stain*, the protagonist Coleman Silk, classics professor and former dean of Athena College, finds himself marginalized through the politically correct machinations of his colleagues, much in the way that Clinton was hounded by rightwing Republicans, and, despite his best efforts to live his life on his own terms, he too falls victim to what Nathaniel Hawthorne (whose work figures prominently in this novel) called "the persecuting spirit" (Hawthorne 1983: 126).

In the several years following the publication of its first installment, Roth's American Trilogy has received an impressive amount of critical interest.[1] With its references to the myths surrounding John F. Kennedy, his tragic and untimely assignation, and the turmoil and upheavals of the late 1960s—a period that, in many ways, continues to define our political landscape—it is not surprising that that the Pulitzer Prize-winning *American Pastoral* stands out as the recipient of most of this attention. On the surface, the novel is about Swede Levov and his attempts to make sense of his daughter Merry's Vietnam War protest bombing of the community's general store and post office, an act of domestic terrorism that killed the town doctor and destroyed the Levovs' comfortable middle-class lives. It is divided into three sections, each with revealing titles. In the first, "Paradise Remembered," the narrator, Zuckerman, recalls his high-school idolizing of the Swede as the all-American pride of his Jewish Newark neighborhood. The narrator reminisces that "through the Swede, the neighborhood entered into a fantasy about itself and about the world," a condition that he later describes as "the happy release into a Swedian innocence" (Roth 1997: 3–4). It is also in this first section of the novel that Zuckerman learns of the Swede's family tragedies. While attending his forty-fifth high-school reunion, Nathan runs into Jerry Levov, Seymour's younger brother, who tells him about Merry's murderous behavior, the family's unsuccessful attempts at finding her, and the Swede's twenty-five-year mourning period over the loss. The real shocker for the narrator is the news that the Swede had died just several days before the reunion. This causes him to fall into reverie, a dream-like reflection on Seymour Levov's life that serves as the gist of the novel. As he listens to the hypnotic rhythms of the Pied Piper's 1944 hit, "Dream," Zuckerman calls up his memories of the Swede and then begins to imagine what his life might actually have been like. "I dreamed a realistic chronicle," the narrator tells us. "I began gazing into his life" (Roth 1997: 89). From this moment on, Zuckerman completely recedes into the background as the narrator, and at no point after this does he reassert himself as the one who is putting together the Swede's story.

"The Fall" and "Paradise Lost," the next two sections of the novel, recount the fall of the house of Levov: the Swede's struggles to find Merry, his wife's inability to come to terms with the tragedy, and the looming breakdown of their marriage. What makes the novel's misfortunes so poignant is its physical, as well as thematic, setting. For Swede Levov, Old Rimrock is a pastoral ideal, a place where he and Dawn can escape their strictly ethnic upbringing—his wife grew up in the strongly Irish Catholic section of Elizabeth, New Jersey—and melt into the de-ethnicized pot of the larger American society. This foregrounding of the pastoral is drawn out by two significant images in the novel. The first is the family's Old Rimrock house. When the Swede first lays eyes on the old stone house, he is smitten with a romanticized sense of social belonging, a feeling that here is where his future family will live out their American dream:

> The stone house was not only engagingly ingenious-looking to his eyes—all the irregularity regularized, a jigsaw puzzle fitted patiently together into this square, solid thing to make a beautiful shelter—but

it looked indestructible, an impregnable house that could never burn to the ground and that had probably been standing there since the country began.

(Roth 1997: 190)

Embedded in this description is the grand promise of the New World. The jigsaw puzzle, the irregular stones, the construction of the many parts into a seemingly indestructible whole all suggest varying aspects of the American dream and the melting-pot philosophy. For the socially marginalized, or ill-fitting, "pieces" of the Levov family—the Jew from Weequahic and the Irish Catholic from Elizabeth—their new rural home becomes for them a means to assimilation into "normal" American society. In this way, the Swede's Old Rimrock habitat is similar to the green light at the end of Daisy Buchanan's dock in *The Great Gatsby*. Seymour Levov, much like Jay Gatsby, reaches out for an idealized version of American life, one that will allow him to escape from any predetermined notions of identity and reinvent himself on his own terms.

The other image that typifies the pastoral ideal is that of Johnny Appleseed. For the Swede, there is no figure more representative of his new life in Old Rimrock than the man who defined himself by journeying throughout America's wilderness. "Johnny Appleseed, that's the man for me," thinks the Swede. "Wasn't a Jew, wasn't an Irish Catholic, wasn't a Protestant Christian—nope, Johnny Appleseed was just a happy American" (Roth 1997: 316). What better myth for the Swede's idealized America than the story of a man who more or less "planted" and nurtured the pastoral onto the national stage. Before Merry's bomb, in the family's salad days, whenever the Swede walked to and from the general store, he imagined himself this legendary American figure, moving across the earth and flinging his arms wide with nature's seeds. These images, of the rustic house and of Johnny Appleseed, reveal the pastoral quest underlying the Swede's transplantation onto the historically rich Old Rimrock soil. And they create a setting that, by contrast, dramatically intensifies the unrealized dreams he harbors.

Unrealized dreams are also the subject of *I Married a Communist*. Zuckerman ruminates on the downfall of another one of his adolescent heroes, Ira Ringold, a working-class stiff who gains celebrity as a 1940s broadcasting icon. Over the course of the novel, Zuckerman recounts his relationship with the radio star, and through his conversations with Murray Ringold, Ira's older brother and the narrator's high-school English teacher, he is able to learn more about his one-time hero. After serving in World War II, Ira becomes involved in leftwing politics and through this connection eventually lands a job in radio dramatization. In this business he meets Eve Frame, also a radio star and a one-time silent-film actress. His marriage to her, his contentious relationship with Eve's daughter with a previous husband, and the various betrayals that make up their relationship—the novel is filled with betrayals, making it the central theme of the book—become the focal point of Zuckerman's novel-length conversation with Murray Ringold.

Whereas a de-ethnicized emersion into white-bread America had been the Swede's pastoral dream, Ira's becomes a socially just and politically progressive America—just substitute the proletariat for rustic shepherds. His tirades against capitalism and his arguments for a working-class utopia become another version of Roth's unattainable pastorals, a realm free from the complexities of daily living. Like the Swede, Ira has a dwelling out in the country (in Ira's case, an old shack in Zinc Town, New Jersey) that serves as his "oasis defense against rage and grief" (Roth 1998: 315). And, as we learn toward the end of the novel, much of Ira's life is the result of his attempts to make himself anew, much like his actress wife. As Murray tells his story to Nathan, he describes how Eve Frame, née Chava Fromkin, was a self-hating Jew desperate to recreate herself as an aristocratic Gentile (in many ways anticipating what Coleman Silk will try to do in *The Human Stain*): "All she's trying to do is get away from where she began, and that is no crime. To launch yourself undisturbed by the past into America—that's your choice" (Roth 1998: 158). The free, unanchored self is indeed an American ideal, and, for young Zuckerman, that ideal of America became flesh in the form of Ira Ringold. This was especially the case during his first summer visit to the rustic Zinc Town dwelling:

> I had never before known anyone whose life was so intimately circumscribed by so much American history, who was personally familiar with so much American geography, who had confronted, face to face, so much American lowlife. ... For me, on those nights up in the shack, the America that was my inheritance manifested itself in the form of Ira Ringold.
>
> (Roth 1998: 189)

Much like Swede Levov with his Old Rimrock house and his Johnny Appleseed fantasies, Ira and his colorful life—his humble beginnings as a ditch digger, his bumming across America during the Great Depression, his plainspoken impersonation of Abe Lincoln, his uncompromising dedication to the common working man, his unadorned Walden-like retreat—become a stand-in for an idealized America, one that epitomizes serenity and simplicity.

However, attempts at capturing this Edenic ideal are elusive at best, self-deluding at worst. This is the message that comes through loud and clear in the American Trilogy. One of the pivotal events in *The Human Stain* occurs when Coleman Silk receives the anonymous letter that Delphine Roux has supposedly sent to him. In it she states that "everybody knows" what is going on in Coleman's life. However, as Zuckerman emphatically asserts, such a presumption of absolute knowledge is an insidious ruse. By refusing the possibility of any ambiguity, one denies the very essence of lived experience:

> Because we don't know, do we? … *Nobody* knows, Professor Roux. "Everyone knows" is the invocation of the cliché and the beginning of the banalization of experience, and it's the solemnity and the sense of authority that people have in voicing the cliché that's so insufferable. What we know is that, in an unclichéd way, nobody knows anything. You *can't* know anything. The things you *know* you don't know. Intention? Motive? Consequence? Meaning? All that we don't know is astonishing. Even more astonishing is what passes for knowing.
>
> (Roth 2000: 208–9)

This not knowing is for Roth one of the indelible "stains" of existence. Any attempt at ignoring the contradictions or imperfections that make up our daily experience is tantamount to denying the very core of humanity. To *live* is to be in a constant state of epistemological flux.

In *American Pastoral*, the Swede's attempts to create an existence free from the ethnic, religious, and economic baggage of his past rests on the assumption of individual, as well as national, certainty. Swede is nothing less than the merging of the personal and the political. His quest for an unambiguous and uncomplicated life parallels his nation's attempts at retaining the façade of innocence, even in the face of civil and international embroilment (e.g., the assassination of Kennedy, the Vietnam War, the race riots of the 1960s). In this way, "The Fall" and "Paradise Lost" could just as well describe America during the 1960s. It is no accident that Zuckerman says of the Swede at one point, "But of course. He is our Kennedy" (Roth 1997: 83), and that the president's assassination is alluded to no less than three other times in the novel. And the motives and desires that underlie the "American dream" are never pure, nor can they ever be definitively understood. This is the conclusion that Zuckerman reaches with Seymour Levov. Try as he might, he is never able to grasp fully the Swede's consciousness, to understand what makes him tick. Yet, there is something encouraging, even empowering, about this admission of incomprehensibility. In confessing his ignorance of Swede's motives,

Zuckerman concludes "that getting people right is not what living is all about anyway. It's getting them wrong that is living, getting them wrong and wrong and wrong and then, on careful reconsideration, getting them wrong again. That's how we know we're alive: we're wrong" (Roth 1997: 35). Zuckerman's words here bear a striking resemblance to his comments on Delphine Roux's "everybody knows" letter. Feeling comfortable in the certainty of your knowledge runs counter to reality and denies the more "human" and less predictable side of experience.

The pastoral is a state of mind that cannot account for conflict, contradiction, or uncertainty, as Swede Levov so tragically learns. After Merry throws her bomb, many around the former high-school superstar point out the fallacy of his Old Rimrock dreams. The Swede's adopted home is further demythologized by his straight-shooting glove-making father, Lou. Even before Merry's bomb, Lou tries to disabuse his son of any idealized notions of Old Rimrock, especially as it stands for an assimilated and homogenized America free of ethnic strife or prejudice:

> You're dreaming. I wonder if you even know where this is. Let's be candid with each other about this—this narrow, bigoted area. The Klan thrived out here in the twenties. Did you know that? ... They wouldn't give a Jew the time of day. I'm talking to you, son, about bigots. Not about the goose step even—just about hate.
>
> (Roth 1997: 309)

His brother Jerry puts the matter even more bluntly. In a diatribe against Swede's worldview, taking up approximately nine pages of the text, Jerry spews forth a scathing indictment that stands as the centerpiece of Roth's pastoral critique:

> You wanted Miss America? Well, you've got her, with a vengeance— she's your daughter! ... You longed to belong like everybody else to the United States of America? Well, you do now, big boy, thanks to your daughter. The reality of this place is right up in your kisser now. With the help of your daughter you're as deep in the shit as a man can get, the real American crazy shit. America amok! America amuck!
>
> (Roth 1997: 277)

Jerry argues that in attempting to live out the "perfect" American life, his brother has in essence lived on the terms of others. The reality of the Swede, the inner self that strives for excellence, has always been concealed in a nationalistic fantasy. "And that is why, to this day," Jerry charges, "nobody knows who you are. You are unrevealed—that is the story, Seymour, *unrevealed*" (Roth 1997: 276).

Coleman Silk, too, hides himself behind a "pastoral" mask, but one that is deeply invested in the denial of racial memory. Just as the Swede attempts to erase the traces of his Jewish ethnicity, so does Coleman try to rid himself of the "stain" of American intolerance. Upon enlisting in the Navy, he repudiates his African-American heritage and as a result becomes, in the words of Zuckerman, "the greatest of the great *pioneers* of the I" (Roth 2000: 108). He refuses to subsume his identity within American racial politics, choosing instead to reconstruct it beyond both white power structure and the black community. Coleman Silk becomes not white—as most assume when reading the novel as one of racial passing—but what might more accurately be described as "non(e)-other." Yet, it is this denial of race, this dream of a homogenized American ideal, that marks him as an absence. In words reminiscent of Jerry's accusations of the "unrevealed" Swede, Zuckerman explains his frustrations in trying to get a fix on Coleman and coming up with nothing. "It's something *not* there that beguiles," the narrator confesses at one point, "and it's what's been drawing me all along, the enigmatic *it* that he holds apart as his and no one else's. … There is a blank. That's all I can say" (Roth 2000: 213).

In *American Pastoral*, Zuckerman had been unable to "get it right" with the Swede, and the same can be said of his attempts at understanding Coleman. Indeed, the mystery of Silk is ironically made manifest through what is normally seen as an indelible identifying mark. When he first meets Coleman, Zuckerman notices a "small, Popeye-ish, blue tattoo" on his right upper arm, a mark (or stain) that seems out of keeping with his neighbor's professorial exterior (Roth 2000: 21). Yet, this tattoo, far from signifying anything explicable, has just the opposite effect. It becomes, for Zuckerman, a "tiny symbol, if one were needed, of all the million circumstances of the other fellow's life, of that blizzard of details that constitute the confusion of a human biography—a tiny symbol to remind me why our understanding of people must always be at best slightly wrong" (Roth 2000: 22). It is no accident that the enigmatic symbol was acquired during Silk's stint in the Navy, an occasion that forever exiled him from his African-American past. In attempting to recreate his identity outside of racial history, he becomes, much like the Swede, an empty subject in search of a nonexistent American Eden.

Similarly, in *I Married a Communist*, Ira Ringold's search for an idealized American life is called into question. Much like the Swede and Coleman, Ira longs to escape the ambiguities and complications that could compromise his "pastoral," except for Ira this takes the form of the political. A Communist utopia is the end point of Ira's quest, and at least outwardly, he is unbending in that pursuit. However, a grand irony underlies Ira's attempts at ideological purity. At the same time he is espousing political certainty, he is living a life that betrays ambiguity. His Communist rhetoric and his bourgeois lifestyle certainly do not mesh. As Johnny O'Day, Ira's old army buddy and leftist ideologue, bluntly puts it once his protégé is outed as a member of the Communist Party, Ira's diatribes on the working class and impersonations of Lincoln were nothing more than an empty façade. Much like Jerry Levov does with the Swede, O'Day cuts through his former colleague's pretense. Ira, AKA the *actor* Iron Rinn, was

> [a]lways impersonating and never the real thing. ... Betrayed his revolutionary comrades and betrayed the working class. Sold out. Bought off. Totally the creature of the bourgeoisie. Seduced by fame and money and wealth and power. And pussy, fancy Hollywood pussy. Doesn't retain a vestige of his revolutionary ideology—nothing. An opportunistic stooge.
>
> (Roth 1998: 288)

It is significant that O'Day is the one to question Ira's political commitment. He represents the pure and uncompromising life of a Marxist precisian, and although he embodies an ideological ideal, his life is anything but attractive. Without a family, without real friends, and without a life outside of union organizing, his is the most depersonalized of existences. He, more than anyone else in the novel, is without ambiguity or contradiction. In other words, he is the least "human," and as such, serves as an unappealing foil to the blundering compromises of Ira. In a similar manner, we can read Les Farley in *The Human Stain* as a deadening will to purity. Despite his struggles with posttraumatic stress disorder, he embodies a longing for uncomplicated perfection. This can be most clearly seen in the final pages of the novel when Zuckerman encounters Les ice fishing against a pristine backdrop of sheer whiteness. His secret fishing spot admits no one and is untainted by impurities. The spring underneath the ice, Les tells the narrator, "cleans itself. [It's] all God-made. Nothing man had to do with it. That's why it's clean and that's why I come here. If man has to do with it, stay away from it. That's my motto" (Roth 2000: 360). It is no accident that of all the characters in the novel, Les Farley is the one most closely associated with death, as demonstrated by his stints in Vietnam, his presumed murder of Coleman and Faunia, and, as Zuckerman is unnerved to discover, his wielding of the auger: "The auger out on the ice. The candor of the auger. There could be no more solid embodiment of our hatred than the merciless steel look of that auger out in the middle of nowhere" (Roth 2000: 352).

These tendencies toward ontological or ideological purity, as exemplified through Farley and O'Day, leave no room for human interaction. As Murray tells Zuckerman in *I Married a Communist*, "when you decide to contribute your personal problem to an ideology's agenda, everything that is personal is squeezed out and discarded and all that remains is what is useful to the ideology" (Roth 1998: 261). Despite his best attempts, Ira cannot ultimately live a political absolute, as his brother points out early on: "He was not perfect from the Communist point of view—thank God. The personal he could not renounce. The personal kept bursting out of Ira, militant and single-minded though he would try to be. ... Ira lived everything personally, ... to the hilt, including his contradictions" (Roth 1998: 83). Zuckerman acknowledges this during the last evening of his conversation with Murray, bringing his one-time hero back down to earth by recognizing these contradictions. Ira is more "human" than his political mentor "[b]ecause purity is petrifaction. Because purity is a lie. Because unless you're an ascetic paragon like Johnny O'Day and Jesus Christ, you're urged on by five hundred things" (Roth 1998: 318). In language that sounds strikingly similar to the "everyone knows" passage in *The Human Stain* and the "getting people wrong" comments in *American Pastoral*, Murray sums up his brother this way: "he could never construct [a life] that fit. The enormous wrongness of this guy's effort. But one's errors always rise to the surface, don't they?" to which the narrator replies, "It's all error ... Isn't that what you've been telling me? There's only error. There's the heart of the world. Nobody finds his life. That *is* life" (Roth 1998: 319).

Ira's inability to get it right is reminiscent of Jerry's accusatory words to the Swede, "nobody knows who you are. You are unrevealed" (Roth 1997: 276). And this declaration is central to a thematic understanding of *American Pastoral*. The Swede is an unknown entity not only to his brother, but to the narrator as well. In the novel's opening section, Zuckerman tells the reader that he chances upon the former high school all-star in the summer of 1985, thirty-six years after idolizing him on the football field, and then unexpectedly receives a letter from him ten years later. In the letter the Swede asks the author if he would help him in writing a tribute to his father—a man who suffered "shocks that befell his loved ones" (Roth 1997: 18), but who is now dead—to be published privately for family and friends. They meet in a New York restaurant, and, during the course of the conversation, Zuckerman is unable to extract from Swede any detail surrounding this apparent shock. Instead, the Swede brings up commonplace niceties: pictures of his children, news of his business dealings, innocuous updates on his brother Jerry. Nathan tries to uncover some hidden motives or disturbing memories behind the Swede's request to meet, but instead he finds that "all that rose to the surface was more surface. What he has instead of a being, I thought, is blandness" (Roth 1997: 23). This leaves Zuckerman at a loss to understand the man who had meant so much to him in high school. He is left with nothing more than unanswered questions as he ponders, "what did he do for subjectivity? What *was* the Swede's subjectivity? There had to be a substratum, but its composition was unimaginable" (Roth 1997: 20).

This inability to fathom his high-school hero is analogous to the Swede's own failure to comprehend the reality underlying Old Rimrock and, by association, the idealized America for which it stands. However, Zuckerman's response to his intellectual impotence—a fitting word, given the fact that he has been impaired by prostate surgery—is markedly different from the Swede's. Being unable to know completely what has happened in the man's life, Zuckerman relies on a strategy that serves him well as a writer: He imagines the life of Seymour Levov. Or, put another way, he constructs a history that allows him to comprehend more clearly the enigma of his subject. Almost everything that we know about the Swede's life—the details surrounding Merry's bombing, her flight and disappearance, the family's attempts to cope with her actions, and the Swede's finding her years later as a follower of Jainism—is, as far as we know, the product of Zuckerman's imagination. After hearing Johnny Mercer's "Dream" at his high-school reunion, he figuratively "lift[s] the Swede up onto the stage," and by doing so places the Swede's story at the center of his own (Roth 1997: 88).

When *American Pastoral* was originally published, most critics failed to notice, or at least failed to acknowledge, that the story of the Swede was more or less a fabrication, the result of Zuckerman's nostalgically induced musings. By stating that his narrator "dreamed a realistic chronicle," Roth apparently threw his readers off track by purposefully blurring the boundaries between the "dream" and the "real." As such, the novel becomes more of a narrative on Zuckerman and the ways in which *he* constructs reality, and less of an explanatory tale of the enigmatic Swede. When we realize that the story of Swede Levov is made up or imagined by Zuckerman, then the storyteller, not the story, becomes our primary novelistic focus. And along with this awareness comes the question: What investment does the narrator have in the story he is telling? The same question could be asked of *The Human Stain*. The story of Coleman Silk is also full of gaps, blank spaces, and narrative silences. In recreating the life of his neighbor, the narrator again turns to fiction as a source of "history," a rather appropriate means by which to expose the "unrevealed" object. And what fascinates Zuckerman about both figures is their desire to embody the pastoral. By narrating the lives of these enigmas, Zuckerman reveals just as much, if not more, about American historiography than he does the subjects of his stories.

Roth himself recognizes as false any assumptions of "purity" or "innocence" that might accompany his country's history (particularly in his lifetime), and acknowledges the politically mixed motives inherent in our national identity. In an interview with the French newspaper *Le Figaro*, he balks at the suggestion that the United States "lost her innocence" after the 9/11 attacks: "What innocence? From 1668 to 1865 this country had slavery; and from 1865 to 1955 was a society existing under brutal segregation. I don't really know what these people [who called America innocent] are talking about" (Leith 2002: 21). In other words, Roth is able to admit what Swede Levov, Ira Ringold, and Coleman Silk cannot: the ambiguity underlying the American project. Their attempts to discover their own American pastoral—a paradise free of ethnic, economic, and political complications—prevent any awareness of the unflattering or even malignant characteristics of their surroundings. These three protagonists serve in a long line of American literary figures whose failure to grasp the ambiguous nature of existence leads to his downfall. Much like Hawthorne's Goodman Brown, who will not admit the darker side of the human heart; much like Melville's Ahab, who must know without any doubt the reality behind the pasteboard mask; and much like Fitzgerald's Jay Gatsby, who refuses to see the more sordid reality behind the green lights of Daisy's dock, Swede, Ira, and Coleman attempt to live an idealized American life.

However, instead of the pastoral, all three find its antithesis, what Zuckerman calls "the indigenous American berserk" (Roth 1997: 86). Merry's bomb awakens Swede to the turmoil of the 1960s, but in a more general sense, it illustrates the fictitiousness of any mythologized national Eden. Coleman's desire for a life free of racial complications is ironically undermined by accusations of his own racism. And Ira's dreams of both a just America and a comfortable bourgeois marriage are turned upside down after he is branded a Communist, especially after "the whole irrational frenzy" of the gossip media take a hold of his and Eve's lives. What the novels in Roth's American Trilogy clearly illustrate is the more troubling side of the American dream. In *American Pastoral*, after Zuckerman attends his forty-fifth high-school reunion, he lies awake in bed, alone and in the dark, composing a speech on what America was like for his graduating class of 1950. In many ways, it reads as a "golden age" tribute to the immediate post-Depression, post-war era, a romanticized meditation on what his country once was. It is significant to note, however, that Zuckerman never gives that speech, and that what seems sensible to him as a late-night rumination never makes it to the light of day. Instead, he "dreamed a realistic chronicle" by reimagining the life of an all-American hero. With more than just a slight ironic twist on Tolstoy's assessment of Ivan Ilych, Zuckerman reveals that "Swede Levov's life ... had been most simple and most ordinary and therefore just great, right in the American grain" (Roth 1997: 31). The "simple" and "ordinary" are given heroic treatment in Weequahic's "household Apollo" (Roth 1997: 4), and in the figure of the Swede we see what is arguably both the promise and the problem of our post-World War II culture.

The ambiguous construct of the American dream is given a similar treatment in the final pages of *I Married a Communist*. After Zuckerman concludes his six-night conversation with Murray Ringold, he heads out to the deck of his country house and stretches out on the chaise lounge. There, he looks up at the clear evening sky and remembers that as a child uncertain about death, his mother reassured him by telling him that when people die they "go up to the sky and live on forever as gleaming stars." He then, in an extended yet highly moving passage that concludes the novel, imagines that all of the principals in Iron Rinn's drama, now dead, are there above him fixed in the peaceful sky, where

> [t]here are no longer mistakes for Eve or Ira to make. There is no betrayal. There is no idealism. There are no falsehoods. There is neither conscience nor its absence. ... There is just the furnace of Ira and the furnace of Eve burning at twenty million degrees. ... What you see from this silent rostrum up on my mountain on a night as splendidly clear as that night ... is that universe into which error does not obtrude. You see the inconceivable: the colossal spectacle of no antagonism. You see with your own eyes the vast brain of time, a galaxy of fire set by no human hand.
>
> The stars are indispensable.
>
> (Roth 1998: 322–3)

Here, looking up into the pristine night sky, the narrator takes the pastoral to new heights. Such perfection is a dream, beyond human reach, but, as the last line of the novel suggests, its possibility is nonetheless necessary. The ideal may be out there on some an ethereal plane, but just as prominent is Nathan Zuckerman, standing on the dance floor of his high-school reunion, listening to Johnny Mercer's "Dream," or in his living room dancing with Coleman, the "snub-nosed, goat-footed Pan," to the rhythms of "Bewitched, Bothered, and Bewildered" (Roth 2000: 25). And so too is the *possibility* of the American dream. Despite the fact that Roth has been critiquing it throughout his career, he has nonetheless acknowledged that our national identity is wrapped up in the hopeful as well as the tragic. The pastoral may be an untenable realm for his protagonists, but it is one whose pull is keenly felt. "The stars are indispensable": For Philip Roth, such a statement could just as well stand as a bittersweet epitaph to the aspirations of an entire nation.

Notes

1 For a complete listing of resources on Philip Roth, visit the Philip Roth Society's bibliography and research guide at www.rothsociety.org.

References

Hawthorne, N. (1983) *The Scarlet Letter*, ed. Millicent Bell, New York: Library of America.

Leith, S. (2002) "Philip Roth Attacks 'Orgy of Narcissism' Post-September 11," *Daily Telegraph*, October 5, p. 21.

Roth, P. (1997) *American Pastoral*, Boston, Mass.: Houghton Mifflin.

—— (1998) *I Married a Communist*, Boston, Mass.: Houghton Mifflin

—— (2000) *The Human Stain*, Boston, Mass.: Houghton Mifflin.

—— (2000) "Zuckerman's Alter Brain: Interview with Charles McGrath," *New York Times Book Review*, May 7, pp. 8, 10.

—— (2003) Interview with David Remnick: *Philip Roth at 70*, dir. Deborah Lee. Broadcast BBC4, March 19.

10 Skating on a shit field

Tim O'Brien and the topography of trauma

Brian Jarvis

Over the past twenty years, two of the most conspicuous trends in the humanities have been the "turn to trauma" and the "spatial turn." "Trauma" and "space" have each been the site of an exciting inter-disciplinary convergence involving literary and film studies, history and cultural geography, psychoanalysis and feminism. At the same time, and somewhat surprisingly, there has been relatively little exploration of the intersections *between* trauma and space. Of course there have been excep-tions (Pierre Nora's pioneering work on *lieux de mémoire* [1996–98], Geoffrey Hartman's readings of place in Wordsworth [2004] and Anne Whitehead's study of landscape in contemporary fiction [2004]) but, in general terms, trauma has been conceived as a matter of time. Trauma theory, especially where it intersects with Holocaust studies, has dis-played a marked preoccupation with crises in temporality and historio-graphy, memory and moments. It would be well beyond the scope of this essay to offer an explanatory model for the spatial crises of trauma, but I do intend to gesture towards the ways in which trauma might *take place*. In literary representation, trauma appears as an event horizon that folds geographical referents into itself. The traumatic experience devours space and confuses coordinates through a cascade of displace-ments that prohibit (en)closure and jeopardize the very concept of a coherent topography. Consequently, in place of a lucid mapping of trauma, I intend to offer a cautionary traumatology of topos through a close reading of spaces in Tim O'Brien's Vietnam novel *The Things They Carried* ([1990] 1991).

Inter faeces et urinam nascimur

Vietnam Vietnam Vietnam, we've all been there.

(Herr 1978: 207)

Whenever a man dreams of a place or a country and says to himself, while he is dreaming: "this place is familiar to me, I've been here before" we may interpret that place as being his mother's genitals or body.

(Freud 2003b: 64)

The first place that is mapped by O'Brien is the first place. "In country" is rendered as a gynecological geography. No women carry babies in *The Things They Carried*, but the maternal imago haunts a landscape of fecund jungle, intrauterine tunnels and invaginating fox holes, swamps, rivers and a shit field. Following a journey over water, the tour of duty is simultaneously sutured with the primal displacement of birth trauma and thalassic regression (the psychoanalytical term for dreams of oceans and smaller inland seas that might symbolize life in the womb):

All around you, everywhere, the whole dark countryside came alive. You'd hear a strange hum in your ears ... Like the night had its own voice—that hum in your ears—and in the hours after midnight you'd swear you were walking through some kind of soft black protoplasm, Vietnam, the blood and the flesh.

(O'Brien 1991: 217).

The more dead bodies it claims, the more this devouring womb comes to life. Vietnam, the vampyress, sucks soldiers down into the blood-soaked soil, the undergrowth, the rice paddies and primeval swamp. In the opening title story, "The Things They Carried," Alpha Company is ordered to explore the "elaborate tunnel complexes in the Than Khe area south of Chu Lai" (O'Brien 1991: 9). After stripping off his gear, a lone soldier "crawl[s] in headfirst ... you had to wiggle in—ass and elbows—a swallowed-up feeling" (O'Brien 1991: 10). Confinement is followed, if lucky, by a subsequent surfacing "filthy, but alive" (O'Brien 1991: 11). The rest of the men avoid "facing the hole," but cannot help imagining "the tunnel walls squeezing in" (O'Brien 1991: 9–10). When one of his men fails to surface, platoon leader Jimmy Cross imagines a tunnel collapse which then elides with a fantasy about his girlfriend, Martha: "The stresses and the fractures, the quick collapse, the two of them buried alive under all that weight. Dense, crushing love ... his love was too much for him, he felt paralyzed, he wanted to sleep inside her lungs and breathe her blood and be smothered" (O'Brien 1991: 10).

To escape from the dark continent of 'Nam's interior, Cross dreams of uterine flight back to his American sweetheart. We are not told Martha's surname, but perhaps, given O'Brien's extravagant psychoanalytical self-consciousness, it might be Bernays (the maiden name of Martha Freud, whose courtship with Sigmund, like that of Martha and Jimmy Cross, began with the exchange of love letters).

In the Than Khe tunnels, Cross's missing soldier, Lee Strunk, returns. Later, however, the platoon is devastated by the loss of another man, Kiowa, in the key location for O'Brien's mapping of Vietnam as the monstrous feminine. This site is introduced in the traumatized recollections of Norman Bowker as he drives round his hometown lake, "hopelessly round and round" (O'Brien 1991: 146), whilst compulsively replaying memories of his inability to save Kiowa from drowning in a "shit field." Bowker recalls that after the October monsoons, the Song Tra Bong, "a slow flat muddy river … overflowed its banks and the land turned into a deep, thick muck … Like quicksand, almost, except the stink was incredible" (O'Brien 1991: 142–3). On night patrol, in torrential rain, Alpha Company make camp in this "deep, oozy soup" despite the rising slime and olfactory offensive: "a dead-fish smell—but it was something else, too. Finally somebody figured it out. What this was, it was a shit field. The village toilet. No indoor plumbing" (O'Brien 1991: 145). When the company comes under mortar fire, the "[t]he field [starts] boiling … earth bubbled" (O'Brien 1991: 147). Kiowa is wounded and Bowker tries forlornly to save him from drowning: "he grabbed Kiowa by the boot and tried to pull him out. He pulled hard but Kiowa was gone" (O'Brien 1991: 148). Bowker manages, slowly and painfully, to extract himself from the earth, caked in muck and with the taste of shit fresh in his mouth. The psychogeography of this scene suggests antipodal birth traumas in the *anus mundi*: one "newborn" survives to be haunted by meconium aspiration (when a baby swallows its own feces during labor), but the other undergoes a rectal absorption which recalls Freud's "cloaca theory" (a misconception amongst some children that women have only one pelvic orifice and birth occurs through the anus). Following an intensive search the next day, a second anal parturition takes place in which three men pull Kiowa's dead body out of the shit field by his feet: a breach extraction with the stillborn coated in the "bluish-green" slime of mother earth's *decidua* (O'Brien 1991: 172). In the "Notes" that follow "Speaking of Courage," Bowker's story becomes "O'Brien's" (as character-narrator), and the shit field becomes an abject geographical microcosm for the war itself: "For twenty years this field had embodied all the waste that was Vietnam, all the vulgarity and horror" (O'Brien 1991: 186).

In *Male Fantasies*, Klaus Theweleit examines the literature of the Freikorps (various paramilitary groups formed in Germany by veterans of World War I) and uncovers the recurring image of an "anthropomorphized body of Mother Earth that devours, flows and erupts"

(Theweleit 1987: 238). This conceit is so conspicuous in interwar fascist writing that Theweleit contends "[t]his is no longer a matter of war. The war simply creates a means for expressing the desire for—and fear of—being swallowed up by the earth" (1987: 239). The fantasy of the oral mother projected onto the battlefield is part of a generalized gender anxiety apparent within the libidinal economy of war. Military power seeks to colonize the soldier's gender identity and to develop a militarized body that must be permanently hard and function with mechanical efficiency. The skin is replaced by armor and spontaneous movements exchanged for precise geometrical patterns. This paradigm entails a pathologizing of the nonmilitary corpus: anything "soft," or "wet" is

> negativized to such an extent that they [become] the physical manifestations of all that [is] terrifying … all the hybrid substances that were produced by the body and flowed on, in, over, and out of the body: the floods and stickiness of sucking kisses; the swamps of the vagina, with their slime and mire; the pap and slime of male semen; the film of sweat that settles on the stomach, thighs, and in the anal crevice, and that turns two pelvic regions into a sub-tropical landscape.
>
> (Theweleit 1987: 410)

The secret enemy is the anima (a term from Jungian psychoanalysis that signifies the femininity which is typically repressed in the male unconscious). The soldier, trained to be at war with physical and psychological manifestations of the feminine, carries around his own occupied territories. The hyperbolic masculinity imposed by military discipline ensures that trauma is inseparable from the corporeal cartographies of gender identity.

Indian country

> The words that cannot be uttered, the scenes that cannot be recalled, the tears that cannot be shed—everything will be swallowed along with the trauma that led to the loss. Swallowed and preserved. Inexpressible mourning erects a secret tomb inside the subject. Reconstituted from the memories of words, scenes, and affects, the objective correlative of the loss is buried alive in the crypt as a full-fledged person, complete with its own topography.
>
> (Abraham and Torok 1994: 130)

A traumatic crisis in cartography and gender identity is evident in "Sweetheart of the Song Tra Bong." When Mary Anne Bell audaciously visits her boyfriend, Mark Fossie, in 'Nam, she undergoes a dramatic metamorphosis from all-American girl to predatory Amazonian. Fresh from "Cleveland Heights Senior High," Mary Anne initially boosts morale and entertains the troops (O'Brien 1991: 90). Gradually, however, she stops being something to look at and starts to look for herself: at the wounds and the weapons, the Vietnamese people and the jungle. She stops using makeup, removes her jewelry, cuts her hair short and eventually joins the Green Berets on ambush. Her boyfriend complains that her body is changing: it has become "foreign somehow—too stiff in places, too firm where the softness used to be" (O'Brien 1991: 94). Fossie suspects infidelity, and his suspicions are founded although Mary Anne has not been unfaithful with another soldier; rather, she has been seduced by the Land itself: "[s]ometimes I want to eat this place. Vietnam. I want to swallow the whole country—the dirt, the death—I just want to eat it and have it there inside me" (O'Brien 1991: 103). Whilst the male soldiers dread incorporation, Mary Anne goes deeper and dissolves into myth:

> [She] was still somewhere out there in the dark … Late at night, when the Greenies were out on ambush, the rain forest seemed to stare at them … She had crossed to the other side. She was part of the land. She was wearing her culottes, her pink sweater, and a necklace of human tongues.
>
> (O'Brien 1991: 107)

Mary Anne's distinctive accessory recalls the taking of body parts—ears, fingers, even heads—as trophies by US soldiers in Vietnam. However, when the necklace first appears, its wearer is singing in a "foreign tongue" which echoes Fossie's earlier complaint regarding Mary Anne's "foreign body." When the innocent all-American girl arrives in 'Nam, she is pure red, white and blue: "long white legs and blue eyes and a complexion like strawberry ice cream" (O'Brien 1991: 90). Mary Anne's subsequent transformation into primitive killer is accompanied by a stripping of her national and racial identity that is perhaps hinted at by the place name with which the "Sweetheart" is associated: as an adjective, *bong* means "snow white" but as a verb it signifies the act of "peeling." The ex-Snow White darkens her skin with charcoal for camouflage and exchanges Cleveland Heights for an "exotic smokehouse" that reeks of "joss sticks and incense," where the windows dance with bright "yellows" in time to "bamboo flutes and drums and chimes" and Mary Anne's own incomprehensible chanting (O'Brien 1991: 102). In the Dragon Lady's lair, patriarchal and colonialist topographies are superimposed. US versions of Vietnam, in fiction and film, frequently indulge in Orientalist mappings of East and West as mythical antipodes: feminine and masculine, irrational and rational, primitive and civilized. A retreat into geographical mysticism "discovers" Vietnam as an Eastern "Garden of Evil" (O'Brien 1991: 76).

In *The Things They Carried*, Vietnam is colonized as primeval shit field in a topography which is both Orientalist and Gothic. O'Brien marshals an inventory of gothic topoi: the body in danger, possession and haunting, ghosts and secrets, and uncanny elisions between inside and outside, living and dead, womb and tomb. The centripetal shit field might be approached as a "crypt," as defined by Abraham and Torok in their Gothic revision of classical psychoanalysis. Although "the crypt marks a definite place in the topography" it is not easily located since it is always "encrypted" and seeks to disguise even the fact of its own existence (Abraham and Torok 1994: 159). The source of the crypt might not even be a trauma experienced directly by the subject. Traumatic experience that is not properly buried can be inherited and "travel" as a "transgenerational phantom": "what haunts are not the dead, but the gaps left within us by the secrets of others" (Abraham and Torok 1994: 171). Nicholas Rand has speculated that the hauntings of ancestral specters might not only be a family affair, but could involve "the phantomatic return of shameful secrets on the level of ... the community, and possibly even entire nations" (Abraham and Torok 1994: 169).

When Kiowa is claimed by the shit field, Azar responds ironically: "Like those old cowboy movies. One more redskin bites the dirt" (O'Brien 1991: 165). But is it only one? Kiowa is the name of a tribe, and Vietnam was known colloquially as "Indian country." In *Dispatches*, Michael Herr complains that American soldiers had "all seen too many movies, stayed too long in Television city" (1978: 201). However, the conceit that framed the Vietcong as Red (Communist) Indians was not merely a postmodern simulacrum. The military tactics adopted in Indochina to win what Richard Slotkin called the "last great Indian War" mirrored the genocidal strategies adopted against Native Americans: targeting civilian settlements, environmental devastation, and gestural relocation (2000: 562). The Military Assistance Program that justified excursions in Southeast Asia was legitimated by "politically acceptable precedents such as the US Army's role in developing the American West" (cited in Chomsky 1970: 120). Intervention in Indochina was accompanied by distant echoes of frontier mythology as well as Freikorps iconography: the "Red Wave" threatening to flood the Fatherland that Theweleit finds repeatedly in interwar German literature resonates with US Cold War demonology and domino theory.

According to Derrida, there is always "a crypt within a crypt, a name within a name, a body within the body" (1986: xxvii). Are there other bodies buried alongside and even inside Kiowa's corpse? Is O'Brien's shit field a mass grave? Alpha Company spend hours trawling the shit field to find Kiowa's body. Alternatively, Abraham and Torok's investigative method—the textual excavations of cryptonomy—seeks not "a metonymy of things but a metonymy of words" (Abraham and Torok 1986: 19). When Kiowa disappears into the earth, Bowker can still see a body part protruding: "There was a knee" (O'Brien 1991: 148). The conjunction here of "wounded" Indian and "knee" might be read as a "crypt-effect" in which the last major armed conflict between Native Americans and the US Army surfaces. The Wounded Knee massacre (1890) was linked to the rise of the Ghost Dance. This intertribal visionary movement responded to westward expansion with an apocalyptic vision of the land being reborn. In the spring, the earth would be covered with a new soil that would bury all white men whilst the Ghost Dancers were taken up into the air. When they returned to a regenerated earth, all evil would be washed away and the ghosts of their ancestors would join them. There are ghosts of the Ghost Dance in O'Brien's shit field and elsewhere in *The Things They Carried*. In "Style," for example, when a teenage Vietnamese girl with "black hair and brown skin" (O'Brien 1991: 135) dances in a "weird ritual" after the traumatic loss of her family and ancestral village. The Ghost Dance movement was integral to Kiowa culture from 1894 to 1916 and involved a syncretic blend of tribal folklore, peyotism (a native American religion and sacramental ritual involving the hallucinogenic peyote button) and Christian resurrection. In this context it is noteworthy that O'Brien's Kiowa is a devout Christian whose commanding officer—Jimmy Cross—carries the Savior's initials, as well as the instrument of His death and subsequent resurrection.

According to the Ghost Dance vision, Christ's second coming would be accompanied by the return of the bison. The buffalo was a sacred creature ranked just below the eagle and the Sun in Kiowa mythology. The buffalo doctors were the Kiowa's most revered medicine men and renowned for their ability to treat wounds inflicted in combat. In May 1971, at the Dellums Committee Hearings on War Crimes in Vietnam, Captain Robert Johnson replied as follows to the question: "What did 'Indian Country' refer to?" "I guess it means different things to different people. It's like there are savages out there, there are gooks out there. In the same way we slaughtered the Indian's buffalo, we would slaughter the water buffalo in Vietnam" (Johnson 1971). In "How to Tell a True War Story," Rat Kiley methodically murders a water buffalo. Starting with the "right front knee" he then shoots the animal in the ear, hindquarters, hump, flanks, mouth, tail, ribs, belly, nose and throat, but, remarkably, it survives. Throughout this assault, the buffalo makes no sound and hardly moves aside from its rolling eyes which are "shiny black and dumb" (O'Brien

1991: 76). The conjunction here of "buffalo" and "soldier" conjures a second transgenerational phantom. "Buffalo soldiers," a nickname given to African Americans in the US Army, was coined by the Kiowa tribe when they encountered the 10th Cavalry Regiment in western Kansas in the late 1860s. The name is said to be inspired partly by a resemblance between African-American hair and the bison's mane but also by shared characteristics of strength, endurance, and great patience. There are no African-American soldiers in *The Things They Carried*, but Rat Kiley's assault on the water buffalo threatens to open crypts in which the historical traumas of white violence and black suffering are buried. Kiley's sadistic and systematic violence is a response to the loss of his friend, Curt Lemon, who stepped on a booby trap and was blown to pieces. The destruction of the buffalo mirrors Lemon's fragmentation into parts left "hanging" in a tree (O'Brien 1991: 78). The instant before the explosion, Lemon's face appears "suddenly brown and shining" (O'Brien 1991: 69 and repeated later on, 1991: 79) as he steps into a dazzling sunlight that seems to "[come] around him and [lift] him up and [suck] him high into a tree" (1991: 69). The image of a "kid" with a brown face claimed by the *"fatal whiteness* of that light" and left hanging from a tree might be read as a phantomatic passing that signposts a long history of execution and lynching (O'Brien 1991: 79, my italics). Alternatively, the images of a young warrior ascending in light might take us back to the Kiowa and their most sacred ritual: The Sun Dance was situated by a sacred tree and involved the ceremonial slaughter of a buffalo with one shot, or arrow, since a bloody kill was considered an ill omen.

Curt Lemon's messy dismemberment takes place on a "trail junction" that intersects with the anagram buried in Rat Kiley's name (trail key) (O'Brien 1991: 69). Following his attack on the buffalo, Kiley breaks down in tears as though in cryptic confirmation of Herr's assertion that "Vietnam was where the Trail of Tears was headed all along" (Herr 1978: 94). Kiley tries "to say something, but then cradled his rifle and went off by himself" (O'Brien 1991: 76). Abraham and Torok speculate that "those who carry a tomb within themselves ... carry one—or many secrets" (O'Brien 1991: 158, 172). Typically, O'Brien's characters are walking mausoleums of inexpressible mourning: "they all carried ghosts" (1991: 9). Alongside the ghost of the pre-Oedipal mother, the topography of trauma in *The Things They Carried* is haunted by the specter of racial guilt (the white man's other burden). A cryptic trail of words, buried alive, takes us metonymically from the combat zones of Vietnam to Wounded Knee, the Trail of Tears, buffalo trails, and Colonel Charles Lynch's infamous walnut tree. Cryptonomic crossings between Asian, Native American and African-American experience are buried in the Gothic melting pot of a shit field.

The topography of trauma is fractured by secrets: the crypt that cracks open to reveal other crypts. Where does this cascading end?

Fiduciary markings in a shit field

> They would often discard things along the route of march. Purely for comfort they would throw away rations … no matter because by nightfall the resupply choppers would arrive with more of the same, then a day or two later still more, fresh watermelons and ammunition and sunglasses and woolen sweaters—the resources were stunning— sparklers for the Fourth of July, colored eggs for Easter—it was the great American war chest … they carried like freight trains; they carried it on their backs and shoulders—and for all the ambiguities of Vietnam, all the mysteries and unknowns, there was at least the single abiding certainty that they would never be at a loss for things to carry.
>
> (O'Brien 1991: 13–14)

> One never escapes the economy of war.
>
> (Derrida 1978: 148)

Just prior to his assault, Rat Kiley opens up "a can of C rations, pork and beans" and offers some to the buffalo (O'Brien 1991: 75). When it refuses, Kiley begins the precise and mechanistic disassembly of the creature: knee, ear, hump, mouth, tail, nose. This procedure recalls a scene in "On the Rainy River," where "O'Brien" details working in a factory before he was drafted:

> an Armour meatpacking plant in my hometown of Worthington, Minnesota. The plant specialized in pork products, and for eight hours a day I stood on a quarter-mile assembly line—more properly, a disassembly line—removing blood clots from the necks of dead pigs … To remove the stuff I used a kind of water gun.
>
> (O'Brien 1991: 41–2).

In a lecture delivered a few years after World War II, Heidegger asserted that, in the twentieth century, agriculture had become "a motorized food industry, the same thing in its essence as the production of corpses in the gas chambers and the extermination camps" (cited in Farias 1989: 287). In the late nineteenth century, the extermination of around 30 million North American bison had more to do with industry than agriculture. Although, like Mary Anne in 'Nam, the hunters might remove tongues as trophies or delicacies, buffalo were not killed for their meat. Skins were flayed for clothing, rugs and industrial machine belts, but the motive force behind the slaughter was the development and efficiency of transport infra-structure. The railroad companies financed the culling of buffalo because the huge herds delayed and sometimes damaged trains. At the same time, by cutting off food supply, this slaughter was a de-facto contribution to the genocide of the Plains Indians.

According to industrial folklore, Henry Ford received inspiration for the assembly-line manufacture of automobiles whilst in a Chicago slaughter-house watching a conveyor belt carrying animal carcasses. Following the inaugural opening of the moving assembly line in Dearborn and Buffalo in 1913, the droves of North American bison were replaced by over 15 mil-lion black Model Ts. Whether the Chicago slaughterhouse story is apoc-ryphal or not, the design of Ford's assembly lines augmented the "armory system" used by the US War Department in the nineteenth century at Harper's Ferry and Springfield. Subsequently, the Model T was adapted and used as a patrol car by the British who purchased around 20,000 vehicles in the first fully industrialized war. The mobilization of industrial capacity for military production in World War I witnessed a fundamental transformation in weaponry, tactics, and logistics. The war was won and lost in the factories manufacturing mechanical, metallurgical, and chemical components for long-range artillery and machine-guns (like the revolving Hotchkiss canon used at Wounded Knee), aircraft, tanks and submarines. World War I escalated integration between industry and the military thus diminishing the distance between factory floor and battlefield. Movements in the factory were choreographed with martial discipline whilst soldiers' bodies, like those tied to assembly lines, were increasingly fused with heavy machinery. The mechanization and dismantling of soldiers' bodies in Europe was mirrored, in America, by Fordist labor and fantasy. In *My Life and Work* (1923), Ford calculated that the manufacture of a Model T required 7,882 distinct operations but only 949 of these required "able-bodied" workers: "670 could be filled by legless men, 2,637 by one-legged men, two by armless men, 715 by one-armed and ten by blind men" (cited in Seltzer 1998: 69).

Prominently displayed amongst the body parts in Mary Anne's lair is a poster advertising an offer to "ASSEMBLE YOUR OWN GOOK!!" (O'Brien 1991: 102). The most gruesome dismemberment in *The Things They Carried* takes place when Curt Lemon steps on a booby trap. Coincidentally, Cora Lemon sold the Wayside Inn, in Sudbury, to Henry Ford in 1923, and he used the grounds as the site for a Mary-Martha Chapel (named for his mother and mother-in-law, but these biblical sisters also share names with the two adult female characters in O'Brien's novel). Ford went on to build a series of six Mary-Martha chapels in an extension of the principle of seriality he cherished in his factory-temples. Assembly line manufacture is driven by a deathly repetition compulsion that converts human into machine and thus "restore(s) the inanimate state" (Freud 2003a: 83). Like Freud's trauma patients, Ford "implacably insist[ed] that every repetition be exactly the same" (Freud 2003a: 76). The roots of modern trauma theory lie of course in *Beyond the Pleasure Principle* ([1920] 2003a). In Freud's Great War novella, the topography of Europe's battlefields is mapped onto internecine psychic warfare. Classical psychoanalysis was radically revised during and immediately after World War I in a period when Freud realized that even noncombatants had become "a tiny cog within the vast war machine" (Freud 2005: 169). Near the beginning of *Beyond the Pleasure Principle*, Freud notes that the "terrible war that has only just ended gave rise to a great many such disorders [traumatic neuroses]" (2003a: 50). The incessant repetitions displayed by war veterans disrupted classical psychoanalysis by hinting at the existence of previously unmapped and possibly unmappable psychic spaces. Freud's exploration of these spaces in pursuit of the death drive was haunted by military metaphor. Throughout *Beyond the Pleasure Principle* the reader encounters tropes of "wounding" and "strikes," "combat" and "mobilization," "constant bombardment" (Freud 2003a: 65) and the "barrage of stimuli" (2003a: 68). Freud maps psychic topography as trench warfare in which "one group of drives goes storming ahead ... another goes rushing back" (Freud 2003a: 81). In this internecine warfare, there are "sentinels ... standing guard" (Freud 2003a: 64) along with "protective shields," "barriers" and "screens" (2003a: 64, 74), but ultimately the defenses are "breached" by the "myrmidons of death" (2003a: 79).

The final lines of *Beyond the Pleasure Principle*—"it was never a sin to limp" (Freud 2003a: 192)—allude both to scripture and the plight of those wounded veterans returning from the war. In "Speaking of Courage," 'Nam veteran Norman Bowker replays his traumatic memory of Kiowa's loss in a shit field whilst cruising round the lake that borders his hometown. Bowker remembers Vietnam as a "shithole" in which he acquired scatological expertise: "He knew shit. It was his specialty. The smell, in particular, but also the varieties of texture and taste" (O'Brien 1991: 144). Excrement was a subject in which soldiers in Vietnam were given ample opportunities to acquire expertise: from sanitation in the field to the construction and maintenance of slit-trench latrines and outhouses in camps and LZs (landing zones), from burning *scybala* (hardened masses of feces) to detecting Vietcong booby traps that were often coated in feces to increase the probability of infected wounds. Bowker tries to counter coprophagy in two ways: He opens his lips "very slightly" whilst swimming in his hometown lake and he stops for a "Mama Burger" at an A&W drive-in (O'Brien 1991: 152). Whilst ordering this fast-food product of the motorized food industry, Bowker experiences an auditory hallucination in which an intercom voice dubs scripted service-sector dialogue with military jargon: "Repeat: one Mama, one fries, one small beer. Fire for effect. Stand by" (O'Brien 1991: 150). In the "Notes" that follow "Speaking of Courage," O'Brien informs us that Bowker committed suicide—an act which literalizes the death drive latent in the vet's compulsive circling of his hometown lake. Bowker's suicide note offers the following: "It's almost like I got killed over in 'Nam … That night when Kiowa got wasted, I sort of sank into the sewage with him … Feels like I'm still in deep shit" (O'Brien 1991: 155). Given the extravagantly self-conscious Freudianism displayed elsewhere in *The Things They Carried*, it seems permissible to read the shit field as not only a crypt but also a safe full of dirty money. For Freud, as modernist anti-Midas, all money was filthy lucre. Psychoanalysis invokes a range of case histories alongside literary, mythological, and anthropological examples, to confirm the folkloric equation between money and feces. The shit field is the dead center to O'Brien's topography of trauma because it is what the US war machine was mobilized to protect. The financial costs of the Vietnam War were worth incurring to ensure long-term access to overseas market in Southeast Asia. South Vietnam was flooded by American soldiers, carried by and carrying machines as well as an array of goods and mass culture. The PXs (post exchanges) were overflowing, the barracks and hooches boasted refrigerators, sound systems and televisions whilst the air waves carried rock 'n' roll and US pop culture. The title story of O'Brien's novel compiles an exhaustive inventory of the things carried by US soldiers and manufactured by US industry: the steel helmets, boots, flak jackets, ponchos, M60s, M16s, M79s, ammunition, bombs, mines, binoculars, radios, canned food. Dominique Laporte suggests that "the site of power must distance itself from the site of shit" (2000: 42). Conversely, *The Things They Carried* constructs a *cloaca maxima*, or symbolic sewer, that carries dirty money from a rural shit field in Southeast Asia to America's industrial heartlands and back again.

Alpha Company carry the burden of overproduction in a bloated and militarized permanent war economy. One of the architects and originator of the term "permanent war economy," Charles E. Wilson, Eisenhower's Secretary of Defense, used his tenure to maximize synergy between military, industry, and government. Wilson was convinced that World War II had pulled the US economy out of the Great Depression and that "preparedness" was the key to maintaining national security, industrial growth, and economic vitality. Before he took over at the Pentagon, Wilson was President of General Motors (GM) and earned the Medal of Merit for directing GM's massive contribution to the war effort. In "Speaking of

Courage," Bowker drives his "father's big Chevy," a model first assembled by GM in 1923 at the East Develan plant in Buffalo which Wilson converted to defense production in World War II. Although Bowker, unlike Kiowa, survives Vietnam, he is followed back to America by the "terrible killing power of that shit field ... The filth seemed to erase identities, transforming the men into identical copies of a single soldier ... interchangeable units" (O'Brien 1991: 158, 164). Bowker carries his trauma whilst being carried by a component part in the permanent war economy that produces the preconditions for wide scale traumatic experience.

Impossible geographies

> If dead ground could come back and haunt you the way dead people do ...
>
> (Herr 1978: 11)

In "To Speculate—On Freud," Derrida poses the critical question confronting any topography of trauma: "Where are we?" (Derrida 1987: 290). This question haunts the final page of *The Things They Carried*. At a frozen pond in Minnesota (the Dakota Indian term for "cloudy water"), the dead are miraculously resurrected: "I can see Kiowa, too, and Ted Lavender and Curt Lemon, and sometimes I can even see Timmy skating with Linda under the yellow floodlights. I'm young and happy. I'll never die" (O'Brien 1991: 236). The regression, or retreat, here is threatened by traumatic eruptions. Just beneath the surface of the aseptic and deodorizing ice, a field of shit is still boiling: "the shells made deep slushy craters, opening up all those years of waste, centuries worth, and the smell came bubbling out of the earth" (O'Brien 1991: 147). The topography of trauma is recursive and shows no respect for borders. The shit field cannot be skated on or over since it cracks open into a fecalized crypt of birth trauma, gender crisis and racial guilt, industrialized battlefields and militarized factories. But does this answer Derrida's question? And how sure can one's footing be in a shit field? Perhaps my own scatter-bombing, or even muck-spreading, has ignored the possibility that sometimes a shit field is just a shit field? By dumping so much on this site, do we risk flushing away the phenomenological materiality, the shittiness and fundamental thingness of things? If we sketch map a place as the site of multiple traumas, a *mise en abyme* of crypts within crypts, do we reduce it, perversely, to a utopia (etymologically, a nonplace)? Perhaps the critic at this point must also partially retreat. Cathy Caruth has argued that the traumatized "carry an impossible history within them, or they become themselves the symptom of a history that they cannot possess" (1995: 5). Following

Caruth, we might propose that *The Things They Carried* itself carries but cannot possess the impossible place of trauma. "They carried the land itself—Vietnam, the place, the soil—a powdery orange-red dust that covered their boots and fatigues and faces. They carried the sky. The whole atmosphere, they carried it, the humidity, the monsoons, the stink of fungus and decay, all of it, they carried gravity" (O'Brien 1991: 13).

References

Abraham, N. and Torok, M. (1986) *The Wolf Man's Magic Word: A Cryptonymy*, Minneapolis, Minn.: University of Minnesota Press.

——(1994) *The Shell and the Kernel: Renewals of Psychoanalysis*, Chicago, Ill.: University of Chicago Press.

Caruth, C. (1995) *Trauma: Explorations in Memory*, Baltimore, Md.: Johns Hopkins University Press.

Chomsky, N. (1970) *For Reasons of State*, New York: Pantheon.

Derrida, J. (1978) "Violence and Metaphysics," in *Writing and Difference*, Chicago, Ill.: Chicago University Press.

——(1986) "Fors," foreword to N. Abraham and M. Torok, *The Wolf Man's Magic Word: A Cryptonymy*, Minneapolis, Minn.: University of Minnesota Press, pp. xi–xlviii.

——(1987) "To Speculate—on Freud" in *The Post Card: From Socrates to Freud and Beyond*, Chicago, Ill.: Chicago University Press, pp. 257–410.

Farias, V. (1989) *Heidegger and Nazism*, Philadelphia, Penn.: Temple University Press.

Freud, S. ([1920] 2003a) *Beyond the Pleasure Principle and Other Writings*, London: Penguin.

——(2003b) "The Uncanny" in *The Uncanny*, London: Penguin, pp. 121–240.

——(2005) "Timely Reflections on War and Death" in *On Murder, Mourning and Melancholia*, London: Penguin, pp. 167–94.

Hartman, G. and O'Hara, D. T. (eds) (2004) *The Geoffrey Hartman Reader*, New York: Fordham University Press.

Herr, M. (1978) *Dispatches*, London: Picador.

Johnson, R. (1971) "Statement of Robert B. Johnson, Capt, US Army, West Point, Class of 1965" offered at the Dellums Committee Hearings on War Crimes in Vietnam, April–May 1971. Online. Available at http://members.aol.com/warlibrary/vwch1e.htm (accessed May 5, 2007).

Laporte, D. (2000) *History of Shit*, Cambridge, Mass.: MIT Press.

Nora, P. (ed.) (1996–8) *Realms of Memory: The Construction of the French Past*, Vols I–III, New York: Columbia University Press.

O'Brien, T. ([1990] 1991) *The Things They Carried*, London: Flamingo.

Seltzer, M. (1998) *Serial Killers: Death and Life in America's Wound Culture*, London: Routledge.

Slotkin, R. (2000) *Regeneration through Violence: the Mythology of the American Frontier 1600–1800*, Norman, Okla.: University of Oklahoma Press.

Theweleit, K. (1987) *Male Fantasies I: Women, Floods, Bodies, History*, Cambridge: Polity.

Whitehead, A. (2004) *Trauma Fiction*, Edinburgh: Edinburgh University Press.

Part IV
Sex images

11 A painful progress
Queer fiction and the American protest literature tradition

Zoe Trodd

Imagination ... recycles bits and pieces from the world and reassembles them into visions ... In this world, there is a kind of painful progress. Longing for what we've left behind, and dreaming ahead.

(Kushner 1993: 21)

On April 25, 1993, Lani Ka'ahumanu faced the crowd at the March on Washington for lesbian, gay, bisexual, and transgender rights. Society, she said, was based on a series of "simple either/or divisions," but should embrace something "fluid—ambiguous—subversive." Explaining that the bisexual and transgender movements offered such a vision, with their "fluid social, sexual and gender dynamic," she added that the recognition of "bisexual orientation and transgender issues" presented a challenge to "assumptions not previously explored within the politics of gay liberation." What would it take, asked Ka'ahumanu, "for the gayristocracy to realize that bisexual, lesbian, transgender, and gay people are in this together?" (1993: 36). The preamble to the March's platform had offered a similar vision of unity-amid-difference, announcing "that our quest for social justice fundamentally links us to the struggles against racism and sexism, class bias, economic injustice, and religious intolerance" (Blasius 1994: 175). Then, trying to forge that shared "quest," numerous speakers used the term "queer." The term allowed for differences to be understood within a common queerness: not a substitute for other self-identifications, it was an extension of them.

This moment in 1993 made visible an ongoing shift from the rhetoric and politics of first-wave gay liberation, to that of the so-called "Queer Nineties." In 1990, Douglas Crimp and Adam Rolston had announced a "second wave" of "gay radicals" and heralded AIDS activists as "direct heirs to the early radical tradition of gay liberation" (1990: 98), including 1970s groups like the Gay Liberation Front (GLF). But these new radicals were also "rejuvenators of the gay movement," added Crimp and Rolston, for that movement had "in the intervening decades become an assimila-tionist civil rights lobby" (1990: 98).[1]

In fact, while the Queer Nineties saw the American mainstream appro-priate gay culture (part of a new trend to adapt minority cultures as a "kick," like "gangsta rap," according to Nadine Milde [2001: 136]), and mainstream reform groups focus their energies on the question of same-sex marriage, the AIDS crisis did reconfigure the movement and produce Crimp and Rolston's "rejuvenators." The epidemic demanded alliances between different social groups, and these alliances highlighted the myriad differences of class and race. Transgender issues began to resonate within these struggles, and, in 1992, Leslie Feinberg published the pamphlet, "Transgender Liberation: A Movement Whose Time Has Come." That same year saw the founding of Transgender Nation, which helped fuse the transgender movement celebrated by Ka'ahumanu at the March. The newly visible transgendered subject was then understood as further chal-lenging the foundation of gender and sexuality binaries.

In addition, the AIDS crisis galvanized activists into a more confronta-tional protest style. ACT UP performed street theater and political funerals, and the Lesbian Avengers took a similarly theatrical approach. Queer Nation, founded in March 1990 by activists from ACT UP, were equally "in your face." They offered same-sex kiss-ins and the slogan "We're Here. We're Queer. Get Used to It." Queer Nation was perhaps "the first wave of activists to embrace the retrofuture/classic contemporary styles of post-modernism," claimed activist scholars Allan Bérubé and Jeffrey Escoffier in 1991 (1991: 14). Echoing Crimp and Rolston's claim that a new generation of activists were both heirs to and transformers of the old movement, Bérubé and Escoffier explained that Queer Nation was building an "identity from old and new elements—borrowing styles and tactics from popular culture, communities of color, hippies, AIDS activists, the antinuclear movement, MTV, feminists, and early gay liberationists" (1991: 14).

One "old" element reconfigured by Queer Nation was the epithet "queer." Appropriating the slur, like speakers at the March, Queer Nation embraced it as a term that might forge a more inclusive gay, lesbian, bisexual, and transgender community—beyond that "gayristocracy," as Ka'ahumanu put it. "Queer," which represented any social position that opposed oppressive gender and sexual norms, then became an intellectual term. Offering a scholarly counterpart to the social activism of ACT UP, scho-lars such as Michael Warner and Eve Kosofsky Sedgwick developed queer theory. For these scholars, queer praxis didn't mean seeking a *new* identity but rather refusing to accept any stable identity at all. Judith Butler embraced the chance to rethink ontological identity constructions and suggested that feminists had reified gender dynamics by constructing women as coherent subjects. In 1990, she proposed that—without fixed identities—a "new configuration of politics would surely emerge from the old" (Butler 1990: 190). The following year Diana Fuss noted that "queer" embraced "what gets left out of the inside/outside, heterosexual/homosexual opposition" (1991: 2), and in 1993, Rosemary Hennessy argued that "queer" challenged the "obvious categories (man, woman, latina, jew, butch, femme), oppositions (man vs. woman, heterosexual vs. homosexual), or equations (gender = sex) upon which conventional notions of sexuality and identity rely" (1993: 964).

But while it was comprised of the "left out" fragments, "queer" also suggested to scholars "possibilities for organizing around a fracturing of identity" (Sedgwick 1993: 27). "Queer" moved "against both assimilationist politics and separatist identity definitions," explained Sedgwick (1993: 28), while Crimp insisted that "remaking identities" must "result in a broadening of alliances rather than an exacerbation of antagonisms" (1992: 16). Echoing Queer Nation, and anticipating the March's platform, Crimp called for a "collective political struggle" (1992: 13–14).

Reflecting and developing queer activism and queer theory was the decade's queer fiction. In 1992, Anne Waldman demanded "an enlightened poetics, an androgynous poetics ... a poetics of transformation beyond gender" (Waldman 2004: 326). She insisted that "the page not be empty female awaiting penetration by dark phallic ink-juice," and added: "Turn the language body upside down. What does it look like?" (Waldman 2004: 327). In the year that followed, two semi-autobiographical novels took up Waldman's call, combining activists' message of multiple and unified queer visibilities and the academy's theorization of multiple and unified queer identities.

Dorothy Allison's *Bastard Out of Carolina* (1992) and Leslie Feinberg's *Stone Butch Blues* (1993) mixed different protest voices to create what Waldman termed "a utopian creative field ... a transsexual literature, a transgendered literature" (2004: 327). Free from "essentialist arrogance" *and* the reduction to "a purely negative stance" (Nicholson 1992: 65), the bastard radicalisms of Allison and Feinberg were identities built from "old and new elements" (as Queer Nation activists put it with reference to their group). Reconfiguring the protest literature tradition for the Queer Nineties, just as activists and scholars had reconfigured the gay liberation movement and its theoretical framework, Allison and Feinberg expressed faith in a kind of painful progress.

In hope of a remade life: Allison and the reconfiguration of trash

Bone begins life with three variations on her given name. No one had "bothered to discuss how Anne would be spelled," she explains in the opening of *Bastard Out of Carolina*, "so it wound up spelled three different ways on the form" (Allison 1992: 2–3). But, as though the universe is compensating for this surplus, Bone is then denied a paternal name: Ruth wasn't sure and Granny refused to speak it, so "the clerk got mad" and there she was—"certified a bastard" and labeled "no-good, lazy, shiftless" (Allison 1992: 3).

Bone struggles to claim an identity beyond the red stamp of "illegitimate" on her birth certificate. She observes that her sister Reese, who knows something about her father, can "choose something different for herself and be someone else altogether" (Allison 1992: 59), while Bone has no easily accessible material for self-reinvention. Trying to read and discover herself nonetheless, Bone finds only blankness—as symbolized when she keeps her "face blank" (Allison 1992: 27) upon hearing about her possible ancestry, or when she gazes in her mother's mirror and sees an "unreadable" face, eyes "blank" and "empty" (1992: 208). Throughout the novel, such blankness is associated with lost characters, like her rapist stepfather Glen (whose image in a photograph is "empty" and without "details" [Allison 1992: 43]), while Raylene, Bone's lesbian aunt and rescuer, defies such blankness: she has "scars behind one ear" (1992: 179) that indicate a storied past.

Bone's journey is toward that storied self—what Allison calls elsewhere "the hope of a remade life" (1994: 219). Seeking an escape from the essentializing stamp on her certificate, Bone reaches for a fluidly constructed identity. Overnarrated by the label "illegitimate," so that all other life plots are erased and she is left a mere blank, she tries to seize control and renarrate herself and her world: she claims she is "Roseanne Carter from Atlanta" (Allison 1992: 67), tells Reese a horror story to prevent her from "flagging down strangers" (1992: 75), narrates tales "of boys and girls gruesomely raped" (1992: 119), seizes upon the plots of gospel lyrics, and engages in a series of sexual fantasies. The theme of story telling runs throughout the novel, encompassing Shannon's stories of "little children" (Allison 1992: 157), Granny's stories, which make "no distinction between what she knew to be true and what she had only heard told" (1992: 26), and even Alma's scrapbook.

Janet Zandy explains this process of story telling as a "way of locating oneself, a way of finding a home in an inhospitable universe" (1990: 2). Narration, Zandy notes, is a way of "certifying one's humanity, linking generations, and denying oblivion" (1990: 3), and the characters' story telling in *Bastard* does create a series of unofficial histories that move beyond the official stamp on Bone's certificate, the clerk's assertion that "'[t]he facts have been established,'" and society's collective dismissal of the Boatwrights as "'[s]ome people'" (Allison 1992: 4–5). The characters' unofficial histories deny "oblivion" and reach instead for the self-certification of humanity.

The characters' impulses toward story telling also reflect Allison's own conviction that "if you can step back from your life and look at it as a story, you can revise it … alter the plot" (Lewis 2006: 60). Like Bone, who manages Glen's violence by imagining people watching it, Allison senses that seeing your life "as a narrative is a very powerful act" (Lewis 2006: 60). She crafted stories as a child, remembering that she'd say: "I'll tell you a story and maybe you'll believe me" (Allison 1995: 3). She explains that she wanted to tell these stories—and later to write fiction—in order to draw in the audience until it imagines itself "like my characters." Then she would have "come closer to knowing myself as real" (Allison 1994: 4). For Allison, story telling can "alter the plot" of the teller's life through locating this "real" self.

In addition, the presence of the "real" challenges what she terms "the acceptable myths and theories of both mainstream society and a lesbian-feminist interpretation." Story telling is part of Allison's "fight [against] broad generalizations from every theoretical viewpoint" (1994: 15): acknowledging that she has been "hated as a lesbian both by 'society' and by the intimate world of my extended family," Allison knows that she has "also been hated … by lesbians for behavior and sexual practices shaped in large part by class" (1994: 23). Her story telling is an attempt to understand what she calls "the politics of *they*, why human beings fear and stigmatize the different while secretly dreading that they might be one of the different themselves" (Allison 1994: 35).

To escape from the "politics of *they*"—the essentializing categories of gender, sexuality, and class—Allison appropriates and transforms auto-biographical material: remembering her childhood in South Carolina, she explained in 1994 that "[w]e were the *they* everyone talks about—the ungrateful poor" (Allison 1994: 3), and referred to "the complicated, painful story of how my mama had, and had not, saved me" (1994: 34) (the story of *Bastard Out of Carolina*). Challenging her own identity stamp—*white trash*—Allison made the decision to "show you my aunts in their drunken rages, my uncles in their meanness," as she noted in a 1992 interview. She explained: "that's exactly who we are said to be. That's what white trash is all about." But she wanted to "show you those people as larger than that contemptible myth … human beings instead of fold-up, mean, cardboard figures" (Hollibaugh 1992: 16). Using autobiographical fiction to debunk these myths, Allison makes her work "the *condensed and reinvented* experience of a cross-eyed working-class lesbian … who has made the decision to live … on the page … for me and mine" (1988: 12, emphasis added).

But unlike Allison, Bone repeatedly makes the mistake of seeking an entirely new identity; that "purely negative stance" critiqued by Nicholson.

Allison condenses and reinvents her own experience, while Bone builds her identity on a series of myths. She imagines Mrs. Parsons is her grand-mother because she looks like "a granny you'd read about" (Allison 1992: 55), spends time "looking for something … magical" (1992: 207), wants to be "more like the girls in storybooks" (1992: 206), and at one point even desires a lie about her father, just to hear "the story Mama would have told" (1992: 27). Bone's is the hope of a life remade from dreams: "I closed my eyes and tried to make up a story for myself," she notes toward the end of the novel; "pretended that Daddy Glen had … gotten a cross-country trucking job that would pay him lots of money but keep him away from home … I fell asleep there dreaming, loving the dream" (Allison 1992: 263). This iden-tity-creation out of myths, lies, and dreams has already been questioned as ominous when Glen attempts to say something "often enough" and therefore "make it so" (Allison 1992: 44)—to make reality conform to fantasy—and sure enough Bone learns (and mourns) that she can never be "that … storybook girlchild" (1992: 208), or that she is no Scarlett O'Hara (1992: 206).

Only from Raylene does Bone grasp what Butler terms a "radical invention, albeit one that employs and deploys culturally existent and culturally imagin-able conventions" (1987: 139). Raylene teaches Bone a different method of identity-creation—one that embraces three elements of 1990s queer theory and activism. First, she suggests reaching across the divide between self and other to find an empathetic unity. Echoing Crimp's hope for a "broadening of alliances," Raylene asks that Bone transform *they* into the "culturally imagin-able," as Butler puts it. When Bone sees a bus with "children pressed against the windows staring at me hatefully" and glares back, Raylene tells her: "'You don't know who those children are … You're making up stories about those people. Make up a story where you have to live in their house, be one of their family … Look at it from the other side for a while" (Allison 1992: 262). In fact, Raylene's instruction to look "from the other side" was repeated by Allison in 1994, when she suggested "telling the truth" while simultaneously remembering that there are "truths other than your own" (1994: 177).

Second, Raylene excavates capitalist, heterosexual, and patriarchal categories but doesn't transcend them. Offering what Butler calls a "dis-solution of binary restrictions through the proliferation of genders" (1987: 136), rather than existing outside binary categories of gender and sexu-ality, Raylene's lesbian subjectivity is multiple and shifting. Always "com-fortable with herself" (Allison 1992: 182), she embraces cultural norms for both female and male identity (she once lived as a man and called herself Ray and now wears women's clothing; she is maternal and has no children of her own). In Raylene is "the postmodern insight that identity is con-structed, flexible, and multiple" (Best and Kellner 1997: 174), and the avoidance of any complicity "with the oppressive categories" (Jagose 1994: 7).

This is an important example for Bone, who herself has a keen perception that gender identity is constructed and flexible. Told early on that she has a "man-type part ... [r]ock-hard and nasty" (Allison 1992: 54), she wants to play "mean sisters," who do "everything their brothers do" only "first and fastest and meanest" (1992: 212). Or, upon seeing another child, Bone observes that she might be "a very pretty boy or a very fierce girl" (Allison 1992: 84). But beyond Raylene, Bone's models of flexible gender identity are then nonexistent. Anney and the others seem "born to mother, nurse, and clean up after the men" (Allison 1992: 23), and the novel's male characters are infantilized by this system. Ruth explains that Glen doesn't like Bone because he's "'jealous ... wanting more of your mama than you, wanting to be her baby more than her husband'" (Allison 1992: 123), and even after raping Bone, Glen sobs "like a little boy" (1992: 288).

Finally, in addition to giving Bone a lesson in empathetic imagination and providing her with a model of gender proliferation, Raylene embraces "what gets left out" (1991: 2), as Fuss puts it. She helps Bone to build her "own identity from old ... elements" (Bérubé and Escoffier 1991: 14) (in the words of Queer Nation activists). Bone has been seeking a new identity with which to erase the essentializing stamp on her certificate, but Raylene's life revolves around the recycling of *old* elements. Like Allison, Raylene condenses and reinvents: Out of the Greenville River comes trash that she makes into treasure. She sells what she finds, thereby maintaining a better lifestyle than that of her married sisters. Raylene's reconfiguration of society's fragments is echoed by the novel's theme of smashed parts— played out in the destruction of the Woolworth's store and Aunt Alma's home, and symbolized by Anney's face in the final pages, which looks like a "cracked white plate" (Allison 1992: 309).

Allison's own process of reclaiming her childhood through the bastard genre of fictionalized autobiography suggests her sympathy for this process of reconfiguring the past's fragments. "We had generations before us to teach us that nothing ever changed," she explained in 1994. "I wanted to run away from ... who we had been" (1994: 18–19). But what hides behind that impulse, Allison continued, "is the conviction that the life you have lived, the person you are, is valueless ... that change itself is not possible" (1994: 19–20). Instead Allison decided that she wanted to "break the heart of the world and heal it," to "write in such a way as to literally remake the world" (1994: 212). Allison's "hope of a remade life" (1994: 219) is that of a shattered and remade world.

Bone's original sensibility had been toward a similar rehabilitation of fragments: From her uncles she stole things "that they didn't really care about—old tools, pieces of chain, and broken engine parts," and "a broken jackknife ... that I taped back together" (Allison 1992: 23). But after moving from school to school, she loses touch with the impulse to make trash into treasure, feeling like a "box that goes missing and then turns up but you realize you never needed anything in it anyway" (1992: 65). Now she encounters a reminder of that past self in Raylene's house, with its "shelves full of oddities" and "old tools" (Allison 1992: 181). With Raylene's encouragement, she pulls from the river "a Betsy Wetsy doll ... baby-carriage covers, tricycle wheels ... jump-rope handles" (Allison 1992: 181–2); symbols of her childhood past before Glen. She also finds and appropriates the hooks, which are not for "mountain climbing" as Grey suggests (Allison 1992: 184) but for "trawling" (1992: 186): for uncovering the river's past from its depths rather than scaling unknown heights.

The challenge is therefore to see her experience with Raylene as a signal to reconfigure the fragments of herself: to sew herself back together as a kind of "Frankenstein's monster," echoing the game she plays with her cousins (Allison 1992: 210). Like the dream of being pulled from the river and sewed back together out of different people's body parts, "just to make up one reasonable body" (Allison 1992: 187), Bone might piece together a multivalent identity from the pieces of her own story—crafting Butler's "radical invention, albeit one that employs [the] culturally existent" (1987: 139). Sure enough, she remembers Raylene's rehabilitation of fragments when she encounters a different kind of trash at Woolworth's (the "junk" of "stale candy," "makeup," and shoes, all "tawdry and useless"). Recalling Raylene's shelves, she finally knows they had been "worth something" (Allison 1992: 224–5).

Bone is given another chance at self-reconfiguration when Anney returns with a new birth certificate. This time, finally, it doesn't say "illegitimate"; instead the "bottom third" is "blank, unmarked, unstamped" (Allison 1992: 309). Bone, no longer labeled a bastard, is free to fill in the blank space with a self-defined identity. She might remain "cut off at the root," her hold on life "as fragile as a seed in the wind," as Allison put it elsewhere while describing individuals without pasts (1995: 12). But she also might fill that blank space with the treasure of her life's trashed fragments. For, while Anney lights out for new territories in California or Florida, Bone entwines her fingers with Raylene's and imagines a remade life: "I was already who I was going to be" (Allison 1992: 309).

The long run: Feinberg and the reconfiguration of protest history

Jess Goldberg's body in *Stone Butch Blues* represents what Sandy Stone refers to as "a hotly contested site of cultural inscription"—a "battlefield" where the "epistemologies of white male medical practice, the rage of

radical feminist theories and the chaos of lived gendered experience" meet
(1991: 295). A transgendered "butch" and self-described "he-she," Jess
exists on "the gender borders at the close of the twentieth century" (Stone
1991: 295). The decision to leave unfinished the transition from female to
male further locates Jess within this liminal space. As Jay Prosser observes:
"Jess turns back in her transition, thus refusing the refuge of fully becoming the other sex and the closure promised by the transsexual plot" (1995:
489). In addition, Prosser explains, "the unsituatedness of the subject's
gender (transgender)" is "reflected by the unsituatedness of the text's form
as in between the genres of fiction and autobiography (trans-genre)" (1995: 489).
Stone Butch Blues, like *Bastard Out of Carolina*, is a bastard text, resisting
categorization as either fiction or autobiography. In fact, the book is "a very
thinly veiled disguised autobiography," Feinberg admitted in an interview
(also paraphrasing Allison to note that fiction is "less than autobiography
but more than lies" [Horwitz 1994: 13]): just as Jess almost passes as a
man but stops short, so the autobiography only partially passes as fiction.
This double borderland of genre and gender seems to leave Jess stranded,
as though forever caught in the blank space of Bone's final birth certificate.

This blankness might be debilitating, for as Stone explains, "[i]t is difficult to generate a counterdiscourse if one is programmed to disappear,"
and the "highest purpose of the transsexual is to erase him/herself, to fade
into the 'normal' population" (1991: 295). While looking in the mirror,
Jess witnesses this disappearance of self. In a scene that echoes looking-
glass moments in the protest writings of William Apess, Ralph Ellison,
James Baldwin, and Mary Crow Dog, Jess can't recognize the image
reflected back: "What I saw reflected in the mirror was not a man, but I
couldn't recognize the he-she," Jess notes. "I hadn't just believed that
passing would hide me. I hoped that it would allow me to express the part
of myself that didn't seem to be a woman" (Feinberg 1993: 222).

The moment dramatizes attempts by queer theorists and activists to
debunk "simple either/or divisions," as Ka'ahumanu put it at the March,
and reflects Feinberg's interest in the theoretical framework of the 1990s:
"I had read many works of gender theory in the early 1990's," Feinberg
explained in 1996, adding that this led to the desire "to write the kind of
gender theory that we all live" (Peters 1996: 11). *Stone Butch Blues* is a love-
story and a protest against police violence, but also an exploration of
biology as destiny and a literary contribution to the queer theory debates
of the 1990s. Jess asks: "Who was I now—woman or man?" and feels there
should be more choice than this; that the question "could never be
answered if it had to be asked" (Feinberg 1993: 222). This valuing of
choice echoes Marjorie Garber's concept of a "'third' ... space of possibility ... which questions binary thinking" [1991: 11]) and signals Jess' desire

for a place beyond gender borders—"borders that will never be home" (Feinberg 1993: 11).

Yet, like Allison's Raylene—and in an echo of queer theorists who proposed a proliferation of identities rather than a "purely negative stance" (Nicholson 1992: 65)—Jess seeks not to escape but instead collapse the binary categories of gender and sexuality. In a dream Jess doesn't "feel like a woman or a man" and likes how this is "different" (Feinberg 1993: 143): Blankness becomes an empowering liminality. Journeying away from "a heterosexist world that must measure every word, every act against itself," as Waldman put it (2004: 327), Jess moves toward Waldman's imagined place where "we are not defined by our sexual positions as men or women in bed or on the page" (2004: 327).

Like Allison, Feinberg broke from the identity-based gay liberation movement of the 1970s and found Waldman's "androgynous poetics." In addition, like Allison, Feinberg fashioned this newly shifting subjectivity from old elements—writing herself into blankness with the past's ink. The mirror moment in *Stone Butch Blues* foregrounds the question of the *past* for queer theorists and activists of the 1990s: the challenge of "building ... from old and new elements," in the words of Bérubé and Escoffier (1991: 14) and of being what Crimp and Rolston called "direct heirs" to but also "rejuvenators" of the movement (1990: 98). Observing the image in the mirror, Jess adds: "I didn't get to explore being a he-she, though. I simply became a he—a man without a past" (Feinberg 1993: 222). This loss of one's past, as part of the process of self-erasure, "is known as *constructing a plausible history*," Stone explains; "learning to lie effectively about one's past" (1991: 295). But Feinberg restores the past by engaging its protest tradition. While Allison suggests reconfiguring the cast-off fragments of one's *own* past into treasure, Feinberg explores the process by which America's *collective* protest past is salvaged and reused. Feinberg explained in 1998 that *Stone* "was a stepping stone," intended to provide the "language and concepts to talk about ... transgendered lives" without which it was "harder for people to look at a broader historical political view" (Bowen 1998: 19), and in the novel this "broader historical political view" is that of American protest.

The novel journeys through past and present protest movements in the direction of a new protest voice that "sings its wisdom" as Waldman put it in an echo of Walt Whitman (2004: 327). For example, Feinberg echoes Whitman too. In *Leaves of Grass*, Whitman had anticipated Jess' unanswerable question: "I too am untranslatable," he wrote; "There is that in me ... I do not know what it is ... It is not in any dictionary" (1881: 193). Toward the end of the novel, Feinberg echoes Whitman again. "Failing to fetch me at first keep encouraged / Missing me one place search another," he had written. "I stop somewhere waiting for you" (1881: 195). Discovering history and a community, Jess now tells a new group of friends: "I've been searching for you all for such a long time. I can't believe I've finally found you" (Feinberg 1993: 266). One of these friends is called Esperanza—"it means hope," she explains, and Jess concludes that it is "possible to still hope" (Feinberg 1993: 266), echoing Whitman's call to encouragement.

Feinberg also explores W. E. B. Du Bois' concept of double-consciousness. As a child, Jess observes water fountains labelled "Colored" and "White," and later reads a passage from Du Bois' *The Souls of Black Folk* (1903): "It is a peculiar sensation, this double consciousness, this sense of always looking at oneself through the eyes of others" (Feinberg 1993: 178). Gay liberationists had long proposed that staying in the "closet" was akin to racial "passing," sometimes alluding to Du Bois' book: "Nothing is more pathetic as a Black who denies his culture and tries to pass for white … unless it's one of our Gay brothers who denies his Gayness to get along in the straight plastic culture," wrote a journalist for the *San Francisco Free Press* in 1969; "Luckily for the souls of Black folk they have awakened to their beauty and cultural integrity in time" (Teal 1971: 34). And, after taking male hormones to pass as a man, Feinberg's Jess understands the meaning of Du Bois' words: "I could see my *passing* self, but even I could no longer see the more complicated me beneath the surface," Jess notes (Feinberg 1993: 222, emphasis added).

As well, Jess reads about Black Power and Women's Liberation and encounters a biography of Mother Jones, Martin Luther King Jr.'s "I Have a Dream" speech, James Baldwin's essays, and Malcolm X's "The Ballot and the Bullet." The book touches on anti-Vietnam War activism and the American Indian Movement, and, toward the end of the novel, Jess' friends make cookies for AIDS patients and offer to teach Jess "an old slave dance" (Feinberg 1993: 266). Feinberg then echoes calls by queer activists and theorists to open up gay civil rights to class analysis when Jess applies past experience in the organized labor movement to the gay liberation movement. Finally, Jess is given a book called *Gay American History* and soon afterwards finds a voice: "I needed to speak too" (Feinberg 1993: 296).

Addressing a rally at Christopher Street, Jess brings together all these encounters with protest movements of the past and present and calls for queer unity across identity differences: "'part of me feels so connected to you all … There's lots of us who are on the outside and we don't want to be … Couldn't the *we* be bigger?'" (Feinberg 1993: 296). Awakened to a new activist identity by the history of activism, Jess tells Duffy: "'I want to know about history. I have all this new information about people like me down the ages, but I don't know anything about the ages'" (Feinberg 1993: 299).

Restoring the weight of personal and collective history to the theories, activism, and literature of the Queer Nineties, Feinberg and Allison forged what Nicholson calls "a discourse that recognizes itself as historically situated" (1992: 65), and entered a tradition of intellectual *bricolage* in protest writing; images and language stored across time, then transformed by new contexts into a living protest legacy. Salvaging pieces of earlier reform movements, protest writers have long offered historical memory in place of national amnesia, and protest voices when silence equaled death. Then, confirming that history mattered, in 1996 Feinberg published the book *Transgender Warriors: Making History from Joan of Arc to Dennis Rodman*, adding in 2003 that queer activists might work by the light of the past to build their movement:

> I believe that the experience not only of the struggles against slavery but also the struggles of the last century or more … have shown that those who … have a firm grasp on the economic and social reins of power, have never let go without a fight.
>
> (Conlan 2003: 6)

In conversation with this palpable past, seeking what Allison termed a "remade life," queer writers of the 1990s found a kind of painful progress.[2]

Notes

1 For the "Queer Nineties" see Garber (1994), and McGarry and Wasserman (1998).
2 For more 1990s scholars excavating gay history, see Beemyn (1997), Blasius and Phelan (1997), Rupp (1999), and Warren (1997).

References

Allison, D. (1988) *Trash*, Ithaca, NY: Firebrand.
—— (1992) *Bastard Out of Carolina*, New York: Dutton.
—— (1994) *Skin*, Ithaca, NY: Firebrand.
—— (1995) *Two or Three Things I Know for Sure*, New York: Dutton.
Beemyn, B. (1997) *Creating a Place for Ourselves*, New York: Routledge.
Bérubé, A. and Escoffier, J. (1991) "Queer/Nation," *Outlook* 11: 13–15.
Best, S. and Kellner, D. (1997) *The Postmodern Turn*, New York: Guilford Press.
Blasius, M. and Phelan, S. (1997) *We Are Everywhere*, New York: Routledge.
Bowen, G. (1998) "Transgendered Warrriors," *Lambda Book Report*, 6 (6): 19.
Butler, J. (1987) "Variations on Sex and Gender," in S. Benhabib and D. Cornell (eds), *Feminism as Critique*, Minneapolis, Minn.: University of Minnesota Press, pp. 125–42.
—— (1990) *Gender Trouble*, New York: Routledge.

A painful progress   163

Conlan, M. (2003) "Leslie Feinberg," *Zenger's*, June 19: 6–7.

Crimp, D. (1992) "Right On, Girlfriend!" *Social Text*, 33: 2–18.

Crimp, D. and Rolston, A. (1990) *AIDS Demo/Graphics*, Seattle, Wash.: Bay Press.

Feinberg, L. (1993) *Stone Butch Blues*, Ithaca, NY: Firebrand.

Fuss, D. (1991) "Inside/Out," in *Inside/Out*, New York: Routledge, pp. 1–10.

Garber, L. (ed.) (1994) *Tilting the Tower*, New York: Routledge.

Garber, M. (1991) *Vested Interests*, New York: Routledge.

Hennessy, R. (1993) "Queer Theory," *Signs* 18 (4): 964–79.

Hollibaugh, A. (1992) "Telling a Mean Story: Amber Hollibaugh Interviews Dorothy Allison," *Women's Review of Books*, July: 16–17.

Horwitz, K. (1994) "Politics and Gender: An Interview with Leslie Feinberg," *FTM Newsletter* 26: 13–14.

Jagose, A. (1994) *Lesbian Utopics*, New York: Routledge.

Ka'ahumanu, L. (1993) "How I Spent My Two Week Vacation Being a Token Bisexual," *Anything That Moves*, 6: 32–6.

Kushner, T. (1992) *Angels in America*, London: Nick Hern.

Lewis, M. (2006) "Marina Lewis Talks With Dorothy Allison," *Other Voices* 19 (45): 54–60.

McGarry, M. and Wasserman, F. (1998) *Becoming Visible*, New York: Penguin Studio.

Milde, N. (2001) "Pop Goes the Queerness, or (Homo)Sexuality and Its Metaphors," *Amerikastudien*, 46 (1): 135–50.

National Steering Committee for the March on Washington, "Platform of the 1993 March on Washington," April 25, in M. Blasius (1994) *Gay and Lesbian Politics: Sexuality and the Emergence of a New Ethic*. Philadelphia: Temple University Press, pp. 175–178.

Nicholson, L. (1992) "Feminism and the Politics of Postmodernism," *Boundary 2*, 19 (2): 51–69.

Peters, J. (1996) "Making Connection: An Interview with Leslie Feinberg," *Southern Hemisphere* 7: 11.

Prosser, J. (1995), "No Place Like Home: The Transgendered Narrative of Leslie Feinberg's *Stone Butch Blues*," *Modern Fiction Studies* 4: 483–514.

Rupp, L. J. (1999) *A Desired Past*, Chicago, Ill.: University of Chicago Press.

Sedgwick, E. K. (1993) *Tendencies*, Durham, NC: Duke University Press.

Stone, S. (1991) "The Empire Strikes Back: A Posttranssexual Manifesto," in K. Straub and J. Epstein (eds), *Body Guards*, New York: Routledge, pp. 280–304.

Teal, D. (1971) *The Gay Militants*, New York: Stonewall Inn.

Waldman, A. (2004) "Feminafesto," in A. Waldman and L. Birman (eds), *Civil Disobediences*, Minneapolis, Minn.: Coffee House Press, pp. 326–7.

Warren, N. P. (1997) "How Real Is Our Sense of History?" *Quest*, October: 14–17.

Whitman, W. (1881) *Leaves of Grass*, in E. Greenspan (2004) *Walt Whitman's Song of Myself: A Sourcebook and Critical Edition*, New York: Routledge.

Zandy, J. (1990) *Calling Home*, New Brunswick, NJ: Rutgers University Press.

12 Regular Lolitas

The afterlives of an American adolescent

Kasia Boddy

How's her daughter Rita?
A regular Lolita.

Allan Sherman, "Sarah Jackman" (1962)

Moi, je m'appelle Lolita

Alizée, "Moi ... Lolita" (2000)

Naomi Wolf began *Promiscuities*, her 1997 "secret history of women's desire," by "reconstructing the 'libraries' of adolescence" that she and her girlfriends "plundered for sexual information and imagery" in the late 1970s. In a list that includes magazines, ranging from *Seventeen* to *Penthouse* and self-help books such as *Our Bodies, Ourselves*, only one novel is mentioned: *Lolita*.

> The book scared us in several ways. Humbert's physical revulsion with the grown woman, Lolita's mother, and his fascination with the child's body, gave us a sense of foreboding. Was this how grown men really felt? Was this book perverse or merely honest? ... Were we already, at sixteen, in decline?
>
> (Wolf 1998: 201)

Wolf recounts how she and her friends gathered in the bathroom for "sessions of literary criticism":

> As the water hissed and the bathroom grew comfortably steamy, we would talk about what we'd been reading. ... In the case of *Lolita*, we read the more lurid lines out loud. "There would have been a sultan, his face expressing great agony (belied, as it were, by his molding caress), helping a callipygian slave child to climb a column of onyx. ... There would have been a fire opal dissolving within a ripple-ringed

pool, a last throb, a last dab of color, stinging red, smarting pink, a sigh, a wincing child," I intoned. Sandy cracked up. The revolting quality of the image, for us, was reinforced by the photograph on the back of the book of Nabokov, the bald, and in our eyes, ancient man. The revulsion we felt for the narrator also had a quality of revenge.

(Wolf 1998: 201–2)

Naomi and Sandy are not the only readers to have responded so strongly to Nabokov's prose and subject matter, or to seek revenge. Since *Lolita* was published in 1955, many have agonized over the fact that his eponymous heroine had neither much of a life nor, in Humbert Humbert's hands, much of a literary memorial. Wolf ends her account by stating (contra Lo herself) that "if somebody wrote up her life," it would now be believed (1998: 202). Indeed, she might have added, it would be warmly welcomed.

Late-twentieth-century literary rewritings often begin with a sense that some character in a novel other than the narrator or main protagonist has been unfairly neglected and that restorative justice is needed. The case for doing this with *Lolita* was strengthened by the fact that Humbert takes great pride in ignoring the real Dolores Haze. Richard Rorty famously described him as a "monster of incuriosity" (1989: 161). "Lolita" (rather than Dolores) is Humbert's "own creation," having, he freely admits, "no will, no consciousness—indeed, no life of her own" (Nabokov 1995: 62). In saying this, he seems to be issuing a challenge.

But there is perhaps another reason why so many have been drawn to the novel that Nabokov described as a record of his "love affair" with the English language (1995: 316). Since its publication, *Lolita* has been universally praised for its virtuoso style and erudite literary game-playing. To make even a passing allusion to *Lolita* is to share in these qualities; references to the novel accrued cultural capital for late-twentieth-century novelists. Often this was simply a matter of mentioning lepidoptery, tennis, chess, or motels. Sometimes, a key scene was reworked. For example, Jack Gladney's attempt to kill Willie Mink in Don De Lillo's *White Noise* was a parody of Humbert Humbert's murder of Clare Quilty (DeLillo 1985: Chapter 39). The most "quoted" scene in *Lolita*, however, is the lap scene—in which Humbert, with the girl sitting on his "tense, tortured, surreptitiously labouring lap," fantasizes his way to an orgasm (Nabokov 1995: 60). Most of the novels I discuss below contain a version of this scene—Nabokov himself even re-enacts it with Dumbert Dumbert and Dolly in *Look at the Harlequins!* (Nabokov 1974: 143).

Beyond discrete images and scenes, the most imitated aspect of *Lolita* is its narrative voice. Naomi and her friends may have been disturbed by the way that "great art seemed to make what happened to [the girl], if not good, at least understandable" (Wolf 1998: 200), but, for many readers, Nabokov's great achievement lay in conveying the subjective life of a "monster." Humbert's arch tone spawned many imitators in the 1990s, most notably and controversially the narrator of Bret Easton Ellis's *American Psycho* (1991).

Critics and novelists looking for metaphors of exploitation and violation were also drawn to Nabokov's novel. Reading *Lolita* in late-1990s Tehran, Amar Nafisi and her pupils interpret the relationship between Humbert and Lo as an allegory for the workings of a repressive state—"the truth of Iran's past" is "as immaterial to those who appropriated it as the truth of Lolita's is to Humbert" (Nafisi 2004: 37). Salman Rushdie's going-to-America-in-the-nineties novel, *Fury*, meanwhile, used incest to represent civil war. Professor Salanka's young (but not underage) lover Mila Milo is drawn to his "cushioned lap" because she had been sexually abused by her novelist-father (Rushdie 2001: 132–3). "Milo" is really Milošević, and we are encouraged to relate his fucking his daughter to his namesake's fucking his country during the Yugoslav and Kosovo wars of the 1990s. Another professor, this time of Sanskrit, features in Lee Siegel's *Love in a Dead Language* (1999). Although Leopold Roth has many other (obvious) literary ancestors, he is also a bit of a Humbert Humbert. Instead of a lost childhood love, he had a daughter called Leila who was twelve when she was murdered, and his *inamorata* is a college student called Lalita Gupta; "Lolita with an A+" he says (Siegel 1999: 12). As Humbert makes Lolita a symbol of American virgin soil, Lalita embodies Indian exoticism for Roth. Like Humbert, he is punished. Ruined by accusations of sexual harassment, Roth dies when a ten-pound Sanskrit–English dictionary falls on his head.

These revisionist *Lolitas* treat the sexual relationship between Dolores and Humbert as, most interestingly, metaphoric. During the 1990s, however, another group of novels emerged that deliberately rejected metaphor. Such works can be read in the context of several developments: renewed psychoanalytic interest in traumatic memory and a consequently increased visibility for the victims of child abuse; feminist antipornography activism; and, in response, a "new feminist" rejection of censorship and "puritanism."

In *Feminism Unmodified* (1987) Catherine MacKinnon had declared the existence of "a whole shadow world of previously invisible silent abuse": "Rape, battery, sexual harassment, forced prostitution, and the sexual abuse of children emerge as common and systematic. ... Thirty-eight percent of little girls are sexually molested inside or outside the family" (MacKinnon 1987: 169). While MacKinnon's precise statistics were debated, few in the 1990s challenged her conclusion—that sexual abuse was a common, rather than rare, childhood experience (Freyd 1996: 36–8).

America was facing a "national emergency," declared a 1990 US government panel of childcare experts (Hacking 1991: 257). Soon, critical studies
with titles such as *Too Scared to Cry* and *Unchained Memories* (Terr 1990 and
1994) were sharing shelf space with bestselling memoirs of "psychic trauma
in childhood" such as Kathryn Harrison's *The Kiss*, an analysis of the
aftereffects of her father's "wet, insistent, exploring" tongue (Harrison
1997: 68). Similar themes informed numerous novels including Dorothy
Allison's *Bastard Out of Carolina* (1992) and *Push* (1996) by Sapphire, in
which a sixteen-year-old gets pregnant with her father's child, twice.
MacKinnon's reading of *Lolita* as primarily about "the tragedy of child
abuse" (Roiphe 1993: 144) became the norm as literary critics began to
publish what Timothy MacCracken describes as "Lo-centric" accounts of
Nabokov's novel (2001: 130–4). Noting the ubiquity of the term "Lolita"
in everyday speech, Elizabeth Patnoe asked why the definition was not "a
molested adolescent girl instead of a 'seductive' one?" (1995: 83).

In 1996, the US Congress passed the Child Pornography Prevention
Act, which broadened the definition of child pornography to include not
only pornographic images made using actual children but also images
merely appearing to involve children. In a widely publicized case,
Oklahoma used the Act to prosecute a video store for renting out the 1979
Oscar-winning adaptation of Günter Grass's novel, *The Tin Drum*. This
happened just as Adrian Lyne was completing a film adaptation of *Lolita*,
and, despite careful editing under legal advice, the movie was unable to
secure a distributor for over a year (Adler 2001: 241). Both Lyne's film
and its parent novel found themselves repeatedly cited in debates on the
competing claims of protection against pornography and free speech.
Speculating that Nabokov's book might have contributed toward social
tolerance of pedophilia, an argument also put forward by Martin Mawyer
of the Christian Action Network (Kauffman 1998: 19–20), Norman
Podhoretz suggested that "we might have been better off if even a masterpiece like *Lolita* had never been published." "Protection against the
pollution of the moral and cultural environment" was more important
than art (Podhoretz 1997: 35). But with *Lolita*, it was too late—the "masterpiece" *had* been published. What then to do?

Emily Prager's *Roger Fishbite* (1999) offers a direct rewriting. Lucky
Linderhof (L.L. instead of H.H.) tells her story as she awaits psychiatric
evaluation in the New York Department of Corrections, Juvenile Division. It
is the eve of her fifteenth birthday, and she has murdered her sexually
predatory stepfather. Lucky's account is full of references to other abused children. Her schoolfriends are all either neglected or psychologically abused
in some way and on television she can hardly escape stories about JonBenet
Ramsay, the six-year-old beauty queen who was thought to have been

murdered (the media speculated—falsely, it turned out) by her stepfather, and about Amy Fisher, the teenager who shot her lover's wife and who was known as the "Lethal Lolita" (Prager 1999: 51, 67, 39). And that is not all: "on what seemed to be a child abuse channel, the announcer told of newborns being kidnapped, newborns in garbage bins, a little boy beaten to death during toilet training, an eleven-year-old who had never been bathed, and children stabbing children in New Jersey" (Prager 1999: 111–12).

Prager's novel sticks closely to many aspects of Nabokov's (mainly to reverse them). Lucky's mother dies in an absurd road accident, and her stepfather, Roger Fishbite, conceals the information, before attempting to have sex with her at a motel at Lake Innuendo. Part I leads up to the first sexual encounter; Part II is their road trip. Lucky remembers "Dadee. Dad-ee. Dada. Dad" (1999: 53) and, just as Humbert had defined "nymphets" (Nabokov 1995: 16–17), she gives a definition of "dirty old men":

> Is every man a dirty old man? Oh no! Were that true then little girls would have no rest and certainly go mad. No, this is a special man, a man for whom a Catholic school uniform, even on a mannequin, does more than a whole album of grown-up girl nudes. A man whom Carter's white underpants titillate worlds beyond the classiest catalogue of frilly lingerie. ...
>
> You can recognize such men only if you are or have been that Carter's-wearing girl. They do not have looks in common. There is no body type that gives them away. Just a certain nervous obsessiveness about their manner that only an expert would notice.
>
> (Prager 1999: 13–14)

Fishbite resembles Humbert Humbert in various other ways: He is devoted to his typewriter; indeed his room has all "the trappings ... of a private detective" (Prager 1999: 10). Yet, it is clear that here it is Lucky, with her Manhattan private school education, who is the sophisticate. She may look like Britney Spears in the video for "Baby One More Time" (1999), but Lucky savors the novels of Henry Fielding and drops French phrases into her daily chat. Fishbite, meanwhile, is a Texan whose "conversation consisted entirely of sports scores and the doings of celebrities recounted from gossip columns which he pursued with unnatural intensity" (Prager 1999: 128) and whose idea of a road trip is to take his prey to airport motels in the tri-state area. He has no double; instead she does—a child actress/ model called Evie Naif, with whom Fishy two-times her.

Although Prager makes clear that the 1990s media is completely saturated with sex, and although Lucky claims she "never felt much like a child," we are certainly meant to believe that "the end of innocence" is still a meaningful moment; placed on Dad-ee's lap, Lucky doesn't really understand why, all of a sudden, it is "not all that comfortable" (Prager 1999: 37). Her reaction is initially self-destructive—after her mother's death, she starts cutting her legs (Prager 1999: 161), and when she finds out that Fishy has taken Evie to Disneyworld, she follows with a gun. Although aiming at her rival, Lucky ends up shooting Fishbite in the heart—as if Amy Fisher had, more properly, fired at her lover Joey Buttafuoco instead of his wife, Mary Jo.

Although Prager wants us to believe that Lucky is literate and literary, she doesn't really develop this to any great extent. Lucky addresses us as "Dear Readers and Watchers of tabloid TV and press" (Prager 1999: 6), and, for all that she claims to enjoy Fielding, her understanding of life seems rather to be informed by that staple of daytime 1990s television, the talk show: "Was I in love with him? … Warma Moneytree says young girls can't yet love in that way. Sally Jesse agrees. Ricki Lake disagrees. Jerry Springer wants to chew on it. Geraldo is outraged by the question. Montel Williams abstains. Barbara Walters is a definite no" (Prager 1999: 130).

Unlike Nabokov, Prager is not interested in arguing that television (and mass culture generally) somehow victimizes Lucky again. Lucky's daily diet of talk shows has turned her, in her own eyes anyway, into "a strong feminist type" (Prager 1999: 38). She starts a protest group, WHINE (World's Hapless Infants, Notice Everyone! [Prager 1999: 180]) and organizes street theatre about the child sex industry in Thailand. At the corrections facility she becomes famous as "the first sexual-abused girlchild … to actually murder her abuser" (Prager 1999: 223), and during the trial her news conferences raise 10 million dollars for children's charities. Lucky also ends up with her own talk show, *Baby Talk*—weekdays at 4 P.M.. Prager dedicates the novel to "all the little girls I've met who started life in desperate circumstances. It is their boundless determination and unstoppable joy in life that profoundly influenced this book" (n.p.). Lolita's revenge seems complete.

Avenging Lolita also seems to have been the aim of Nancy J. Jones's "homage to Nabokov," *Molly* (2000). Molly Liddell's story (of sustained abuse by her British college-professor stepfather, the doubly named Dr Richard Richard) emerges when her childhood friend Betsy Thurmont reads her diaries after her death. At the end of the book, Betsy, who was in love with Molly, grows up to found a women's legal-aid service, to help mothers "save their children from abuse." It turns out that "what Dick had done to Molly" is also "what had happened to so many girls I'd met and counseled" (Jones 2000: 244).

While Prager rewrites *Lolita* in order to suggest that sexuality is thrust upon teenagers, for Jones and others—including commentators as various as Naomi Wolf, Camille Paglia, and Elizabeth Wurtzel—thinking about Nabokov's novel provided a way of acknowledging and exploring the complex sexuality of teenage girls. Wurtzel's *Bitch: In Praise of Difficult Women* contains a chapter on teenage sexuality, focusing on the Amy Fisher story. For Wurtzel, the lack of feminist response to the case (the exception was Madonna who identified Joey Buttafuoco as the "real enemy") was diagnostic of 1970s-style feminism's unwillingness to deal with sexuality:

> Amy Fisher made us see that the desexed persona of the proper feminist—which made it impossible for feminism to take up her cause— meant that a number of women who wanted to walk on the wild side that was supposed to be part of the promise of liberation had nowhere to turn.
>
> (Wurtzel 1999: 137)

Keen to stress that the "new proper feminist" must recognize adolescent female sexuality—"teenagers are hormones with legs attached to them, and not much else"—Wurtzel also argued against falling into the trap of the "Lolita syndrome"—that is, assuming that teenage sexuality can be anything other than innocent (Wurtzel 1999: 104). Misinterpreting "Nabokov's beautiful and complicated text," readers had "turned the girl who is the object of perverse desire into the subject of a rapacious sexual appetite" (1999: 104).

Wurtzel's admonition, interestingly, only applied to girls. It is madness, she maintained, to chastise adult women for having affairs with underage boys, because boys' sexuality is so different. "Regardless of what the law says, most thirteen-year-old boys would consider any female willing to have sex with them a gift from above; that attitude may not be good or healthy, but there it is" (Wurtzel 1999: 115). Not everyone agreed. Several novels used allusions to *Lolita* to talk about the sexual exploitation of teenage boys: most explicitly, Donald Harington's 1993 *Ekaterina*, in which an exiled Georgian princess writes novels based on her affairs with a series of twelve-year-old lovers; and Dennis Cooper's *Try* (1994), which details a sexual relationship between a Humbert-like "super aesthete" Roger and his stepson Ziggy, whose hobby is editing *I Apologize*, "A Magazine for the Sexually Abused" (Boddy 1995: 105).

What Wurtzel terms "rapacious sexual appetite" is the quality that websites with names like *Lolitaz* and commentators like Paglia freely celebrated throughout the 1990s. Paglia also wanted to reject what she termed "Infirmary Feminism" in favor of a "revamped feminism" (1994: 111), but she went further than Wurtzel in also rejecting the "sexual borderline" between child and adult. As "conscious, wilful and manipulative as any mature woman," Lolita, she says, "melts" that "artificially drawn" borderline. And, although a man "named her," Paglia continues, "Lolita is not merely a male fantasy. ... she is drawn from life" (1994: 135) This belief forms the premise of Pia Pera's *Lo's Diary* (1999). Pia imagines a different ending to Nabokov's novel. In her version, Lo did not die in childbirth. Instead, expecting her second child, she decides to publish the diary of her years with Humbert. In this version, Lo emerged from the experience unscathed: Humbert Guibert was merely a "bore"; the sex was lousy (but no big deal); and so on.

A more complicated and controversial take on teenage sexuality can be found in A. M. Homes's novel *The End of Alice*. In 1997, it made the British headlines when Jim Harding, Chief Executive of the National Society for the Prevention of Cruelty to Children, denounced it "the most vile and perverted novel I have ever read" (Birkett 1997: 10). Harding asked bookstores not to stock the novel, and, although some followed his advice, the titillating publicity, as in all such cases, fuelled both curiosity and sales.

The novel presents the correspondence between a bored and depressed nineteen-year-old student and a prisoner who was convicted of the brutal murder and sexual assault of a twelve-year-old girl, Alice Somerfield, twenty-three years earlier. Unlike Nabokov, Homes does not allow her pedophile to die but forces him to experience incarceration; indeed, she details its brutalities. The teenaged correspondent sends him letters about her obsession with, and seduction of, Matthew, a twelve-year-old boy whom she tutors in the Nabokovian games of tennis and sex.

The prisoner is determined to view the girl as a kindred spirit in sexual exploration. Initially, the novel goes along with this, suggesting that perverse sexual fantasy and, to some extent, sexual predatoriness is ubiquitous. Matt's parents both have "crushlettes" on the girl; the prisoner is repeatedly raped; and Alice too, it is suggested, not only had sexual desires but probably a sexual past. The girl's letters prompt the prisoner to remember his encounters with Alice, and, finally, we are presented with a kind of a confession. At this point, it becomes clear that sex between a nineteen-year-old girl and a twelve-year-old boy is not the same as sex between a thirty-year-old man and a twelve-year-old girl—even though both are, initially at least, consensual.

The behavior of all these characters is accounted for as post-traumatic acting out. It turns out that the teenaged girl lives on the street where Alice grew up. "Your influence is everywhere," she tells the prisoner, "And it's not only me, it's all the mothers and all the girls. Everyone is afraid" (Homes 1996: 167). She says she was attracted to Matthew simply because he was "someone who didn't scare me" (Homes 1996: 169). And, while

Nabokov, a great opponent of Freudianism, simply presents H.H.'s pedo-philia as a fact, Homes's child-abuser turns out himself to be the victim of childhood sexual abuse, the memory of which gradually emerges. Since Homes is keen to challenge all taboos, the perpetrator of that abuse is his (just-released-from-psychiatric-hospital) mother, who forces him to mas-turbate her violently in a bathtub. (He is so small, it feels like a pool.) After they get out, she starts menstruating and, not understanding where the blood is coming from, he thinks he has hurt her. Soon afterwards, she dies, and he feels he has murdered her. This is the primal scene that will be repeated many years later with Alice Somerfield. When she discovers that she's menstruating, she becomes hysterical, and the narrator kills her. The end of Alice's childhood is the end of Alice.

Homes acknowledged several influences on *The End of Alice:* a biography of Lewis Carroll in which she discovered that "Alice was a very powerful little girl"; psychoanalytic research into the way "girls approaching ado-lescence" experience a loss of self that makes them vulnerable to abuse (Brown and Gilligan 1992: 2); the concept of "moral pornography" from *The Sadeian Woman*, by her former teacher Angela Carter; and, of course, Nabokov's *Lolita*.

Revisiting *Lolita*, said Homes, allowed her to explore "how the language of literature, how explicitness, had moved forward" since 1955 (Boddy 1996). Prager's narrator refused to describe sex at all, arguing that "I must stop here lest I join the illustrious company of titillators and muddy my intent" (1999: 113). Humbert too dismissed the idea that he was a porno-grapher: "I am not concerned with so-called 'sex' at all. Anybody can imagine those elements of animality" (Nabokov 1995: 134). For Homes, the problem was that many readers refused to do that imagining.

> I overheard this comment in a cafe where somebody said, "I don't think he slept with her." What do you say? She didn't believe that Humbert had slept with Lolita. And I was appalled. How can you read that and think that? There is some subtlety to it but he's also pretty clear. He told her, "look, if you don't do this I'm going to send you off forever." I wanted to write something where you couldn't deny it, you couldn't read it and pretend that this wasn't happening.
>
> (Boddy 1996)

Joining "the company of titillators" for Homes was a conscious act of "moral pornography"—pornography, that is, in the service of a moral argument—a method of forcing readers (like the nineteen-year-old corre-spondent) to think about the ways in which their desires overlap with those of the "pervert" before, ultimately, provoking them to recognize the difference between fantasy and the "deeper cord" of perversion (Prager 1999: 187).

And there were perhaps other reasons why Homes wanted to take on the point of view of the pedophile rather than his victim. One might have been to develop a feminist perspective rather different from that of Jones and Prager. Homes—whose first name is Amy although she prefers to be known by the gender-free initials, A.M. so as, she claims, "not be bound by the personal sound or cultural connotations of Amy"—has often spoken about what she sees as the restrictive conventions of accepted notions of women's fiction—books "written by women, very domestic kind of stories. … for an audience that was basically women" (Boddy 1996). Unlike most of the writers discussed here, Homes did not want to be closely identified with her characters; rather, she wanted precisely to disrupt that possibility—to write not from the perspective of the girl or the young woman but from that of "a 53-year-old man in jail" (Crewdson 1996: 39). When the teenaged girl first writes to the pedophile, he responds, "what interested me about this well-typed tome was the willingness of its author to transcend, to flirt, outside her chosen category or group" (Homes 1996: 13). For Homes, rewriting *Lolita* was a way both of rejecting the constraints of literary identity politics and of displaying her virtuosity as a novelist. "Women are not supposed to do things that are not very, very nice, and now they're doing them" (Boddy 1996).

At the end of Nabokov's novel, Humbert Humbert recognizes that because of his love for Lolita, he has become an artist. Although "mentally" he found her to be "a disgustingly conventional little girl," she was nevertheless his muse (Nabokov 1995: 148). While the 1990s Lolitas often tell their own stories, they do not, on the whole, become artists. Most writers are happy for them to remain conventional (if not disgusting) and thus representative rather than exceptional teenaged girls. Prager's supposedly well-read Lucky tells her story with verve but ends up fronting a chat show. Pera's Lo hands over her diary to her editor with the warning that her impressions of "that time" are "definitely less literary" than those of her tormentor (Pera 1999: 1). Molly's diary is equally unliterary, and Betsy's retelling fairly pedestrian, but, in case we worry that girls can't ever write, Jones has her heroine encounter Sylvia Plath on her cross-country journey, allowing an allusion to Plath's poem "Daddy." Mostly, though, the "conventional" vocabulary of the girls is again contrasted to the lyrical waxings of Humbert's descendants. Siegel's Lalita moans about "fuckin' bureaucracy"; Professor Roth responds with a paragraph on "her precious use of the present participle" (Siegel 1999: 15). The prisoner-narrator of *The End of Alice* rarely quotes his teenaged correspondent's letters, arguing that her prose style needs his extensive reworking. He complains about her punctuation (too many exclamation marks), her vocabulary ("stinted, stilted language of youth" [Homes 1996: 29]), and her imagery (the "false poetry of the overly undereducated" [1996: 165]). Of course, this says a lot about his "disease" (Homes 1996: 15)—he refers to her as one of his "characters" (1996: 96)—but it also says something about what Homes will or will not allow for her teenager. As in *Lolita*, the girl's voice and personality emerge occasionally in brief direction quotation, but nothing the prisoner quotes contradicts his stylistic assessment. She writes things like *"Matt bought Doc Martens. Took Matt to Tower. Wash Sq. Pak. Ate falafel, bab ganoush. Matt had an egg cream"* (Homes 1996: 108), and the prisoner responds with tirades against the "imbecilic nature of her communication" (1996: 114). "Her language, the words she uses are brainless, convey nothing" (Homes 1996: 108). No wonder, then, that the girl's words make up less than three pages of the book.

One of the tenets of Humbert's philosophy of pedophilia (and one that is echoed by his imitators) is that adult women are rather revolting. While the novels described here express outrage on the behalf of the girl victims of such pedophiles, most share Humbert's antipathy to their absent and "collusive" mothers, more interested in their shiny houses than their troubled daughters (Karlyn 2004: 82). Charlotte Haze (especially as played by Shelley Winters in the first film adaptation by Stanley Kubrick in 1962) epitomised the "plasticmom" that so many of these works present as the story's second villain (Pera 1999: 83). Carolyn Burnham (Annette Bening) updated the role in Sam Mendes's 1999 film *American Beauty* (Karlyn 2004: 74). Her frustrated husband (played by Kevin Spacey) is called Lester Burnham, an anagram of "Humbert learns"—and, indeed, he has progressed enough to refrain from having sex with his daughter's classmate. There is, however, no suggestion that his wife learns anything.

In many of the novels I discuss, to kill these women off and so transcend their suburban ways is to enact a fantasy that their daughters share with their husbands. Only Homes provides a mother who seems to take care of her child. From the nineteen-year-old's letters, the prisoner constructs an image of her mother as one of the "last lost generation of homemakers, trained to be deaf, dumb, and blind. They stay in the house, floating from room to room, cans of Endust and Lemon Pledge in hand" (Homes 1996: 83). So far, so "plasticmom." But even the prisoner has to acknowledge that although she remains a limited suburbanite (believing that happiness might be found in shopping and a trip to Europe), the girl's mother is not blind. She eventually unearths the pedophile's letters and promises to find her daughter someone to "talk to … about this" (Homes 1996: 247). In the 1990s, there was no shortage of willing listeners.

References

Adler, A. (2001) "The Perverse Law of Child Pornography," *Columbia Law Review*, 101 (2) (March): 209–73.

Allison, D. (1992) *Bastard Out of Carolina*, New York: Dutton.

Birkett, D. (1997) "The End of Childhood," *The Guardian*, October 28, pp. 10–11.

Boddy, K. (1995) "Conversation with Dennis Cooper," *Critical Quarterly*, 37 (3): 103–15.

—— (1996) Unpublished interview with A. M. Homes.

Brown, L. M. and Gilligan, C. (1992) *Meeting at the Crossroads: Women's Psychology and Girls' Development*, Cambridge, Mass.: Harvard University Press.

Carter, A. (1979) *The Sadeian Woman*, London: Virago Press.

Cooper, D. (1994) *Try*, London: Serpent's Tail.

Crewdson, G. (1996) "A. M. Homes in Wonder Land," *Bomb*, 55 (spring): 38–42.

DeLillo, D. (1985) *White Noise*, London: Picador.

Ellis, B. E. (1991) *American Psycho*, London: Picador.

Freyd, J. (1996) *Betrayal Trauma: The Logic of Forgetting Childhood Sexual Abuse*, Cambridge, Mass.: Harvard University Press.

Hacking, I. (1991) "The Making and Molding of Child Abuse," *Critical Inquiry*, 17 (2): 253–88.

Harington, D. (1993) *Ekaterina*, New York: Harcourt Brace & Co.

Harrison, K. (1997) *The Kiss*, New York: Random House.

Homes, A. M. (1996) *The End of Alice*, New York: Scribner.

Jones, N. J. (2000) *Molly*, New York: Crown Publishers.

Karlyn, K. R. (2004) "'Too Close for Comfort': *American Beauty* and the Incest Motif," *Cinema Journal*, 44 (1): 69–93.

Kauffman, L. S. (1998) *Bad Girls and Sick Boys: Fantasies in Contemporary Art and Culture*, Berkeley, Calif.: University of California Press.

MacKinnon, C. A. (1987) *Feminism Unmodified: Discourses on Life and Law*, Cambridge, Mass.: Harvard University Press.

McCracken, T. (2001) "Lolita Talks Back: Giving Voice to the Object," in Mica Howe and Sarah Appleton Aguiar (eds), *He Said, She Says: An RSVP to the Male Text*, Madison, N.J.: Fairleigh Dickinson University Press, pp. 128–42.

Nafisi, A. (2004) *Reading Lolita in Tehran: A Memoir in Books*, London: Fourth Estate.

Nabokov, V. (1974) *Look at the Harlequins!* New York: Vintage.

—— (1995) *The Annotated Lolita*, Harmondsworth: Penguin.

Paglia, C. (1994) *Vamps and Tramps*, New York: Vintage.

Patnoe, E. (1995) "Lolita Misrepresented, Lolita Reclaimed: Disclosing Doubles," *College Literature*, 22 (2): 81–104.

Pera, P. (1999) *Lo's Diary*, trans. Ann Goldstein, New York: Foxrock.

Podhoretz, N. (1997) "Lolita, My Mother-in-Law, the Marquis de Sade, and Larry Flynt," *Commentary*, 103 (4): 23–35.

Prager, E. (1999) *Roger Fishbite*, London: Chatto & Windus.

Roiphe, K. (1993) *The Morning After: Sex, Fear and Feminism*, New York: Little, Brown & Co.

Rorty, R. (1989) "The Barber of Kasbeam: Nabokov on Cruelty," in *Contingency, Irony and Solidarity*, Cambridge: Cambridge University Press, pp. 141–68.

176   *Kasia Boddy*

Rushdie, S. (2001) *Fury*, London: Jonathan Cape.
Sapphire (1996) *Push*, New York: Alfred A. Knopf.
Siegel, L. (1999) *Love in a Dead Language*, Chicago, Ill.: University of Chicago Press.
Terr, L. (1990) *Too Scared To Cry: Psychic Trauma in Childhood*, New York: Harper & Row.
—— (1994), *Unchained Memories: True Stories of Traumatic Memories, Lost and Found*, New York: Basic Books.
Wolf, N. (1998) *Promiscuities: A Secret History of Female Desire*, London: Vintage.
Wurtzel, E. (1999) *Bitch: In Praise of Difficult Women*, London: Quartet.

13 *Glamorama*, *Fight Club*, and the terror of narcissistic abjection

Alex E. Blazer

> The mannequin springs grotesquely to life in the freezing room, screeching, arching its body up, again and again, lifting itself off the examination table, tendons in its neck straining, and purple foam starts pouring out of its anus, which also has a wire, larger, thicker, inserted into it. Bunched around the wheels on the table legs are white towels spotted heavily with blood, some of it black. What looks like an intestine is slowly emerging, of its own accord, from another, wider slit across the mannequin's belly.
>
> (Ellis 2000: 323)

> This is the greatest moment of our life.
>   The lye clinging in the exact shape of Tyler's kiss is a bonfire or a branding iron or an atomic pile meltdown on my hand at the end of a long, long road I picture miles away from me. Tyler tells me to come back and be with him. My hand is leaving, tiny and on the horizon at the end of the road.
>
> (Palahniuk 2005: 74)

Images of bodies being tortured and blown up fill the pages of Bret Easton Ellis's *Glamorama* (1998), a schizophrenic tale, in narrative if not also in mind, that merges the worlds of celebrity culture and international terrorism. Images of bodies battering each other and destroying themselves comprise Chuck Palahniuk's *Fight Club* ([1996] 2005), another story of mental dissociation that finds its white-collar office-working narrator in an underground fight club cum anti-capitalist terrorist organization. On the one hand, the human body in these two novels is exalted as ideal—the perfect face atop the model's body, the powerful, potent and primal machine of raw masculinity—while on the other, the body is a dummy subjected to humanity's most debased and vicious cruelties. Per Serritslev Petersen asserts that *Glamorama* and *Fight Club* function as pretexts for 9/11: The postmodern apocalyptic imagination is realized by real-life terrorist events. By contrast, this examination looks at how the two novels portray an abreaction of unconscious corporeal anxiety created by living in a culture that valorizes an unending barrage of glitzy images and faddy products in an attempt to deny the routinely bland cerebral labor that divorces its denizens from the physical world. These books spring from a "me" generation of narcissists in part because we have been inculcated by the media's egotistic ideology in its unfailing quest to hock products through lifestyle imagery. Moreover, these stories portray the dark underside of contemporary narcissism, a primal anxiety that one's self does not measure up to the culture's doctrinal dream. Full of themselves, yet terrified of the very thing that absorbs them, the idealized, consumerist body becomes the site of a primal war between narcissistic pleasure—perfectly sculpted bodies greeted with onlookers' admiration and lovers' sexual gratification—and abject pain—those same model bodies being beaten up and ripped open, apart. *Glamorama* and *Fight Club* present narcissistic narrators simultaneously hollowed out and devoured by a culture of empty images and endless consumption. When their narcissism is left bereft, they turn to terrorism to annihilate the images and products that haunt them.

Glamorous abjection

Whereas Ellis's first killer tome, *American Psycho* (1991), shows the mind of a young Wall Street executive being psychotically leveled by his name-brand consumer culture in which goods are god and people are things to be collected and killed, *Glamorama* follows another deteriorating psyche, this one belonging to a fashion model and minor celebrity on the New York scene of glamorous glitterati. The novel's vain anti-hero, Victor Ward, is so terrified of his lack of immortality, existence, and control over his own life that death works through his unconscious. Victor's death-invested narcissism triggers a psychotic break with reality, in which he becomes the true center of the universe (he's followed around by two film crews that script his life) that is fragmenting, if not wholly decomposing. As his image-conscious mental world disintegrates, Victor becomes caught in a conspiracy of models-turned-terrorists who jaunt around Europe dismembering and blowing up people. Narcissism takes a deadly turn in *Glamorama*, an apogee of abasement and abjection that exposes the death—by dismemberment— wish that underlies our body image- and celebrity-obsessed culture.

Victor is utterly consumed by the pursuit of his self-image—a girlfriend tells him, "A mirror's your best friend" (Ellis 2000: 116)—and media hype, especially praising propaganda that sells his image. As "It" cover boy of the month, according to that seminal subscription *YouthQuake* magazine, he's the pretty-boy face who is opening a club for moneyman Damien Nutchs Ross while vying for a part in *Flatliners II*. In his private life, he juggles sleeping with his girlfriend (supermodel Chloe Byrnes), his boss's fiancée

(Lauren Hynde—his girlfriend's best friend, and his own ex-girlfriend from college that he now cannot remember going out with at the time), and eventually pursues a would-be ex-flame from college (Jamie Fields) all the while conniving to open a club of his own behind Damien's back. Victor's life consists of a flurried haze of publicity and parties, congress and conspiracy.

His character fits the *Diagnostic and Statistical Manual of Mental Disorders* (*DSM-IV*) criteria for narcissistic personality disorder. Victor (1) "has a grandiose sense of self-importance," (2) "is preoccupied with fantasies of unlimited success [and] beauty," (3) "believes that he … is 'special' and unique and … should associate with other special or high-status people," (4) "requires excessive admiration," (5) "has a sense of entitlement," (6) "is interpersonally exploitative," (7) "lacks empathy," (8) "is often envious of others," and (9) "shows arrogant, haughty behaviors or attitudes" (American Psychiatric Association 2000: 717). While the *DSM-IV* lists personality traits, Freud's analysis suggests how Victor's psyche could be structured. In "On Narcissism: An Introduction," Freud differentiates between two forms of narcissism, the primary narcissism every human psyche has, which is constituted by the desire for self-preservation, and secondary narcissism, an aberrant extreme of primary narcissism. The pathological, schizophrenic narcissist is one who can invest emotional and sexual energy only in himself, his own ego rather than others in the world: "The libido that has been withdrawn from the external world has been directed to the ego and thus gives rise to an attitude which may be called narcissism" (1991: 5). The psyche of the current "It" boy has been taught by his glamorous lifestyle and cult of celebrity media that he is the center of the world, so much so that he manipulates and exploits everyone in his life without a second thought. Moreover, when we first meet him, he fakes an orgasm with Alison because he's focusing on a photo of Alison, Damien, Chloe, and himself. Soon after, he bluffs his way out of intercourse with Chloe in order to watch a music video and gaze at a framed photo of himself taken by fashion photographer Herb Ritts. While he does eventually have sex, Victor is fundamentally portrayed as a narcissist invested only in his self-image, sexually and emotionally.

In order to launch the club, Victor must create the perfect event which will induce celebrity participation and thus reap glowing MTV and *Entertainment Tonight* coverage for the ogling public, all while being himself attended by a reporter from *Details* magazine who is doing a puff piece on him. Confirming the stars' attendance through their bevy of public-relations people as well as the stars' own petty desires to be seen in the trendiest place possible proves a Herculean effort. However, what truly installs cataclysmic angst in Victor's façade are some spots on the wall of the club:

"Specks—all over the third panel, see?—no, *that* one—the second one up from the floor and I wanted to point this out to someone yesterday but a photo shoot intervened and Yaki Nakamari or whatever the hell the designer's name is—a master craftsman *not*—mistook me for someone else so I couldn't register the complaint, but, gentlemen—and ladies—there they are: *specks*, annoying, tiny specks, and they *don't* look accidental but like they were somehow done by a machine—so I don't want a lot of description, just the story, streamlined, no frills, the lowdown: who, what, where, when and don't leave out why, though I'm getting the distinct impression by the looks on your sorry faces that *why* won't get answered—now, come on, goddamnit, what's the *story?*"

(Ellis 2000: 5; author's italics)

Although his conscious mind rejects the epiphany of his beautiful body's limited immortality, Victor unconsciously realizes that the spotlight life he has chosen will necessarily end in lighting his ever-growing spots. Outwardly, Victor possesses the ideal celebrity lifestyle: a hard body coupled with a perfect face that can sell underwear and magazines as well as open clubs. But his spotless exterior quickly shows signs of cracking. Not only does the club wall have specks but his life—his psyche—is falling apart.

In the first part of *Glamorama*, the chapter numbers count down from 33 to 0, as if it is a time bomb ticking down from the initial specks in Victor's world to the complete psychological undoing of Victor's own body through the return of his repressed death-invested psyche. As the opening of the club approaches, Victor cannot deal with Damien, Alison, Lauren, the *Details* reporter, the club opening, and his secret club: He fragments. The opening night party is marked by the refrain in Victor's mind: "*We'll slide down the surface of things*" (Ellis 2000: 164; author's italics). Victor's narcissistic subjectivity collapses under the body image that will no longer support him. Victor's narcissism devolves into paranoia. In order to maintain its self-importance, his psyche creates not one but two delusional worlds, both of which relieve him of doing anything about the real problems with the real people in his real life.

In one hallucinatory world, Victor is "acting" in two rival movies with two crews, one American and one French, thus unbosoming the psychotically deteriorating Victor from the burden of existence, of free will. The films not only determine his actions but also script his fate. Although Victor needs to be told what to do because narcissism no longer sustains, his psyche nonetheless requires narcissistic reinforcement. The solution: living life as if it were a film in which you are the star. The problem with this solution: life's specks, its spectacular uncertainties, return in delusion as apocalyptic annihilators. The death that undergirds Victor's obsessive investment in the imaginary body rends even his narcissism apart as the two crews cannot exist simultaneously in his mind. One must be blown apart and destroyed in order to function without ambivalence.

The other part of Victor's delusion involves terrorism. Victor is pursued by the manipulative machinations of the elusive figure of Palakon, a man who is working for and against Victor's father's presidential bid and asks Victor to travel to Europe to seek out a former Camden classmate, Jamie Fields, a double or triple agent working for and against a terrorist organization run by the former, foremost, and first male model. Bobby Hughes enlists current models to bomb fashionable and political venues in Europe because models have the perfect cover: They are always traveling to the trendiest and glitziest spots in this mediated Western civilization but are considered too dumb by security forces to pose a risk. Moreover, models are highly manipulable, sacrificing free will for imaginary validation:

> How did he recruit people? ...It was only models...and famous models...He wasn't interested in anyone else. ...He would use the fact that as a model all you do all day is stand around and do what other people tell you to do. ...He preyed on that...and we listened...and it was an analogy that made sense...in the end...when he asked...things of us...and it wasn't hard to recruit people...everyone wanted to be around us...everyone wanted to be movie stars...and in the end, basically, everyone was a sociopath...
>
> (Ellis 2000: 352, author's ellipses)

Victor loses not only his intellectual self-consciousness to the pursuit of his self-image but also his affective inwardness. Death wreaks havoc on his psyche. From this point on, Victor's inner death is externalized via a series of increasingly grotesque tortures, as illustrated by this chapter's epigraph, and bombings described in the most minute detail of corporeal abasement:

> The extent of the destruction is a blur and its aftermath somehow feels beside the point. The point is the bomb itself, its placement, its activation—that's the statement. ... It's not the legs blown off, the skulls crushed, the people bleeding to death in minutes. The uprooted asphalt, the blackened trees, the benches splattered with gore, some of it burned—all of this matters just as much. It's really about the will to accomplish this destruction and not about the outcome, because that's just decoration.
>
> (Ellis 2000: 337)

In her seminal work, *Powers of Horror: An Essay on Abjection*, Julia Kristeva describes a subject akin to Victor's psychological experience: "On the edge of non-existence and hallucination, of a reality that, if I acknowledge it, annihilates me. There, abject and abjection are my safeguards. The primers of my culture" (1982: 2). Victor's glittered existence constitutes a dazed and confused *Dasein* that threatens to nullify his subjectivity completely: In the world of celebrity, Victor is all style and no substance, all image and no inwardness. Shallowness reveals a more fundamental emptiness. Glamorous images offer hallucinatory self-inflation that ultimately proves unrealistic. The specks in the club wall symbolize the abreaction of Victor's mind: the image-conscious narcissist is beginning to anxiously realize that his real life, his unconscious subjectivity, is being annihilated by acute vacuity. The abject is first and foremost the recognition of primal annihilation, *self*-annihilation—from the inside out. Because Victor has interpellated the cultural value of superficial body image into the core of his subjectivity, the horrific destruction of the body becomes a wake-up call urging Victor to change his life, his very being. The kind of gore Victor imagines witnessing is unspeakable and unimaginable until his degenerating psyche needs to imagine it and is compelled to speak it in order to verify that it (his psyche) has not been totally subsumed by the perfect body image. Abject—disemboweled, dismembered—bodies in *Glamorama* serve as avatars of Victor's anxiety regarding the hyper-imaginary world that constitutes his being. Furthermore, abjection provides Victor his only link to the real world. Without existential pain or grotesque dismemberment, Victor would float off into the ether of glitz.

Bobby embodies Victor's obliterating ambivalence. Victor desires Bobby's body of work even as he is terrorized by Bobby's work of death. On the one hand, he admires Bobby's image; he wants to be just like Bobby, a pioneer in the industry. He craves the sense of control that Bobby wields over his corporeal and contingent life, the lives of his gang members, and Victor's life. On the other, Bobby represents the death which once lurked inside Victor's narcissism and rots his mind until no idealized body image can contain its abject wish. This inner limit of decay seeks externalization, and it compels an eyewitness, Victor, to be subjected to an excess of terrorism and torture, destruction and dismemberment. The life of the mind will be experienced through the delusions of ripped-open bodies. As the oblivious mind awakens to its own narcissistic self-destruction, real-life hard bodies are replaced by hallucinatory exploding bodies. The narcissistic ideal tears itself asunder in an onslaught of abjection. Bobby turns on Victor, plants a biological bomb that melts his girlfriend Chloe from the inside out and then attempts to kill him. Victor's delusional world is at war with itself. His breakdown breaks down until he finds balance by dropping out of the glitterati scene, enrolling in law school and helping out with his father's presidential bid. However, such stability remains relative and uncertain for in the end Victor nonetheless still thinks himself a spy.

Through the psychologically debilitated character of Victor Ward, the novel *Glamorama* mediates body image into bodily fragmentation as, for instance, the beautiful body of a Calvin Klein advertisement is supplanted by a body blown to bits by a bomb. The body is a thing to be viewed, devoured, and destroyed, most notably for the spectacle of film, which enlists our most pathological of narcissisms. The ultimate goal of terrorism is more psychological than physical, and the psychotic unbinding of Victor's mind embodies terrorism at its canniest best. Victor becomes a model terrorist subject to the destructive will of another model terrorist in his own mind precisely because he is terrified of who he has become by worshiping the impossibly speckless images flitting across the pages and screens of his culture. Although he unconsciously knows that death works inside him, from within the void that embodies his self-image, he can do nothing but devolve into disillusioned delusion.

Abject resurrection

While Bret Easton Ellis's *Glamorama* criticizes how the image-conscious 1990s creates a celebrity-driven culture of narcissists and then proceeds to drive one particular narcissist insane through the impossibility of bodily perfection, Chuck Palahniuk's *Fight Club* reveals how the office space of a bureaucratized life, though certainly not as hyperaware of image as *Glamorama*, nonetheless annihilates subjectivity, specifically masculinity. If *Glamorama* destroys bodies because of a fundamental anxiety regarding body image in a world devoted to image consumption, then *Fight Club* destroys bodies because of a fundamental anxiety regarding masculinity in a world that substitutes consumerism for potency.

Fight Club's unnamed narrator, who eventually proves himself to be as unreliable as Victor Ward, has a white-collar job (car recall coordinator) and a pleasant, upscale condo. At first glance, it would appear as if he is living the American Dream. Not only has he fulfilled his desires by pur-chasing just the right decor for his home, but his interior design satiates his interiority by providing respite and relief from the everyday problems of the world:

> You buy furniture. You tell yourself, this is the last sofa I will ever need in my life. Buy the sofa, then for a couple years you're satisfied that no matter what goes wrong, at least you've got your sofa issue

handled. Then the right set of dishes. Then the perfect bed. The drapes. The rug.

(Palahniuk 2005: 44)

Despite a bevy of posh and comforting appliances, despite a job traveling the country, he is fundamentally alienated from his home, his labor, his lifestyle, his very existence. Whereas Victor's initial sense of anxiety occurs with the wall-defiling specks, we are introduced to the narrator's core conflict when he is bear-hugged by the castrated and breast-befitted Bob at a testicular-cancer support-group meeting and mandated to cry, which he does and in the process realizes two things: First, everything he has done is "trash" and, second, he is "lost inside" (Palahniuk 2005: 17). Enveloped by a gelded cancer patient, the narrator weeps with the unconscious recognition that his life spent laboring for soothing stuff has existentially emasculated him and his entire generation. He traded both agency and virility for the comforts of commodity fetishism. The narrator's interest in collecting creature comforts in order to stave off the harsh realities of life escalates into libidinal desire: "And I wasn't the only slave to my nesting instinct. The people I know who used to sit in the bathroom with pornography, now they sit in the bathroom with their IKEA furniture catalogue" (Palahniuk 2005: 43). Moreover, the narrator's particular form of commodity fetishism not only turns products into pornography in which the desire for consummation with another human being is supplanted by the desire for consumption of decor but also transforms masculinity into maternity. If a real man is one who has power and potency, constitution and control, then the man who is consumed by his covey of goods and compelled to build them into a womb in the world is either a baby or a girl. Just as the narrator was engulfed by castration, his life has been usurped by his possessions: "Then you're trapped in your lovely nest, and the things you used to own, now they own you" (Palahniuk 2005: 44).

Similarly, the narrator's job siphons off his power. In the first place, the job forces him to spend days, if not weeks, in the air and on the road, away from his homey safety nest, which creates a fundamental paradox: The narrator works a job to assemble a domicile in which he cannot comfortably dwell because of his job. Rather than relaxing at home, he wakes up at airport after airport until he is so disconnected from missed connections that he is "nowhere" (Palahniuk 2005: 33). While the good stuff remains at home, he lives a "tiny life" of travel products and "single-serving," "miniature," and "do-it-yourself" cuisine onboard and in terminals. Meanwhile, he must squeeze his "single-use" friendships into the time between boarding and deplaning. The narrator's subjectivity is diminished by his business travels. Anxiety intensifies into abject, annihilating thinking: "Every takeoff and landing, when the plane banked too much to one side, I prayed for a crash. That moment cures my insomnia with narcolepsy when we might die helpless and packed human tobacco in the fuselage" (Palahniuk 2005: 25). As his job alienates him from his life, the narrator wishes for a death that poetically represents the bitter feelings of belittling confinement afforded by his bit trips. Second, the narrator's job itself puts life on the same level of value as commodity. As Car Recall Coordinator, he calculates if his company should issue a safety recall based on the probable cost of lawsuits. His job teaches him that pain and suffering are quantifiable, legal and financial entities—and it keeps him up at night. Hollowed out by both the corporate bottom line that places profit before humanity and the IKEA catalogue that collects his existential and sexual desires, his subjectivity deteriorates to that of an insomniac—a zombie, a dead man going through the motions of life.

While Victor's pathological narcissism is total, the narrator's is more complicated. Although one can validly argue that he was always a narcissist due to his egotistical relationship with his things, one can also make the case that his secondary narcissism does not truly present itself until he realizes that his life, indeed no life, can measure up to the American Dream precisely because the dream is warped and perverts the self. In the former argument, commodity fetishism is an extension of oneself, thus equating with self-love; the latter, by contrast, asserts that the narrator's alienation from commodity fetishism engenders an abreacted resurrection of self so total that it becomes pathological. In either case, the narrator responds to his bereft feeling of subjective destitution by seeking out others, not for intersubjective communion but rather for narcissistic ful-fillment. He adds to his death-dealing job in the insurance industry a self-ish scheme of manipulating care and compassion from the sick and dying. The insomniac narrator becomes a physical malingerer and emotional skulker when he attends support groups—testicular cancer, tuberculosis, leukemia, brain parasites, bowel cancers, organic brain dementia—ostensibly to cure his insomnia. A group cry liberates him from his zombification because it nullifies his job, his nest, his life: "This was freedom. Losing all hope was freedom. ... Look up into the stars and you're gone" (Palahniuk 2005: 22). The narrator does not say that the groups assuage his alienation; rather, they obviate his hope. In other words, he is still invested in his life of deadly goods despite its psychological ramifications. When stuff no longer fills him up, dying people do. He identifies with them and uses their strength to reinvigorate his psyche: "Every evening, I died, and every evening, I was born" (Palahniuk 2005: 22). One can now argue that Bob does not enclose the narrator *simply* with his castration but instead the narrator *also* manipulates himself into this emasculated human being because he wants to be unconditionally mothered as he is in all the other groups he attends.

As a faker, he does not offer support but simply takes it. Skeletal support-group member Chloe wishes for the intersubjectivity of intercourse before she dies, but the narrator can only offer her his repulsion: The members buttress the malingerer's subjectivity but not vice versa. On the outside, from the point of view of the group, the narrator is damaged, dying goods; on the inside, he really is deranged. Although he may have started his journey in the novel with justifiable alienation from the American Dream, he becomes an emotional sycophant when the ideology of commodity fetishism breaks down precisely because he has a demonical need for narcissistic self-fulfillment that is the by-product of being raised in a culture in which goods are designed to effect effusive, infantilizing comfort. Not surprisingly, the faker falls for a faker, but not at first. Marla attends many of the narrator's support groups, even the one for testicular cancer, and they become rival "tourists" on safari, poaching the perishing packs for invaluable affection (Palahniuk 2005: 24). Although she destroys his narcissistic high, she also paradoxically invigorates it. On the one hand, "Marla's lie reflects my lie, and all I can see are lies" (Palahniuk 2005: 23), but on the other, he has now looked out into the world and found a woman who constitutes his mirror image.

As we saw above, Victor imagines Bobby Hughes in order to cede control of his fragmenting life and fractured psyche. The narrator's psyche splits asunder, and his caustic and corroded unconscious of repressed death becomes his alter ego, Tyler Durden, who can rage against the machine that hollowed out his host. The narrator creates, befriends, and becomes Tyler Durden for a number of reasons. It is through Tyler that the narrator can dissociate from himself and have a relationship with Marla, for this narcissist cannot function sexually without such a split. Further, Tyler's rough sex with Marla points to an overcompensation of the narrator's repressed masculinity. Tyler represents the endpoint of the narrator's alienated desires regarding masculinity, occupation, and home. Much like *Glamorama*'s Bobby, Tyler is sculpted and strong, a charismatic, demanding leader rather than a nurturing, infantilizing mother-man deprived of his manhood. Tyler does not immerse the narrator in a dark oblivion of man-breasts; he hits the narrator into refreshed and unwearied consciousness with fists. He fulfills the narrator's desire to break free from and bleed the corporate system: As film projectionist, he sticks it to his middle-manager bosses by splicing pornographic film stills into family features and then extorting them with threats of going public; as waiter, he urinates in the soup of the capitalist elites, teaches the narrator to use his penis to stir the drinks of lawyers, and commands a band of "guerrilla terrorists of the service industry. Dinner party saboteurs" (Palahniuk 2005: 81); as leader of Project Mayhem, he plots to destroy both the world's tallest building, living symbol of the American Dream, and the national museum that serves as the sacrosanct reliquary of the diseased, commodified culture. Moreover, he convinces the narrator that he is more than the stuffing of his nest by blowing up his home, effectively hollowing it out as the "exploded shell of [his] burned-out condo" (Palahniuk 2005: 192). Fight clubs symbolize the narrator's need to destroy himself in order to be born anew and empowered; Tyler's terrorist Project Mayhem represents the narrator's need to demolish the culture of corporate bureaucracy that authorizes the corporeal and psychological death of its citizen-consumers. Tyler replaces those fattening, feminizing IKEA goods with god, the pulsating transcendence of battle in which a copy-center kid can be "a god for ten minutes when you saw him kick the air out of an account representative twice his size then land on the man and pound him limp" (Palahniuk 2005: 49):

> It used to be enough that when I came home angry and knowing that my life wasn't toeing my five-year plan, I could clean my condominium or detail my car. Someday I'd be dead without a scar and there would be a really nice condo and car. Really, really nice, until the dust settled or the next owner. ... Since fight club, I can wiggle half the teeth in my jaw.
>
> (Palahniuk 2005: 49)

Dead products make way for a revolutionary becoming. Tyler and fight club constitute the rebirth of aggressive masculinity that wreaks vengeance upon the consumer society that repressed and infantilized it.

Tyler, fight club, and Project Mayhem comprise, however, a singular transcendence marked by an even more revolting abjection: The narrator's body is fragmenting beneath the blows of his own hand. The cuts and bruises of fight club escalate first to loose teeth, then Tyler's lye brands, and finally a ripped apart face: "The bullet out of Tyler's gun, it tore out my other cheek to give me a jagged smile from ear to ear" (Palahniuk 2005: 207). Through the delusion of Tyler, the narrator maims himself for his commodity fetishism. Through the dream of Tyler, the narrator mangles those who fit the ideal of perfection that he cannot match himself, such as the handsome blonde "mister angel face" whom he destroys so completely because he "was in [the] mood to destroy something beautiful" (Palahniuk 2005: 122). Through the demand of Tyler, the narrator not only bloodies beautiful people but also demolishes his home and ruins museums. Tyler's ideology blossoms not only with corporate cultural criticism but also with bleak death: "Picture this: you on top of the world's tallest building, the whole building taken over by Project Mayhem. Smoke rolling out the windows. Desks falling into the crowds on the street. A real opera of a death, that's what you're going to get" (Palahniuk 2005: 203). Such imagery turns death into an abject art. As narcissist alienated from the culture that made him, the narrator-as-Tyler indulges in the death-work that comprises his unconscious.

According to Tyler's philosophy, only through (self-)destruction and death can one be reborn. Demolish the building to reboot the culture; bomb the condo to awaken the consciousness; kill the body to resurrect the soul: "Only after disaster can we be resurrected" (Palahniuk 2005: 70). While Tyler may talk about resurrection, he certainly luxuriates in destruction. Tyler is ultimately a nihilist; he believes that humanity is worthless and base: "You are not a beautiful and unique snowflake. You are the same decaying organic matter as everyone else, and we are all part of the same compost pile" (Palahniuk 2005: 134). The alienation of narcissism leads to the abjection of self: egotism turns back on itself as psychic devastation, and the perfect life decays into the pitiable refuse. The refusal of one's narcissism turns self-love into self-loathing. The subject becomes nothing more than excrement: "I am the shit and infectious human waste of creation" (Palahniuk 2005: 170). One's inner goods, the product of a deprived narcissism feasting upon itself, are revealed to the outside world as utterly repulsive and revolting.

When the foundations of one's pathological narcissism are threatened, one's entire conception of the world is cracked—with abjection. For all his power and potency, Tyler is nothing more than the narrator's narcissism abjectified. Tyler is born of the narrator's alienation from his own narcis-sism—his egotistical, commodified desires go unfulfilled. Tyler is the nar-rator's abject delusion; that is, Tyler is the narrator's fragmenting narcissistic inwardness splintering itself into the outside world in much the same way as Victor's psychosis spills out into his imagined reality as a surreal film of torture and terrorism. Tyler terrorizes the machine of cor-porate capitalism even as he rages against himself by putting a gun to his own head, the narrator's head. Terrorism in *Fight Club*, as in *Glamorama*, functions as the disastrous revenge of the psyche upon the symbolic order that decimated it. The ultimate goal of terrorism is more psychological than physical, and the psychological regression of Victor and the psychotic splitting of the unnamed narrator embody terrorism at its canniest best. *Glamorama* and *Fight Club* suggest that the media in particular and the bureacratized, corporatized culture in general are the most radical terror-ists of all because they destroy the mind and then the body from the inside out as they create a generation of homicidal narcissists at best or abject schizophrenics at worst. Both novels indict the symbolic order of postmodern culture that evacuates interiority and abjects the psyche.

References

American Psychiatric Association (2000) *Diagnostic and Statistical Manual of Mental Disorders*, 4th edn, Arlington, Va.: American Psychiatric Association.

Ellis, B. E. (2000) *Glamorama*, New York: Vintage-Random.

Freud, S. (1991) "On Narcissism: An Introduction," trans. J. Strachey, in J. Sandler, E. S. Person, and P. Fonagy (eds), *Freud's On Narcissism: An Introduction*, New Haven, Conn.: Yale University Press, pp. 3–32.

Kristeva, J. (1982) *Powers of Horror: An Essay on Abjection*, trans. L. S. Roudiez, New York: Columbia University Press.

Palahniuk, C. ([1996] 2005) *Fight Club*, New York: Norton.

Petersen, P. S. (2005) "9/11 and the 'Problem of Imagination': *Fight Club* and *Glamorama* as Terrorist Pretexts," *Orbis Litterarum*, 60: 133–44.

Part V
Postmodern technologies

14 Beyond the Cold War in Don DeLillo's *Mao II* and *Underworld*

Peter Knight

One of the key questions of the 1990s was what kind of world would emerge with the fall of the Berlin Wall in 1989. The official story promoted by President Bush Sr. and political pundits such as Francis Fukuyama was that the end of the Cold War would usher in a "new world order" that in effect would see the "end of history," a time when sooner or later the whole world would come to realize that Western neoliberal capitalism and democracy was the only game left in town (Bush 1990; Fukuyama 1992). After the titanic clash of rival economic and political ideologies that had structured the Cold War, the prediction was for a convergence to the one remaining viable model, with foreign policy restricted to a mere policing operation. Don DeLillo's two novels of the 1990s, *Mao II* and *Underworld*, present a take on the post-Cold War future that is at odds with the American triumphalism of the official version. In interview, DeLillo expressed his uncertainty about what the collapse of the Soviet empire meant: "We're in between two historical periods, the Cold War and whatever it is that follows it. I'm not sure that this is what follows it. This may just be the interim. I think we're just beginning to wonder what happened, and what didn't happen" (Williams 1997). DeLillo goes on to discuss how the Cold War nuclear threat had paradoxically produced, for all its restrictiveness, a "sense of limits we don't have any more," a "kind of ceiling against which other things were measured" (Williams 1997). Both *Mao II* and *Underworld* portray thematically and formally the disorienting instabilities of this new world order that has no recognizable limits. The two novels explore the psychic damage inflicted by the Cold War and the potentially greater anxiety produced in its aftermath. They focus on the loss of triumphant American nationalism, the threat of deterritorialized terrorism, the loss of historical memory with increasing dominance of technologies of mass mediation; and the role of globalized consumerism in reshaping the world. In sum, they map the shift from secure paranoia of the Cold

War to the insecure paranoia of a postnational age in which everything is connected.

Mao II

Inspired partly by the Salman Rushdie affair, *Mao II* is a novel about a group of terrorists who have taken an obscure Swiss writer hostage in Beirut. Bill Gray is an obsessively reclusive American novelist who has withheld his *magnum opus* from publication in fear of the loss of privacy that the publicity it will bring but who has also recently agreed to be photographed. In a forlorn effort organized by his publisher to free the imprisoned writer, Bill ends up going to London, then Greece and finally Beirut, before succumbing to a terminal injury and illness himself. The prologues of both *Mao II* and *Underworld* begin with crowd scenes in baseball parks in New York, the former at the end of the Cold War and the latter at its beginning. The word "baseball," the narrator of the introductory section of *Mao II* explains, "has resonance if you're American, a sense of shared heart and untranslatable lore" (DeLillo 1991: 9), and the virtuosic prologue of *Underworld* recounts one of the golden moments of American national baseball mythology, the last-minute heroic Bobby Thompson home run that brought triumph to the Brooklyn Dodgers over the New York Giants in the pennant game in 1951. The opening sentences of both novels make a direct appeal to a seemingly lost sense of Americanness. Whereas *Underworld* begins by declaring that radio announcer Russ Hodges (an evangelist of the power of baseball as the potential cement of national identity) "speaks in your voice, American" (DeLillo 1997b: 11), *Mao II* describes a contemporary mass Moonie wedding in Yankee Stadium, with the first sentence announcing that "Here they come, marching into *American* sunlight (DeLillo 1991: 3; emphasis added).

In the eyes of Rodge, the "uneasy" (DeLillo 1991: 3) father of Karen, one of the American brides, these masses from over fifty countries constitute a kind of new nation (1991: 7). Rodge, like the other anxious American parents in the audience, doesn't know what to make of this reconfiguration of American traditions ("Who the hell thought it up? What does it mean?" [DeLillo 1991: 5]), uncertain even whether his daughter is marrying someone who is Korean or Japanese. He finds "a strangeness down there that he never thought to see in a ballpark" (DeLillo 1991: 4). Rodge and his wife Maureen's solid middle-class background no longer provides "assurance," as the Cold War relationship between Them and Us, and the First World and its colonial others, seems to have come blurred. Maybe, Maureen muses as she reflects on the fact that the Moonies have come to the USA on a missionary quest, "they think we've sunk to the status of a less developed country" (DeLillo 1991: 5), a mistake that is easy to make given that in the audience there are also "city nomads more strange to her than herdsmen in the Sahel, who at least turn up on the documentary channel" (1991: 4).

With its seemingly automatic portrayal of terrorists as Middle Easterners, and its repeated depiction of foreign crowds as violent, chaotic forces that are at odds with Bill's classically American insistence on rugged, cantankerous individualism, it might seem at first that *Mao II* betrays a fearful sense of nostalgia and xenophobia (see Hardack 2004). The geopolitical certainties of the Cold War are eroded with the emergence of new postnational dangers such as deterritorialized terrorism, inspired by an apocalyptic "chant for world-shattering rupture" (DeLillo 1991: 16); Rodge "can't tell if it is English or some other unknown language" (1991: 15). If, as the prologue of *Mao II* concludes, "the future belongs to crowds" (DeLillo 1991: 16), it seems to be a future that will not be comfortingly American, unlike the twentieth century, in Henry Luce's famous declaration. In contrast to Bill's cult of the novelist as a lone voice of opposition, one of the terrorist intermediaries he encounters informs Bill that the "cult of Mao" was also the "cult of the book, a call to unity, a summoning of crowds where everyone dressed and thought alike" (DeLillo 1991: 162). Bill's foreign interlocutor guesses that, as both an American and a resolutely modernist writer, "this is what you fear, that history is passing into the hands of the crowd" (DeLillo 1991: 162).

However, *Mao II* also suggests that the source of these disorienting changes is very much homegrown. The "strangeness down there" that Rodge finds in the ballpark mass wedding results not merely from the translation of an emblematically American space into an alien one but also from the way that it turns people into mass-produced copies of one another. Rodge is disturbed by the way that "they take a time-honored event [i.e., a wedding] and repeat it, repeat it, repeat it until something new enters the world" (DeLillo 1991: 4). It is the "set of ready-made terms and empty repetitions," the "loss of scale and intimacy" and the way a "mass of people [are] turned into a sculptured object" that "really scares him" (DeLillo 1991: 7). The idea of endless repetition that removes individuality, particularly through the mass production and consumption of images, is central to DeLillo's work in general and *Mao II* in particular, conjuring up nightmares of totalitarian dehumanization (the novel uses photographs to divide its sections, and includes, for example, a picture of Iranian crowds swarming in front of a vast image of the Ayatollah Khomeini). The mass-wedding ritual in the prologue of *Mao II* contrasts with the closing of the novel, when Brita Nilsson, the photographer who takes Bill's picture, glimpses a spontaneous, joyous wedding party in wartorn Beirut.

The novel's argument about the shared dystopian potential of massed people and mass reproduction is developed in a discussion of Andy Warhol's work. Scott, Bill Gray's faithful caretaker, goes to see Warhol's paintings in New York before meeting up with Brita. He walks past the familiar "electric chair canvases, the repeated news images of car crashes and movie stars" (DeLillo 1991: 20), and is drawn to a silkscreen painting called *Crowd* in which "the crowd itself, the vast mesh of people, was being riven by some fleeting media catastrophe" (DeLillo 1991: 21). In the following room, he comes across Warhol's seemingly countless variations on images of Mao (one series of which forms the illustration on the dust jacket of DeLillo's novel). If, as DeLillo has suggested in interview, "the photographic image is a kind of crowd in itself" (Nadotti 1993: 88), then this room presents a crowd of Maos, the people's leader as an endless copy of himself; not the original Mao, but Mao II. The endless proliferation of Mao's followers in massed gatherings is thus connected to the boundless reproduction of the leader's image. However, the dehumanization through repetition that Rodge finds so unsettling in Yankee stadium is, as Andy Warhol's pop art made manifest, part and parcel of a recognizably American form of mass production and consumption of images.

Even Bill's stubborn, modernist resistance to a future dominated by the spectacle of massed crowds and mass media is compromised, not least because his extreme cult of reclusiveness fans the flames of his own celebrity. When he does finally reluctantly agree, first, to be photographed in Brita's series of photos of writers and, second, to cash in some of his fame in order to promote the campaign to free the Swiss writer, he spirals out of control into alcoholism and a violent death. What he wants to avoid is the mire of celebrity in which "A man cuts himself shaving and someone is signed up to write the biography of the cut. All the material in every life is channeled into the glow" (DeLillo 1991: 44). But that possibility has already deformed his own perception of himself, with his realization in Brita's photo session that "Nature has given way to aura," and that "Already I see myself differently. Twice over or once removed" (DeLillo 1991: 44)—a Bill II that is the twin of Mao II and the billboards for Coke II that are pasted throughout Beirut.

More than anything, Bill fears that the voice of the novelist has already been made redundant by acts of terrorism, as writers become mere cogs in the machine of advertising-driven corporate production:

> There's a curious knot that binds novelists and terrorists. In the West we become famous effigies as our books lose the power to shape and influence. Do you [Brita] ask your novelists how they feel about this? Years ago I used to think it was possible for a novelist to alter the

inner life of the culture. Now bomb-makers and gunmen have taken that territory. They make raids on human consciousness. What writers used to do before we were all incorporated.

(DeLillo 1991: 41)

The terrorists in the novel, however, do not carry out lone acts of heroic individualism. Instead, they too are reliant on the spectacle of media attention, feeding symbiotically off the oxygen of publicity generated by actions such as Bill's protest. They are also organized into cults that turn followers into subservient, deindividualized victims that are serialized copies of their charismatic leaders: "The boys who work near Abu Rashid [the terrorist leader who has kidnapped the Swiss writer] have no face or speech. Their features are identical" (DeLillo 1991: 234). In *Mao II*, terrorism reshapes the world not so much by its direct actions as by its participation in the "society of the spectacle" (Debord 1994), the replacement of direct, authentic experience of reality by secondhand representations that are spread by the pervasive influence of technologies of mass media. History itself becomes merely a disposable commodity like any other: "Terror makes the new future possible. All men one man. Men live in history as never before. He [Rashid] is saying we make and change history minute by minute. History is not the book or the human memory. We do history in the morning and change it after lunch" (DeLillo 1991: 235).

Underworld

Like *Mao II*, *Underworld* also focuses on the way that the increasing dom-inance of the mass media has eroded a sense of direct connection to the fabric of everyday reality and the wider web of history. The novel begins with a sweeping recreation from numerous vantage points of the moments leading up to the "Shot Heard 'Round the World," Bobby Thompson's epic last-minute home run. The rest of the novel, in roughly reverse chronological order, tells the intertwining stories of a host of characters whose lives have crossed at some point with the home-run baseball that was caught by a boy in the crowd and that represents for its subsequent owners a tangible connection to the legendary game. DeLillo presents the 1951 Dodgers–Giants game as an event that was experienced in its full, unmediated richness—"an example of some unrepeatable social phenom-enon"—before the "power of history" was lost to endless television repeti-tions and commodified nostalgia, that "debasing process of frantic repetition that exhausts a contemporary event before it has rounded into coherence" (DeLillo 1997a).

The portrait of a vibrant, diverse community in the Polo Grounds witnessing a momentous sporting triumph is the vanished flipside of the spectacle of mass dehumanization that takes place in Yankee Stadium in *Mao II*. (DeLillo often seems to distinguish between the buzzing diversity of urban crowds and the depressing homogeneity of mass audiences.) The contrast with a golden age of immediacy, participation, and community is also drawn clearly within *Underworld*. Later in the novel, the principal character, Nick Shay (who had been listening to the pennant game on the radio as a teenager in the Bronx, and is now owner of the ball) attends a Dodgers–Giants game in the 1990s with colleagues, but this time he is far removed from the action and excitement, sitting behind glass in a corporate box. (Not only has the aura of historical immediacy been sanitized but also the sense of specific connection with New York: Both the Dodgers and the Giants left their fans stranded when they were moved by their corporate owners to California in 1957.)

In the corporate box, one of Nick's colleagues in the waste-management industry compares Thompson's home run with the Kennedy assassination, another "shot that was heard 'round the world" and that also produced indelible memories:

"When JFK was shot, people went inside. We watched TV in dark rooms and talked on the phone with friends and relatives. We were all separate and alone. But when Thompson hit the homer, people rushed outside. People wanted to be together. Maybe it was the last time people spontaneously went out of their houses for something."

(DeLillo 1997b: 94).

If the Thompson home run was an event experienced together in public as a "momen[t] of binding power" (DeLillo 1997a) for New York and even the entire nation, then the Kennedy assassination marked the emergence of the ersatz and isolated community of a global television audience. For DeLillo, the unrepeatable and more distant memory of the 1951 pennant game takes on a "clarity and intactness that amounts to a moral burnish" (DeLillo 1997a) in comparison with the Kennedy assassination, which by now has dissolved into endless repetitions not of the raw event itself but of its mediated and commodified versions. Previously in his work, DeLillo had retrospectively posited the assassination of President Kennedy in 1963 as the symbolic origin of a society reshaped by its consumption of repeated spectacles of mass-mediated and, thus, routinized violence. Following this line of argument, *Underworld* includes a scene at an art-world party in the 1970s where the Zapruder shaky home movie that captured the assassination is played on a continual loop to a cynical crowd growing numb to its shocking imagery.

The narrative in *Underworld* about the diminishing of historical memory in a culture of "serial replays" (DeLillo 1997a) is further extended through the scenarios involving the "Texas Highway Killer." One of the serial killer's random shootings on the highway is accidentally captured on video by a young girl (the victim, it turns out, was at one time an owner of the Thompson home-run ball). The film clip is then played relentlessly on television. The television audience find themselves compelled to watch the endlessly repeated violent death, the only thing they share being a voyeurism of violence that intrudes into the domestic scene. For DeLillo, the endless repetition of spectacles of violence (for example, a convenience store hold-up caught on a surveillance tape and shown on the evening news) not only robs the original event of its distinctness and reality but also invades the consciousness of the addicted viewer. "And if you view the tape often enough," DeLillo explained in an essay coinciding with the publication of *Underworld*,

> it tends to transform you, to make you a passive variation of the armed robber in his warped act of consumption. It is another set of images for you to want and need and get sick of and need nonetheless, and it separates you from the reality that beats ever more softly in the diminishing world outside the tape.
>
> (DeLillo 1997a)

In short, *Underworld* maps out the gradual historical loss of aura, immediacy, and communal identity over the past half century.

The much-fabled 1951 pennant game is not only significant as a turning point before history lost its "moral burnish." As DeLillo realized while rereading the account of Thompson's home run on the front page of the *New York Times*, it was also a symbolic beginning because it happened the same day that the US Government made public its conclusive discovery that the Soviets were engaged in a nuclear-weapon testing program, a parallel blast that was in effect "heard 'round the world." The 1951 pennant game is, thus, not just the high-water mark for a sense of local community and unmediated experience of history but also the beginning of the end of American innocence and optimism with the loss of the US atomic monopoly and before the paranoia of the Cold War seeped in everywhere. Although not aware of it at the time, it turns out that New York baseball fans in particular and Americans in general are joined together under the shadow of apocalypse: Hoover, in DeLillo's version, informed of the news of the Soviet explosion while at the Polo Grounds, realizes that "All these people formed by language and climate and popular songs and breakfast foods and the jokes they tell and the cars they drive have never had anything in common so much as this, that they are sitting in the furrow of destruction" (DeLillo 1997b: 28).

Underworld explores how anxiety in the Cold War "displaces religious faith" with "radioactivity, the power of alpha particles and the all-knowing systems that shape them, the endless fitted links" (DeLillo 1997b: 241, 251), a chain reaction of fear that extends across the nation. DeLillo's novel devotes many pages to the "secret history" of the nuclear age, to the "hundred plots [that] go underground, to spawn and skein" (1997b: 51). It documents how the "power and intimidation" of the state seeped their way into the "personal bloodstream" of its citizens, from Lenny Bruce's mantra of "We're all gonna die!" during the Cuban Missile Crisis to Sister Edgar's obsessive use of latex gloves to protect her from the "submicroscopic parasites in their soviet socialist protein coats" (DeLillo 1997b: 241). Only after the end of the Cold War does it become apparent how deeply the secrecy and fear had altered people's consciousness. After it is over, it turns out that "everything is true": all the "secrets kept in whitewashed vaults, the half-forgotten plots—they're all out here now, seeping invisibly into the land and air, into the marrowed folds of the bones" (DeLillo 1997b: 244). The secrets of state have literally seeped into the bones of their citizens, with the realization that both the USA and USSR lied about the effect of nuclear experiments involving unfortunate "downwinders": Each country harbors unwitting victims of radiation. Yet, the novel also makes clear that in a sense we were all "downwinders," victims of a pathology of secrecy fuelled by the over-arching military-industrial complex, still unable to escape the terrible legacy of nuclear waste and contamination. The novel also explores how "all technology refers to the bomb" (DeLillo 1997b: 467) in the postwar period, tapping into the underground currents that link civilian and military hardware. The "October 8, 1957" section (published as a separate short story in the *New Yorker* under the title "Sputnik") dwells not just on the shared futuristic language of brand names and weaponry but also on the unsettling physical resemblance between domestic and military products: The adolescent Eric Deming (future nuclear-waste manager) masturbates into a condom "because it had a sleek metallic shimmer, like his favorite weapons system" (DeLillo 1997b: 514); his mother doesn't like one of her Jell-O molds because it was "sort of guided missile-like" (1997b: 515); her loaf of bread is "strontium white" (1997b: 516); and the vacuum cleaner is both ominously and excitingly "satellite-shaped" (1997b: 520).

As much as *Underworld* makes manifest the psychic damage inflicted by the Cold War, it also recognizes that in contrast with the environment of perpetual but unspecific risk we currently inhabit, nuclear paranoia can seem oddly comforting. Visiting a nuclear test site in Kazakhstan, Nick

Shay, for example, feels a "kind of homesickness" (DeLillo 1997b: 793) for the 1950s brandname products left on the shelf of a recreated American home destined for destruction. In a similar fashion, when they meet again after four decades, Klara Sax explains how, as a young woman during the 1960s, she used to watch mysterious lights in the sky and wanted to believe that they were from B-52 bombers carrying their nuclear cargo:

> War scared me alright but those lights, I have to tell you those lights were a complex sensation. Those planes on permanent alert, ever present you know, sweeping the Soviet borders, and I remember sitting out there rocking lightly at anchor in some deserted cove and feeling a sense of awe, a child's sleepy feeling of mystery and danger and beauty.
>
> (DeLillo 1997b: 76)

Looking back from beyond the end of the Cold War (she is now turning those decommissioned planes into an artwork), her past fear comes to seem appealing:

> Now that power is in shatters or tatters and now that those Soviet borders don't even exist in the same way, I think we understand, we look back, we see ourselves more clearly, and them as well. Power meant something thirty, forty years ago. It was stable, it was focused, it was a tangible thing. It was greatness, danger, terror, all those things. And it held us together, the Soviets and us. Maybe it held the world together. You could measure things. You could measure hope and you could measure destruction. Not that I want to bring it back. It's gone, good riddance. But the fact is.
>
> (DeLillo 1997b: 76)

In a postnational age, when the balance of power has become unstable and the source of threat unfocused, Klara expresses a fondness for the certainties of four decades ago, while also recognizing the misery of living under the shadow of nuclear terror. In *Underworld*, this nostalgia is less for the constrictions of the culture of containment of the 1950s than for the more manageable certainties of Cold War anxiety, a paradoxically secure form of paranoia that helped generate an imagined sense of national identity and purpose. "The Cold War is your friend" (DeLillo 1997b: 170), the baseball collector Marvin Lundy comes to understand.

In place of the paranoia engendered by the Bomb, throughout its 827 pages and its half-century span, *Underworld* also explores an underworld of hidden connections that exceeds the bipolar logic of the Cold War and its "ideologies of massive uniformity" (DeLillo 1997b: 786). DeLillo offers glimpses of the increasing interconnectedness of social and economic relationships in the period covered by the novel. Matt Shay (Nick's brother), a systems analyst involved in bomb production, has a moment of insight into those interlocking systems of production and consumption that are developing out of the convergence of military and consumer technology:

> He was thinking about his paranoid episode at the bombhead party the night before. He felt he'd glimpsed some horrific system of connections in which you can't tell the difference between one thing and another, between a soup can and a car bomb, because they are made by the same people in the same way and ultimately refer to the same thing.
>
> (DeLillo 1997b: 446)

During the Vietnam War, Matt experiences another sudden flash of insight, when he notices that "the drums [of Agent Orange] resembled cans of frozen Minute Maid enlarged by crazed strains of DNA" (DeLillo 1997b: 463). What at first appears to be merely a visual resemblance, the product of a bombed-out mind, years later becomes a troubling ethical question as Matt waits for the sun to rise in the desert while contemplating quitting his bomb-related job: "[H]ow can you tell the difference between orange juice and agent orange if the same massive system connects them at levels outside your comprehension?" (DeLillo 1997b: 465). Matt comes to sense that "everything connects in the end, or only seems to, or seems to only because it does" (DeLillo 1997b: 465), uncertain whether his insight into vast interconnectedness is merely a paranoid projection.

His subliminal awareness of interconnectedness is a long way from a traditional Cold War conspiracy theory that finds hidden enemy agents behind every event. It is also a long way from the traditional form of systems-theory analysis in which Matt was trained, since, with the interpenetration of the logic of the market into every last enclave of social life, there is no way to separate out neatly self-contained systems:

> Everything connected at some undisclosed point down the systems line. This caused a certain disquiet. But it was a splendid mystery in a way, a source of wonder, how a brief equation that you tentatively enter on your screen might alter the course of many lives, might cause the blood to rush through the body of a woman on a tram many thousands of miles away, and how do you define this kind of relationship?
>
> (DeLillo 1997b: 409)

What Matt comes to realize (echoed by the inverted chronology and fragmented structure of the novel) is that the chain of cause and effect in a globalized world is virtually impossible to map out. As the popular parable of chaos theory warns, a butterfly flapping its wings in Peru might lead to a typhoon in Japan, but there is no way to predict or even to comprehend the full causal chain that connects the two events. The increasing globalization of the economy in the post-Cold War era has thus meant not a reduction of anxiety but a "certain disquiet" that we now live in an environment of permanent but virtually incalculable risk whose connections span outwards in place and time like a nuclear chain reaction. These shifting, subterranean connections promote what might be termed "insecure paranoia" (Knight 2000). The subliminal perception of multiple connectedness can hardly be said to maintain a stable sense of self, whether personal or national, since it does not conjure up a clearly identifiable enemy, as the secure paranoia of the Cold War had done. As in *Mao II*, the sense of strangeness is an effect of no longer being able to clearly identify what is American and what is foreign.

However, as much as connection leads to a "certain disquiet," it also produces a "source of wonder." Although some of the linkages in *Underworld* are sinister, many others—such as the interest in numerology shared by many characters, especially in the number 13—conjure up a sense of mystical connectedness that cannot be explained away in conspiratorial terms. On one of his trips to track down the missing link in the Thompson home-run saga, the baseball collector Marvin Lundy visits the Conspiracy Theory Café in San Francisco, a place filled with "books, film reels, sound tapes, official government reports in blue binders" (DeLillo 1997b: 319). Given Marvin's predilection for wild conspiratorial theories, it is perhaps surprising that he "waved the place off" as a "series of sterile exercises" (DeLillo 1997b: 319). He does so because he has come to realize that "the well-springs were deeper and less detectable, deeper and shallower both, look at billboards and matchbooks, trademarks on products, birthmarks on bodies, look at the behavior of your pets" (DeLillo 1997b: 319).

The novel is full of strange parallels and intersections, many of which are resonant at a thematic level, and very few of which are visible to the characters involved. Nick and his former lover Klara Sax both visit the Watts Towers in Los Angeles at different times, unbeknown to one another. Or take the example of the Minute Maid drums. The link between weapons and domestic goods, though operating more at an emblematic than a factual level, nevertheless taps into the plausible suggestion that both are part of a larger system of production. But what are we to make of the other references to orange and orange juice in the novel? In passing, we learn that Chuckie Wainwright's ad-agency father is daydreaming about the Minute Maid account on the day he decides to give the baseball to his ungrateful son—who later ends up in Vietnam. While working on the art project in the desert, Klara wears an orange T-shirt. The work of graffiti artist Moonman 157 is scrubbed off the subway trains with orange juice. And in the novel's transcendent ending, the image of the street kid Esmeralda appears on a billboard underneath a poster for—what else?—Minute Maid orange juice.

Taken individually, these and the many other connections in the novel are perhaps no more than the usual thematic concentration of a well-composed work of fiction (DeLillo talked about the well-crafted construction of the text in interview). Taken together, however, they amount to an extended examination of subliminal connectedness. If "everything is connected" is the working principle of conspiracy theory, it is also the founding insight of ecology. In both its form and its thematic content, *Underworld* explores the ecological idea that everything is interrelated, with our waste—whether nuclear or consumer—coming back to haunt us: "waste is the secret history, the underhistory" (DeLillo 1997b: 791) of our world. Given the backwards chronology and the fragmentary narrative structure of *Underworld*, as readers we learn about the connections belatedly, haphazardly and in passing, creating a subliminal sense both of disquiet and wonder. Like the many artists in the novel who are engaged in reclaiming the waste of the Cold War and of consumerism to turn it into art in an effort to "h[o]ld the world together" (DeLillo 1997b: 76) now that the secure paranoia of the Cold War is no longer available, the process of reading *Underworld* becomes a training in an ecological re-envisioning of the world beyond the Cold War.

"In the ruins of the future"

Re-reading DeLillo's novels of the 1990s after the terrorist attacks of September 11, 2001 is an uncanny experience. In addition to its focus on Arab terrorists, *Mao II*, for example, contains discussions of the ominous power of the World Trade Center towers looming over New York (DeLillo 1991: 40), while the cover of *Underworld* is a photo of the Twin Towers, the tops of which are shrouded in a smoke-like cloud, with the silhouette of a bird circling nearby that to our post-9/11 eyes now looks not unlike a plane. If it was only with the demise of the Eastern Bloc that DeLillo could recognize the full significance of the Cold War, then it was only in the light of 9/11 that he could come to realize what the "interim period" of the 1990s were about. The post-Cold War period, he concluded in an essay published just after the attacks (DeLillo 2001) and explored further in the novel *Cosmopolis* (2003), had been dominated by the rise of US-led neoliberal globalization. The "surge of capital markets" had "shaped global consciousness," eroding a sense of historical memory and clear boundaries by "summon[ing] us all to live permanently in the future" (DeLillo 2001). After 9/11, however, DeLillo argued that we had once again entered a period marked by a Manichean struggle, although the world in his view was not divided into West versus East but into an opposition between those who wanted to claim the future and those who want to bring back the past. As with the omnipresent sense of apocalypse in the Cold War, the effects of terrorism—not least because the spectacle of catastrophe was relentlessly repeated on television—have seeped into everybody's consciousness, once again making literal and metaphorical downwinders of us all: "Terror's response is a narrative that has been developing over years, only now becoming inescapable. It is our lives and minds that are occupied now" (DeLillo 2001).

References

Bush, George H. W. (1990) "Toward a New World Order," speech given to joint session of US Congress, September 11.

Debord, Guy (1994) *The Society of the Spectacle*, New York: Zone Books.

DeLillo, Don (1991) *Mao II*, New York: Viking.

—— (1997a) "The Power of History," *New York Times Magazine* September 7, pp. 60–3. Available online at: www.nytimes.com/library/books/090797article3.html (accessed January 10, 2007).

—— (1997b) *Underworld*, New York: Scribner.

—— (2001) "In the Ruins of the Future: Reflections on Terror and Loss in the Shadow of September," *Harper's*, December, pp. 33–40. Reprinted in *The Guardian* (Manchester), December 22. Online. Available at www.guardian.co.uk/Archive/Article/0,4273,4324579,00.html (accessed January 10, 2007).

—— (2003) *Cosmopolis*, New York: Scribner.

Fukuyama, Francis (1992) *The End of History and the Last Man*, New York: Free Press.

Hardack, Richard (2004) "Two's a Crowd: *Mao II*, Coke II and the Politics of Terrorism in Don DeLillo," *Studies in the Novel*, 36 (3): 374–92.

Knight, Peter (2000) *Conspiracy Culture: From the Kennedy Assassination to "The X-Files,"* London: Routledge.

Nadotti, Maria (1993) "An Interview with Don DeLillo," *Salmagundi*, 100: 86–97.

Osteen, Mark (2000) *American Magic and Dread: Don DeLillo's Dialogue with Culture*, Philadelphia, Penn.: University of Pennsylvania Press.

Williams, Richard (1997) "Everything under the Bomb:" Interview with Don DeLillo, *The Guardian* (London), January 10. Online. Available at http://books.guardian.co.uk/reviews/generalfiction/0,96807,00.html (accessed January 10, 2007).

15 Selfless cravings
Addiction and recovery in David Foster Wallace's *Infinite Jest*

Timothy Aubry

David Foster Wallace's aggressively clever 1,079 page novel *Infinite Jest* features many tendencies typical of the postmodern genre: compulsive irony, multiple layers of self-referentiality, seemingly gratuitous displays of wit, bewildering interruptions of the linear narrative, and frequent references, at once deadpan, disaffected, and fond, to popular culture. So relentless are Wallace's various displays of virtuosity that they can, like a precocious adolescent's tricks and gimmicks, weary their audience, but this, I would maintain, is part of the novel's agenda. Wallace treats the excesses of postmodern culture as concomitant with larger trends in contemporary American society, namely, narcissism, self-indulgence, and an addiction to the ephemeral pleasures of popular entertainment. And, while his novel in many ways exemplifies these tendencies, its aim, I would argue, is to overwhelm and oversaturate its readers' desires so as to make them apprehend the need for an alternative set of values, centered around simplicity, empathy, and sincerity, instantiated by Alcoholics Anonymous.

Set in the second decade of the twenty-first century, *Infinite Jest*'s cultural landscape seems an ominous caricature of the late twentieth century. Perhaps the most notable sign that consumer capitalism has colonized new areas of experience is the sale of the calendar to corporations, so that years are now designated as "Year of the Whopper," "Year of the Tucks Medicated Pad," "Year of the Perdue Wonderchicken," and "Year of the Whisper-Quiet Maytag Dishmaster" (Wallace 1996: 223). The President, Johnny Gentle, is a former "lounge singer turned teenybopper throb turned B-movie mainstay" (Wallace 1996: 381). Television has been replaced by an endless variety of cartridges all connected to people's individual entertainment units. The USA has entered a union with its northern and southern neighbors called, in a ludicrous pun, ONAN. Just about every character in the novel is, or has been, addicted to a substance. Several unlucky minor characters encounter the ultimate addiction: a "terminally compelling" short film entitled *Infinite Jest*, so irresistible that viewers are never again able to wrench themselves away from it. Paralleling consumers' addictive tendencies, but at a larger scale, the US Government employs a spectacularly frightening process, which Wallace terms "annulation"—it manages its nuclear waste by throwing even more hazardous waste at it, so as to produce fuel for nuclear fusion, which satisfies the country's energy needs but also produces even more nuclear waste, which is then reinserted into the original process, thus perpetuating the cycle. Annulation is a recursive loop that feeds voraciously on its own products. Significantly, the process is utterly self-referential and cyclical; the material it uses gets endlessly processed and reprocessed. In the novel, annulation serves as a metaphor for just about every problem that Wallace seeks to diagnose within postmodern society. Most notably, the drug addicts he describes engage in a similarly disturbing, circular trajectory; they attempt to soothe their pain by ingesting more substances, which only adds to their pain and thus requires further drug use.

With its cold, self-referential, mechanical facility, annulation also functions as a metaphor for prevailing modes of consciousness and cultural production in contemporary America, which are characterized, according to Wallace, by an amorphous family of traits and affectations, including irony, world-weariness, emotional detachment, nihilism, pastiche, self-referentiality, and technical mastery.[1] Describing the efforts of the teenage character Hal to revive his emotional life, Wallace editorializes: "We are shown how to fashion masks of ennui and jaded irony at a young age where the face is fictile enough to assume the shape of whatever it wears. And then it's stuck there, the weary cynicism that saves us from gooey sentiment and unsophisticated naiveté" (1996: 694). Hal's brother Mario, an aspiring filmmaker discontented with the state of art in America, describes his favorite radio program:

> Mario'd fallen in love with the first Madame Psychosis programs because he felt like he was listening to someone sad read out loud from yellow letters she'd taken out of a shoebox on a rainy P.M., stuff about heartbreak and people you loved dying and US woe, stuff that was real. It is increasingly hard to find valid art that is about stuff that is real in this way.
>
> (Wallace 1996: 592)

In his essay on the relationship between fiction and television, Wallace echoes Mario's sentiment:

> The next real literary "rebels" in this country might well emerge as some weird bunch of *anti*-rebels, born oglers who dare somehow to

back away from ironic watching, who have the childish gall actually to
endorse and instantiate single-entendre principles. Who treat of plain
old untrendy human troubles and emotions in US life with reverence
and conviction. Who eschew self-consciousness and hip fatigue.

(Wallace 1997: 81)

But if Wallace evinces dissatisfaction with the proclivities of postmodern
fiction, he does not seem poised to join the earnest rebels whose emergence he tentatively predicts. As A. O. Scott remarks, Wallace appears
addicted to the reflexive modes of irony that plague his characters; and his
only efforts to escape this addiction involve further doses of irony about his
own irony (Scott 2000: 42).

It is no coincidence that the fatally addictive video cartridge responsible
for destroying hundreds of lives in the near-future setting bears the same
name as Wallace's novel. One could argue that *Infinite Jest* not only
describes the contemporary culture of addiction in the USA but produces,
through its exhilaratingly tortuous narrative, a reading experience that
resembles addiction. The book, in other words, is like a drug. First of all, it
overwhelms the reader encyclopedically with information about tennis,
geopolitics, math, film theory, and often drugs themselves. Wallace makes
several parallels between consuming drugs and consuming information.
He describes Hal, a "robotic" tennis star and marijuana addict, as a consuming machine. His uncle remarks, "The boy reads like a vacuum. Digests
things" (Wallace 1996: 15). And, with its information overload, *Infinite Jest*
places readers into Hal's position, forcing them to process, machine-like,
an onslaught of technical data. Trying to hold together all of the information, trace the linkages between the characters, and disentangle the
various overlapping, mutually informing thematic concerns makes for an
exhausting chore. The effort to synthesize the chaotic material can be
maddening, like a drug temporarily dangerous to the reader's sense of
integrity. Nevertheless, as Frank Cioffi has observed, reading the book is
rarely an unpleasant task, and can become quite the opposite, can
become, like a drug, perversely addictive (Cioffi 2000: 170).

Wallace uses a common device to underscore the addictive quality of his
text: He jumps from one plot line to another, just before major developments occur, so that readers, hooked on several different narratives, are
likely to feel at once divided and addicted as they push through the text in
a compulsive manner. In many moments, Wallace interrupts the progress
of the plot with carefully placed, lengthy, informational endnotes. At times,
these endnotes even usurp the role of the primary narrative, in a decentering fashion, providing fully elaborated scenes composed of dialogue,
plot, and character development, in a form indistinguishable from the

body text. In a slightly different version of this device, Wallace leaves the hero of the novel Don Gately lying on the ground with a gunshot wound he has received defending the Ennet Drug and Alcohol Recovery House against Canadian terrorists and jumps to an audaciously dry technical passage about computer equipment:

> Year of the Depend Adult Undergarment: Interlace TelEntertainment, 932/1864 R.I.S.C. power-TPs w/ or w/o console, Pink$_2$, post-Primestar D.S.S. dissemination, menus and icons, pixel-free InterNet Fax, tri- and quad-modems w/ adjustable baud, post-Web Dissemination-Grids, screens so high-def you might as well be there, cost-effective couture, all-in-one consoles, Yushityu ceramic nanoprocessors, laser chromatography, Virtual-capable media-cars, fiber-optic pulse, digital encoding, killer apps.
>
> (Wallace 1996: 620)

In the very moment Wallace taunts the reader's impatient need for further narrative development with a sudden freeze, he invokes the home-entertainment unit, the primary agent of atomized, self-indulgent addiction in contemporary culture, thus suggesting a continuity between the consumption of mass-media entertainment and the reader's compulsive relationship to *Infinite Jest*.

When he interrupts the progression of the narrative, rendering it all the more compelling, Wallace highlights the fact that plots are often propelled, or at least enhanced, by efforts to suspend them, and he exposes a similar pattern in addiction. Present in many narratives of addiction, including some of those offered in *Infinite Jest*, are decisions to quit for ever, decisions which typically lead to "one more last" binge (Wallace 1996: 19). Hence, like the plot of the novel, the plot of addiction is sustained by repeated attempts to interrupt or eradicate the plot. Such efforts at intervention tend to produce an obsessive, self-conscious meditation upon the very course of the addiction. The problem most addicts have, according to Wallace, is not that they fail to think enough about their problem but that they think too much about it. He remarks: "Most Substance-addicted people are also addicted to thinking, meaning they have a compulsive and unhealthy relationship with their own thinking" (Wallace 1996: 203). Part of the problem of addiction is an incessant reflection upon addiction itself, which only exacerbates the problem, leading to further abuse and further reflection, and thus addiction grows exponentially, in the form of a positive feedback loop. Addiction and metafiction, then, turn out to be peculiarly resonant. By creating and frustrating readerly expectations, by making readers both follow the plot of the novel compulsively and register constantly their own compulsion to follow the plot, Wallace produces an experience that mimes the hyper-self-conscious character of addiction.

Wallace's motive in designing a text that functions as a virtual-addiction apparatus, in my view, is to bring readers into a state of dazzled intellectual fatigue, a state which might make them ready to embrace the salutary simplicity offered by addiction's potential antidote, Alcoholics Anonymous (AA).[2] Described in florid detail by Wallace, AA meetings give alcoholics the opportunity to listen and offer emotional support to each other as they tell the story of their fall into addiction and their subsequent recovery. The idea behind the entire enterprise is that alcoholics are ideally suited to help other alcoholics; identification with people in a similar predicament is a necessary condition for recovery. And for the maintenance of sobriety, nothing is more effective, AA holds, than constant contact with other recovering addicts. Hence, the organization encourages (but does not require) a degree of participation that some might call fanatical, and critics have accused AA of functioning as a substitute addiction, offering a new form of dependence to replace the old one.[3]

In *Infinite Jest*, Wallace acknowledges the validity of such concerns about AA, but he does not treat them as sufficient grounds for dismissing the organization altogether. Much of the novel centers around the experience of Don Gately, a recovering narcotic addict who gradually comes to embrace AA. In one prodigiously long sentence, he describes the process of recovery.

And so you Hang In and stay sober and straight, and out of sheer hand-burned-on-hot-stove terror you heed the improbable-sounding warnings not to stop pounding out the nightly meetings even after the Substance-cravings have left ... you heed the improbable warnings because by now you have no faith in your own sense of what's really improbable and what isn't, since AA seems, improbably enough, to be working, and with no faith in your own senses you're confused, flummoxed, and when people with AA time strongly advise you to keep coming you nod robotically and keep coming ... and like a shock-trained organism without any kind of independent human will you do exactly like you're told ... things seem to get progressively somehow better, inside, for a while, then worse, then even better, then for a while worse in a way that's still better, realer ... and at this point you've started to have an almost classic sort of Blind Faith in the older guys, a Blind Faith in them born not of zealotry or even belief but just of a chilled conviction that you have no faith whatsoever left in yourself; and now if the older guys say Jump you ask them to hold their hand at the desired height, and now they've got you, and you're free.

(Wallace 1996: 350–1)

The sentence confronts head-on the worry that AA demands a sacrifice of agency and does not dismiss this worry so much as situate it within a paradoxical logic whereby a surrender of volition leads to freedom. The temporal experience of reading this page-long sentence mimics the arduous experience of recovering in AA. Its refusal to stop until it reaches the startling final word, "free," suggests that the mechanical form of obedience AA insists upon necessarily leads dialectically to its opposite, to expanded agency, but it also suggests that this result is a foregone conclusion. At the same time, Wallace's sentence encourages, through its overt registration of its own tensions, the reader's interpretive freedom, a freedom to doubt the validity of the final word "free." And yet, such a response may seem too obvious, given the repeated heavy-handed assertions within the sentence that AA is *not* a source of freedom. Terms and phrases, such as "robotically," "shock-trained," and "they've got you," are too overbearing, and a sophisticated reader in search of a less obvious meaning may treat them as ironic or hyperbolic, thus enabling the final word "free" to regain some purchase on its own straightforward sense. The sentence's seesawing valences encourage a recognition that treating its declaration of AA's liberating function as merely ironic represents a facile mode of resolving a more complicated paradox. Hence, the reader, like the AA participant, is, after some serious mental labor, put in a position to choose actively to embrace the positive though paradoxical account of AA's coercive mechanisms as a means of achieving liberation.

This sentence represents Gately's own retrospective interpretation of his recovery process. AA has taught him how to narrate his life in a way that endows him with agency, as the teller and subject of his story. The ability to produce a stable narrative of the self is, it turns out, a key condition for overcoming addiction, which is why AA members spend so much of their time telling and listening to stories about substance abuse. The experience of the addict, as it is represented by Wallace, is almost always a harrowing downward spiral of decisions negated by failures of will, leading to further decisions—each moment of resolution undermined by the subsequent moment, *until* the moment in which the alcoholic joins AA. The apparently unendurable chaos of addiction produces the need for a fixed moral and epistemological system, which AA is willing to offer. AA works to replace the protean, ceaselessly self-subverting and self-destructive logic of addiction with a more predictable narrative whose meaning and conclusion are always the same—a way of placing the addict's multiple contradictory moments and self-accounts within a stable, unambiguous trajectory that leads inevitably to a happy ending characterized by sobriety.[4]

Moreover, AA, in Wallace's depiction, is one of the few places that permit sincere sentiment in an otherwise cold, competitive society, and as such represents a kind of utopian microcosm. The organization discourages tendencies endemic to contemporary society, such as competitive urges, displays of cleverness or irony, and pretenses of invulnerability, because they interfere with the noninvidious forms of empathy and identification vital to the recovery process. Though professedly apolitical, AA operates according to a vehemently anticapitalist economy; the ordinary rules of exchange are suspended. Wallace observes,

> Sobriety in Boston is regarded as less a gift than a sort of cosmic loan. You can't pay the loan back, but you can pay it *forward*, by spreading the message that despite all appearances AA works, spreading this message to the next guy who's tottered in to a meeting.
>
> (Wallace 1996: 344)

AA's philosophy is that the best method for remaining sober is to help someone else get sober. Hence, each act of assistance, each gift, distributes its energy backwards and forwards so that it is not possible to distinguish giver from receiver. The zero-sum game of capitalism is replaced by pragmatic utopianism whereby every act spreads its value in all directions, and self-interest and generosity become symbiotic partners.

Such an idealizing picture of AA is easy to doubt, especially for new members, typically people accustomed to disappointment, victims of all kinds of false promises and deceptions, the most brutal their own, practiced upon themselves. What, then, makes AA participants confide in and trust each other? What enforces their obedience to its protocols? According to Wallace, the motive is desperation: the realization that the alternative to accepting AA's recommendations is a return to the nightmarish world of addiction.

> Boston AA's Sergeant at Arms stood *outside* the orderly meeting halls, in that much-invoked Out There where exciting clubs full of good cheer throbbed gaily below lit signs with neon bottles endlessly pouring. AA's patient enforcer was always and everywhere Out There: it stood casually checking its cuticles in the astringent fluorescence of pharmacies that took forged Talwin scrips for a hefty surcharge, in the onionlight through paper shades in the furnished rooms of strung-out nurses who financed their own cages' maintenance with stolen

pharmaceutical samples, in the isopropyl reek of the storefront offices
of stooped old chain-smoking MD's whose scrip pads were always out
and who needed only to hear "pain" and see cash.

(Wallace 1996: 359)

AA's utopianism is enforced by the threat of extreme suffering just outside
its borders. The organization could easily fall prey to skepticism, but then
again skepticism—toward relationships, toward stable principles, toward
one's promises to oneself—is often what prolongs or exacerbates, if not
causes, addiction. AA offers a series of rituals and an unambiguous narrative structure with a clear moral as an antidote that is antithetical in every
way to the extravagant self-conscious, self-doubting, ironic processes that
constitute addiction. Members adopt AA's system not because it can
nimbly withstand the assaults of their skeptical tendencies but because they
have been exhausted, almost destroyed, by their skeptical tendencies.
Miserable, desperate, drained, they choose, against all odds, to put their
faith in people they barely know and a set of beliefs they can barely swallow, because doing so goes against everything they have ever valued, and
everything they have ever valued has consistently let them down. This is
the experience AA refers to as "hitting bottom."

Infinite Jest is organized around a reductive polarity that divides the
world into two camps: On one side there is drug abuse, irony, excessive
self-obsession, mass-culture entertainment, hedonistic pursuit of pleasure,
and on the other side there is AA-sponsored sobriety, sincerity, empathy,
difficult art, and authentic feeling. The two categories are loose, but
Wallace repeatedly invokes them:

> And so this unites them, nervously, this tentative assemblage of possi-
> ble glimmers of something like hope, this grudging move toward
> maybe acknowledging that this unromantic, unhip, clichéd AA
> thing—so unlikely and unpromising, so much the inverse of what
> they'd come too much to love—might really be able to keep the
> lover's toothy maw at bay.
>
> (Wallace 1996: 350)

Significantly, AA works to exclude all varieties of irony in the interactions
between its members:

> The thing is it has to be the truth to really go over, here [in AA]. It
> can't be a calculated crowd-pleaser, and it has to be the truth
> unslanted, unfortified. And maximally unironic. An ironist in a Boston
> AA meeting is a witch in a church. Irony-free zone. Same with sly

disingenuous manipulative pseudo-sincerity. Sincerity with an ulterior motive is something these tough ravaged people know and fear, all of them trained to remember the coyly sincere, ironic, self-presenting fortifications they'd had to construct in order to carry on Out There, under the ceaseless neon bottle.

(Wallace 1996: 369)

Irony is a "fortification"; it is like an outer layer, a mask on the self, a winking sheen on one's language disavowing its straightforward sense. Drugs too are a fortification, a shield; they offer a basis for disclaiming responsibility for one's behavior. Both drugs and irony, in Wallace's depiction, are *artificial*, injected into one's body or one's words, producing self-division, self-concealment, preventing authentic communication and subverting the unity and transparency of self upon which sincerity and identification are predicated.

Wallace's sympathy for AA's values as an alternative to addiction and irony implies a strain of anti-intellectualism flagrantly at odds with the overtly clever, experimental quality of *Infinite Jest*. Embracing AA's paradigm entails resisting the novel's own rather alluring style. Wallace comically embodies the reader's dilemma in a conventional barroom scene of seduction:

I saw Orin in bars or at post-tournament dances go up to a young lady he would like to pick up and use this fail-safe cross-sectional pick-up Strategy that involved an opening like "Tell me what sort of man you prefer, and then I'll affect the demeanor of that man." Which in a way of course is being almost pathologically open and sincere about the whole picking-up enterprise, but also has this quality of Look-at-Me-Being-So-Totally-Open-And-Sincere-I-Rise-Above-The-Whole-Disingenuous-Posing-Process-Of-Attracting-Someone-,-And-I-Transcend-The-Common-Disingenuity-In-A-Bar-Herd-In-A-Particularly-Hip-And-Witty-Self-Aware-Way-,-And-If-You-Will-Let-Me-Pick-You-Up-I-Will-Not-Only-Keep-Being-This-Wittily-,-Transcendently-Open-,-But-Will-Bring-You-Into-This-World-Of-Social-Falsehood-Transcendence, which of course he cannot do because the whole openness-demeanor thing is *itself* a purposive falsehood; it is a pose of poselessness.

(Wallace 1996: 1048, footnote 269)

Orin's tactics tacitly presuppose the inescapability of self-conscious, manifestly insincere artifice. What distinguishes his efforts from others is simply the brilliance of his pose, revealing an extra layer of apparently undisguised self-consciousness about the manipulative tactics he is deploying, which the narrator reads as yet another layer of manipulation. But Orin's performance generally proves to be successful, and why not? If, after all, artifice is inescapable, why not choose the kind that is cleverly conscious of itself? It is, of course, this consideration that would lead a reader to embrace *Infinite Jest*'s recursive irony. For those, however, who find Orin's tactics and Wallace's metafictional devices to be even slightly tiresome, Wallace offers AA as an alternative paradigm—and one that would seem to be well-suited for Orin's brother Hal, who recognizes that "hip cynical transcendence of sentiment is really some kind of fear of being really human" (Wallace 1996: 694). Indeed, Wallace suggests that Hal's predicament is widely representative: "One of the really American things about Hal, probably, is the way he despises what it is he's really lonely for: this hideous internal self, incontinent of sentiment and need, that pulses and writhes just under the hip empty mask" (1996: 695).

The experience of reading *Infinite Jest* is designed, in my view, to undermine the psychological defenses that forestall the acknowledgement of sentiment and need, and thus to provoke a new perspective on AA's humanistic values. *Infinite Jest* offers irony, deconstructive games, and postmodern fictional tricks, in a seemingly endless process that mimics addiction and can exhaust readers intellectually, make them weary, at least temporarily, of sophistication, and ready to trust the simple and apparently earnest statements Wallace periodically produces, for instance, "that there is such a thing as raw, unalloyed, agendaless kindness" (1996: 203). The complexity of *Infinite Jest* is an absolutely necessary element of the experience I am describing: In order to draw skeptical readers in, challenge and tire their critical capacities, and push them eventually to accept, as a refreshing departure, a perspective whose banality and simplicity is legitimized only by the arduous intellectual process, the journey through difficulty, required to reach that point.

But, if *Infinite Jest* appears to uphold a rigid division between AA's inner sanctity of compassion, trust, and clarity and the cold, chaotic, neon-lit world of addiction Gately calls "Out There," the novel also suggests, at times, that AA is vulnerable to the elements it would like to banish beyond its borders: irony, complexity, artifice, emotional detachment, and skepticism. Indeed, Wallace himself is acutely aware of AA's susceptibility to artifice. He describes members' "saccharin grins" (Wallace 1996: 350) and the "polyesterishly banal" insights AA helps people to achieve (1996: 358). Moreover, new members, he notes, are taught to "Fake It Till You Make It" (Wallace 1996: 369), to repeat clichés they do not believe, to go through the motions of prayer, to affect devotion to AA's tenets until they actually feel devotion—all of which seem to be institutionalized forms of insincerity. And yet, it is on the same page Wallace describes these simulations of sincerity required by AA that he stresses the organization's intolerance of both irony and "sly disingenuous manipulative pseudo-sincerity" (1995: 369).

Not only does *Infinite Jest* challenge the reader's ability to identify authentic instances of sincerity, it exposes the uncertain and multiple meanings that the term "sincerity" mobilizes. Joelle van Dyne, a recovering cocaine addict who wears a veil, in accordance with the protocols of her self-help group, the Union of the Hideously and Improbably Deformed (UHID), defines sincerity rather differently from Don Gately. He questions her need to wear a veil, and she responds, "U.H.I.D.'s First Step is admission of powerlessness over the need to hide. U.H.I.D. allows members to be open about their essential need for concealment" (Wallace 1996: 535). Deconstructing the binary between sincerity and dissimulation, Joelle contends that wearing a veil is more honest than displaying her naked face, because it acknowledges her own sincere desire for dissimulation. Joelle is only one of many characters in the text who adopt ostensibly artificial supplements. Mario, arguably the most sincere character in the book, assumes a prosthetic identity; his multiple disabilities require him to connect a movie camera to his head. Given the multiplicity of artificially enhanced characters in the book, one might wonder, when Hal speculates about the "fear of being really human" (Wallace 1996: 694), what it could possibly mean to be "really human" in the cybernetic world of *Infinite Jest*. Even the phrase "*really* human," with its evocation of enhancement, subverts the natural, "unfortified" character of humanity that Hal would like to reclaim.

AA would hold, pragmatically, that it is the tendency to ask these kinds of questions, and not the problems to which these questions refer, that jeopardizes the operation of trust and identification. Embracing AA's techniques, in other words, requires at least a temporary containment or bracketing of the skeptical modes of consciousness that Wallace aligns with postmodern addiction culture. He describes the moment in which Joelle converts to AA's philosophy while listening to a speaker:

> He's got your autodidact orator's way with emotional dramatic pauses that don't seem affected. Joelle makes another line down the Styrofoam coffee cup with her fingernail and chooses consciously to believe it isn't affected, the story's emotive drama. Her eyes feel sandy from forgetting to blink. This always happens when you don't expect it, when it's a meeting you have to drag yourself to and are all but sure will suck. The speaker's face has lost its color, shape, everything distinctive. Something has taken the tight ratchet in Joelle's belly and

turned it three turns to the good. It's the first time she's felt sure she
wants to keep straight no matter what it means facing.

(Wallace 1996: 710)

Joelle actively suspends her compulsively skeptical thought patterns, her
multiple levels of self-awareness, so that she can trust the speaker's story
and identify with him, despite his deliberate manipulation of his mannerisms. Her motive is desperation; her cocaine habit has stopped just short of
killing her. Other less troubled individuals may not find within themselves
such an obvious motive, which is why Wallace simulates, in *Infinite Jest,* an
overwhelming addictive experience so as to produce for readers a cerebral
version of "hitting bottom," a hint, however remote and theoretical, of the
conditions under which AA's philosophy would become appealing.

Wallace seems to recognize that many readers will be incapable of sur-
rendering their critical capacities in this way. He himself never adopts
an unequivocal position of antiintellectualism. In fact, he persistently
invites consideration of the complexities that AA systematically dis-
regards and points to the inevitable appearance within AA of precisely
the forms of self-consciousness and irony that the organization aims to
exclude. For instance, in a comical and sadistic fashion, he describes one
AA speaker:

> The next Advanced Basics guy summoned by their gleamingly bald
> western-wear chairman to speak is dreadfully, transparently unfunny,
> painfully new but pretending to be at ease, to be an old hand, des-
> perate to amuse and impress them. … He's dying to be liked up there.
> He's performing. … This is not a regular audience. A Boston AA is
> very sensitive to the presence of ego. When the new guy introduces
> himself and makes an ironic gesture and says, "I'm told I've been
> given the Gift of Desperation. I'm looking for the exchange window,"
> it's so clearly unspontaneous, rehearsed.

(Wallace 1996: 367)

With his self-consciousness and his somewhat ingratiating nervous wit, the
speaker is a sad caricature of some of Wallace's own writerly tendencies.
This character introduces certain qualities that violate AA's tacit code, and
everyone in the crowd is embarrassed for him, but ironically enough his
approach provokes precisely the kind of catharsis AA works to facilitate.
Falsely affecting self-assuredness, the speaker exposes his painful vulnerability, eliciting mass empathy, and "the applause when this guy's done has
the relieved feel of a fist unclenching, and their cries of 'Keep Coming!'
are so sincere it's almost painful" (Wallace 1996: 368).

Described with slightly too much mockery to be purely self-congratulatory, this incongruous performance nonetheless represents Wallace's effort to recuperate some of his own propensities, to find a point of reconciliation between AA's insistence on sincerity, empathy, and simplicity, and his text's attachment to irony, intellect, and recursivity. If *Infinite Jest* is structured around what appears to be a strict dichotomy, Wallace invites the reader to transcend this dichotomy so as to make the two sides work together. In this scene, the character's excessive self-consciousness actually promotes empathy. Self-consciousness and irony are a problem for Wallace only insofar as they colonize the mind or the culture with such totality that they completely exclude other more emotive, less culturally privileged forms of expression, such as the kind promoted by AA. Characterizations of postmodernism, such as Fredric Jameson's famous account, tend to presuppose forms of irony and pastiche entirely incompatible with sincerity and authenticity. Offering an alternative, more flexible perspective, Wallace repeatedly dramatizes uncanny moments of alliance, or at least mutual accommodation, between these ostensibly irreconcilable modes. The function of *Infinite Jest*'s interpretive challenges, then, is not to inspire a rejection of either the ironic, detached cynicism that his readers habitually embrace, or the uncritical, sincere display of sentiment that they secretly find appealing but instead to train them to maneuver more readily and more skillfully between the two.

Notes

1 For an exploration of these postmodern trends in late-capitalist America, see Jameson (1991).
2 Ernest Kurtz (1979) provides a thorough historical and theoretical analysis of AA. Nan Robertson (1988) offers an interesting historical/personal account of the organization. See also Alcoholics Anonymous (1976).
3 See, for instance, Sedgwick (1993: 133).
4 Discussing the function of the AA narrative, Edmund B. O'Reilly observes "Telling the story—it may be said that, in a sense, there is really only *one* story in AA—enables the speaker to reconstrue a chaotic, absurd, or violent past as a meaningful, indeed a *necessary*, prelude to the structured, purposeful, and comparatively serene present" (1997: 24).

References

Alcoholics Anonymous (1976) *Alcoholics Anonymous: The Story of How Many Thousands of Men and Women Have Recovered from Alcoholism*, 3rd edn, New York: Alcoholics Anonymous World Services.
Cioffi, F. (2000) "'An Anguish Become Thing': Narrative as Performance in David Foster Wallace's *Infinite Jest*," *Narrative*, 8: 161–81.

Jameson, F. (1991) *Postmodernism, or, The Cultural Logic of Late Capitalism*, Durham, NC: Duke University Press.

Kurtz, E. (1979) *Not-God: A History of Alcoholics Anonymous*, Center City, Minn.: Hazelden Educational Services.

O'Reilly E. B. (1997) *Sobering Tales: Narratives of Alcoholism and Recovery*, Amherst, Mass.: University of Massachusetts Press.

Robertson, N. (1988) *Getting Better: Inside Alcoholics Anonymous*, New York: Morrow.

Scott, A. O. (2000) "The Panic of Influence," *New York Review of Books*, February 10, pp. 39–43.

Sedgwick, E. K. (1993) "Epidemics of the Will," in *Tendencies*, Durham, NC: Duke University Press, pp. 130–42.

Wallace, D. F. (1996) *Infinite Jest*, Boston, Mass.: Little, Brown and Co.

—— (1997) "E Unibus Pluram: Television and US Fiction," in *A Supposedly Fun Thing I'll Never Do Again: Essays and Arguments*, Boston, Mass.: Little, Brown and Co., pp. 21–82.

16 The end of postmodernism
American fiction at the millennium

Stephen J. Burn

In the 1990s, American fiction was torn between the emergence of a generation of writers seeking to move beyond the aesthetics of postmodernism and the prolonged vitality of many writers associated with the original rise of the movement. But while, for several critics, the end of the century seemed to overlap with the end of postmodernism, the pivotal moment, when the twilight of postmodernism shaded into the dawn of whatever lies beyond, is understandably difficult to locate. One of the problems, here, is that there are several competing accounts of the last days of postmodernism, each of which outlines an alternative chronology for the movement's demise.

From the start of the 1990s, critics and writers seemed eager to draw a line under the postmodern era to apparently clear a new imaginative space for fiction. In 1990, William T. Vollmann published a prescient short essay, "American Writing Today: A Diagnosis of the Disease," in which he argued that the "games of stifling breathlessness" associated with postmodernism and structuralism had robbed fiction of its essential weight (Vollmann 1990: 358). But a more systematic attempt to pinpoint the moment of transition came when a seminar series entitled "The End of Postmodernism" was held in Stuttgart in August 1991. Attended by prominent postmodern novelists, such as Barth, Gass, and Federman, the philosophy of the conference was ostensibly to divine what new directions might be possible after postmodernism. Though many of the participants seemed to doubt whether postmodernism had really come to an end, seminar organizer Heide Zeigler argued that its demise could be more or less directly traced to the postmodern fascination with self-reference: metafiction had trivialized the postmodern aesthetic, degenerating into mere "playfulness and narcissism" (Ziegler 1993: 7).

Shortly after, David Foster Wallace, in an important essay on the end of postmodernism, "E Unibus Pluram," also traced the movement's collapse to what he described as the corrosive power of metafiction. Wallace believed that postmodern irony and metafictional strategies had become unworkable because television (the initial target, in Wallace's eyes, of much postmodern fiction) had co-opted these tactics. Wallace saw a group of writers—whose work, he suggested, might be classified as "post-post-modernism" or "image-fiction" (1993: 171)—that he hoped would ulti-mately be able to "reaffirm the idea of art being a living transaction between humans" rather than a narcissistic game of self-reference (McCaffery 1993: 142).

Wallace, Vollmann, and Ziegler are noteworthy indicators of a growing dissatisfaction with postmodernism. But if there is a moment when the movement comes to an end, it seems to be located later in the decade, in or around a twenty-seven-month period bracketed by the publication of Larry McCaffery's *After Yesterday's Crash* in August 1995, and November 1997, when Richard Rorty claimed that we had reached a point where "nobody has the foggiest idea" what postmodernism meant (1997: 13). We find, here, a dense cluster of attempts to smooth down the soil atop the grave of postmodernism: *After Yesterday's Crash* introduced avant-pop as a movement that was more attuned than postmodernism to the America that had been shaped by the massive media expansion of the late twentieth century. In the same year, Lance Olsen and Mark Amerika introduced a volume, provocatively titled *In Memoriam to Postmodernism* that (in terms that closely mirror Wallace's) described avant-pop as an outgrowth of post-modernism, which had become necessary because the "metafictional stra-tegies of postmodernism got totally absorbed by ... mainstream media marketers" (Olsen and Amerika 1995: 2).

Outside the world of literature and its criticism, there were similar attempts: Urban designer Tom Turner introduced the term "post-post-modernism" to designate a period that challenged "the 'anything goes' eclecticism of its predecessor" (1996: v), while art critic Hal Foster argued that the idea of a postmodernism that suggested the possibility of alter-native forms beyond modernism had failed because it had been gradually "emptied by the media" (1996: 206). Finally, Rorty denounced post-modernism as merely a "word that pretends to stand for an idea" in a symposium on the "Most Overrated Idea" (1997: 13).

Clearly something had taken place here. There were too many different attempts to map a route beyond postmodernism in too many disciplines to simply dismiss such efforts. Yet, one of the problems for these accounts is not just that, as Charles B. Harris observed, the corpse of literary post-modernism "remains suspiciously lively" (2002: 1), but that postmodernism had co-opted reports of its demise and bent them toward the end of *more* postmodernism.

The clearest example of postmodernism's absorption of its own decline is to be found in the work of John Barth. A participant at the 1991

Stuttgart seminar, Barth transformed the conference into an example of postmodern fiction with the appropriately paradoxical title, "The End: An Introduction." Barth's story diagnoses the impetus behind the conference (a millennial fascination with "the end of this, the end of that" [Barth 1996: 15]) as a "terminary malady" (1996: 14), and announces incredulously: "And not long ago, believe it or not, there was an international symposium on 'The End of *Post*modernism'—just when we thought we might be beginning to understand what that term describes!" (1996: 14). But this story about endings resists the ending scripted in Stuttgart not just by mocking how premature the idea of the conference was but also by encoding a resistance to, or refusal of, endings in the story's form. The story begins and ends in midsentence, as if to reinforce the narrator-author's belief that he "expect[s] this series to extend ad infinitum" (Barth 1996: 13). This idea is reinforced on the microlevel by the fact that the sentence describing the symposium begins with a conjunction. Both the form and the content of this story react against the notion of clear starts and ends and reach instead toward perpetuity.

The importance of this story as a response to the end of postmodernism for Barth is indicated by the fact that he recognizably reworked the same imaginative material in *Coming Soon!!!* (2001), the novel that preoccupied him for most of the 1990s. Barth structures this millennial novel around a fiction-writing contest between an aging novelist-surrogate for Barth[1] and a young novelist aspirant. The aging writer is a devotee of both print fiction and "literary postmodernism" (Barth 2001: 329), while the younger is a proponent of the "post-postmodern" (2001: 74), an aesthetic based upon his "hypertexted magnum opus" (2001: 362). In tracing this new direction, Barth obliquely reveals that the germ of his novel lies in David Foster Wallace's "Westward the Course of Empire Takes its Way," a novella-length metafictional story that articulates Wallace's critique of metafiction.

In "Westward the Course of Empire Takes its Way" (which parallels Wallace's "E Unibus Pluram"), Wallace follows the students of a creative-writing instructor named Ambrose on their way to the opening of a Funhouse chain of discotheques developed in association with McDonald's. Ambrose is the name of a character from Barth's famous metafictional story, "Lost in the Funhouse," and Wallace's character is a thinly veiled persona for Barth. Ambrose is evidently soon to be superseded by the younger characters who will "divine a nation's post-post-modern ... future" (Wallace 1989: 354), but Wallace's title and the presence of McDonald's connects Barth's metafiction with the progress of both empire and consumer capitalism. On a technical level, however, he attempts to counter the elder writer's influence by employing metafictional strategies to "expose the illusions of metafiction" (McCaffery 1993: 142).

All of this seems to offer a potentially devastating critique of Barth's work, but Wallace's attack funnels into Barth's novel because the post-post-modernism of the younger writer in *Coming Soon!!!* is, Barth tells us, characterized by the tendency to deploy (as Wallace does) "the tradition of the Postmodernist novel ... with a kind of impatience, like a bored virtuoso illusionist warming up for the main event" (Barth 2001: 13) and to appropriate not simply "certain field-identification marks of Postmodernist taletelling but, on occasion, the tellers themselves" (2001: 14). Wallace's attempt to expose the limitations of postmodernism ironically becomes the engine for Barth's postmodern novel, but the end of this conflict is not the end of postmodernism. In Barth's account, the younger writer gives up on his electronic fiction, to leave the aging writer to complete his work. We are driven back to enjoy what the novel calls "postmodern nostalgia" (Barth 2001: 22): Barth quotes Donald Barthelme, alludes to Robert Coover and several of his own works, perhaps as a way of "closing the circle on his own life's work" (Barth 2001: 194–5).

Similar strategies can be located in the works of other postmodernists. Robert Coover, for example, spent much of the 1990s completing his landmark novel, *The Adventures of Lucky Pierre* (2002). Recounting the tale of Pierre, a legendary, but now aging, pornographic actor in a movie-obsessed world named Cinecity, Coover's novel is suffused with and inspired by an elegiac tone that records the passing of postmodernism. While Coover brilliantly rehearses the staples of his brand of postmodernism—shifting ontological layers, subtle self-reflexivity—"a deep melancholia has stolen in" to this work (2002: 402), as Coover's central character reflects "It's over, isn't it" and falls to "Retrospectives, memorials, relics" (2002: 367). Like Barth's movement toward postmodern nostalgia, however, Coover's fascination with relics leads him to embed a subtle catalogue of postmodernism's greatest hits in Cinecity's film titles. William Gaddis's *The Recognitions* (1955) and *Agapē Agape* (2002) are alluded to in the movie *Randy Recognitions* and the film script that includes "our little love feast. Our agape" (Coover 2002: 386). There are also echoes of such works as Italo Calvino's *Invisible Cities* (1974), which is recast as *Invisible Titties* (Coover 2002: 390); Barth's *Giles Goat-Boy* (1966) and short-story collection, *Lost in the Funhouse* (1968), which are melded together in an early Pierre movie, "a goatish knockabout comedy called *Lust in the Funhouse*" (2002: 297); while "*Horsebuns and Whines & Feeling Blue: The Travelling Salesman and the Lonesome Wife*," a film featuring "who else but the master himself, Willie," contains a double pun on William Gass's *Willie Masters' Lonesome Wife* (1968) and *On Being Blue* (1975) (Coover 2002: 366–7).

Coover's and Barth's works, then, are obituaries to postmodernism which paradoxically testify to its continued vitality. But postmodern fiction's peculiar resistance to accounts of its last days should not be considered entirely surprising. Indeed, the year of the Stuttgart seminars, Fredric Jameson began his landmark study, *Postmodernism*, by identifying one of the movement's distinguishing features to be "an inverted millenarianism in which premonitions of the future, catastrophic or redemptive, have been replaced by senses of the end of this or that" (Jameson 1991: 1).[2] Or, consider Barth's contention that a postmodernist should deal "with ultimacy, both technically and thematically" (Barth 1984: 67). A fascination with the new beginnings to be found in endings seems always to have been deeply etched into the core of postmodernism. But what counternarratives existed for the writer who had mastered postmodernism's theoretical toolkit and sought to move beyond its premises? Examples of younger writers finding their material in the same accounts of the end of postmodernism are pretty scarce. One rare exception would be Mark Leyner's short ironic sketch, "Geraldo, Eat Your Avant-Pop Heart Out" (1997). Taking Rorty's rejection of postmodernism as its starting point, Leyner imagines a recovering postmodernist called Alex who appears on Jenny Jones's talk show to discuss why he "believes that his literary career and his personal life have been irreparably damaged by [postmodernism], and who feels defrauded by the academics who promulgated it" in the wake of Rorty's "shocking admission" (Leyner 1997: 11). But Leyner is not satisfied to solely draw on Rorty as a source text; he also incorporates a parody of David Foster Wallace (who concluded "E Unibus Pluram" with a fairly devastating demolition of Leyner's *My Cousin, My Gastroenterologist* [1990]), and his insistence that the postmodernism could not be followed by writing that simply redeployed postmodern irony. Leyner writes:

> *Dissolve back to studio. In the audience, JENNY JONES extends the microphone to a man in his mid-20's with a scruffy beard and a bandana around his head.*[3]
> MAN WITH BANDANA: I'd like to say that this "Alex" is the single worst example of pointless irony in American literature, and this whole heartfelt renunciation of postmodernism is a ploy—it's just more irony.
>
> (Leyner 1997: 11)

But, apart from Leyner, younger writers have been less likely to find their imaginative materials in the literature of last things that so fascinated their predecessors. Instead, there are several notable (and probably more productive) developments from writers who clearly took the achievement of the preceding generation of American postmodernists as their starting point but who branch out in different directions. One significant factor, here, is surely the changing technologies that molded and infiltrated the worlds the respective generations grew up in. The emergent hypertext technologies and the massive distributed networks of the Internet are indisputably important to Barth's *Coming Soon!!!* (which reproduces fake option buttons within the text) and to Coover (who taught hypertext fiction), whose novels have imitated hypertext's form in the looping connections, and branching stories that explore "how entangled the present was with the past" (Coover 1996: 20). But younger writers, such as Carole Maso and Lee Siegel, have performed much more radical experiments with hypertext-influenced form.

Maso, who once dedicated a book to Gaddis, and who, in 1996, argued that "electronic writing" inspired by the new media would "help us to think about ... new worlds" (Maso 1996: 63) is particularly relevant. While attuned to the experiments of postmodernism, Maso has embraced the formal possibilities of hypertext far more strikingly than her precursors. Indeed, Maso considered publishing her 1993 novel *AVA* as a hypertext fiction, and the influence of nonlinear electronic forms upon linear fiction is evident in the shape of the final work.

AVA tells of thirty-nine-year-old Ava Klein lying in a hospital bed on the last day of her life, but the arrangement of her story is significantly divided. On one level, the narrative is radically nonlinear and fragmented (mostly we have just individual sentences, or short paragraphs), encouraging the reader to move between different sections, as if the text were a highly erudite jigsaw puzzle. Such interactivity replicates the workings of hypertext fiction, and Maso self-reflexively celebrates the idea of "literary texts that tolerate all kinds of freedom ... not texts of territory with neat borders" (1993: 113). But this nonlinear form is challenged by the novel's second level of organization: the associative fragments are themselves grouped (like a "text of territory") into three sections arranged into the linear sequence of Morning, Afternoon, and Night. The arrangement of "infinite beginnings, middles and ends" (Maso 1993: 42) that Maso praises seems to be opposed to the linear trisection of the day, but given that the end of the day climaxes in Ava's death, the implication is that the endpoint of such traditional linear schemes is a kind of death, whether literal or figurative.

Lee Siegel is also pertinent, here, as a spectacularly gifted writer whose work imitates the fragmented forms and branching nonlinear connections of hypertext fictions. Siegel's *Love in a Dead Language* (1999) quotes Coover on hypertext, includes fake web pages and also several sections that imitate the interactive dimension of hypertext. Unlike Barth's novel, which admits that it offers only "linear *simulations* of nonlinear effects" (Barth 2001: 237), Siegel—like Maso—presents interactive nonlinear effects. At one point, Siegel presents six fragments that his narrator insists he cannot order, so he encourages "the exacting reader to copy these pages and then cut along their dashed outlines, reconstructing ... a faithful representation of the text" (Siegel 1999: 236). Similarly, he offers elsewhere alternate pages devoted to different chapters, and his narrator informs the reader that "the choice" of which to read first "is yours" (Siegel 1999: 295). But while Siegel's work is a useful example of how new technologies have changed the forms of fiction after postmodernism, *Love in a Dead Language* also illustrates a more substantial element of the backlash against postmodernism.

In many critical reactions, metafiction is treated as, if not entirely co-incident with postmodernism then certainly as the malignant cell coded into the DNA of the movement. For Ziegler, Wallace, Amerika, and Olsen, the problem with postmodernism is the problem of metafiction. Wallace's solution to this problem in "Westward" (and later works) is to attempt a kind of meta-metafiction, and Siegel, arguably with more success, performs a similar maneuver in *Love in a Dead Language*.

Taking Vladimir Nabokov's *Lolita* and *Pale Fire* as a template, Siegel elaborates upon Nabokov's metafiction to tell the self-referential story of Leopold Roth, an aging professor of Indian studies who has fallen in love with Lalita, a student of Indian descent. This kernel story, however, provides an opening for a spectacular series of nested stories, language games, and much metafiction. Roth is meant to be translating Vātsyāyana's *Kāmasūtra*, but he discovers that "Writing about love and sex is not so much writing about love or sex as it is, and cannot escape being, writing about writing" (Siegel 1999: 100). Yet, as Roth's translation and Siegel's text begin to refer to themselves, Siegel embeds the story in a structure that criticizes metafiction. A third of the way through the book, Siegel includes mirrors amongst a list of "narcissistic themes and images" (1999: 117), and he has arranged his text so that mirroring begins to dictate the way the story is related. As Roth, for example, finally makes some progress in his seduction of Lalita, he writes: "It was the happiest moment of my life. That's not really true, but that's how it felt at the time" (Siegel 1999: 190). Then, as the net of repercussions stemming from his affair begins to tighten around him, he writes. "It was the most miserable moment of my life. That's really true, and that's how it felt at the time" (Siegel 1999: 283). The logic of the narrative's development, then, is dictated by the logic of reflection, so that when Roth begins a section "it could not have turned out better" (Siegel 1999: 211), the reader realizes that this must inevitably be followed by a section that begins "it could not have turned out worse" (1999: 213). By structuring his narrative in this way, Siegel manages to dazzle the reader with spirals of recursion, while he simultaneously reveals reading to be a mediated experience *and* criticizes the tendency of self-referential fiction to descend into narcissism.

Siegel and Maso are important writers, but I'd like to conclude by examining two more famous novels that engage with postmodernism's self-referential tendencies, and which bracket the decade, Richard Powers' *The Gold Bug Variations* (1991) and Jonathan Franzen's *The Corrections* (2001). These writers, who have both been described as post-postmodern, have bent the techniques of postmodernism toward different ends than their predecessors.

The author of nine deeply textured novels, Powers' affinities to Pynchon are frequently noted, but he has also written about Barth's *Coming Soon!!!* (Powers 2003) and has singled out Gaddis as the writer who "was the first to make [him] realize that a large-scale work of fiction could be both highly, schematically constructed and deeply, passionately inhabited" (Powers 2005).

While the masterworks of postmodernism clearly provide one of the starting points for Powers' fiction, his treatment of the act of writing, and of literature (and in fact most art forms), is different from what we find in, say, Barth, who privileges language as "the original virtual reality" (Barth 2001: 87). Powers' work is deeply troubled by the question of what the purpose of art may be in a technology-dominated world that seems to have rendered literature obsolete. In his first novel, *Three Farmers on Their Way to a Dance* (1985), Powers begins by worrying that in the modern world "Art can only hope to be an anaesthetic, a placebo" (Powers 1985: 13), but the process of Powers' novels is to demonstrate literature's continuing relevance. The twist to Powers' aesthetic is that he does not select art, or literature, to be praised in isolation but demonstrates how art is situated in what critics have called an ecological relationship with other disciplines.[4] His most-celebrated novel to date, *The Gold Bug Variations*, provides a neat illustration of how such an ecology works.

The Gold Bug Variations begins with a fairly conventional narrative hook: A librarian, Jan O'Deigh, receives news from an ex-lover, Franklin Todd (nominally a graduate student, trying to complete a dissertation on the obscure painter Herri met de Bles), about the death of an older friend, Stuart Ressler, a once-promising geneticist who abandoned science for (initially) mysterious reasons in the 1950s. The novel goes on to excavate O'Deigh and Todd's love affair, to recapitulate Ressler's scientific research (often drifting, in the process, into surprisingly enthralling mini-essays on molecular biology) and to demonstrate a dazzling spectrum of knowledge that ranges from computer programming to obscure Renaissance painters. Within this diverse and eclectic narrative system, Powers subtly and carefully articulates the power literature can, and cannot, have. This is particularly clear in the novel's carefully structured opening.

The text of *The Gold Bug Variations* is framed by an "aria": a poem split into four parts, each of which is composed of four stanzas.[5] Each of the poem's sections introduces one of the principal themes of the novel: music, molecular biology, love, and time. Where does literature fit within this hierarchy of the novel's interests? While literature is implicit in the *form* of this opening sequence, it is curiously absent as a *subject* from the poem itself. Presumably this is Powers' statement of intent, his way of telling the reader that literature will not be the subject of this work of literature (as in pure metafiction) but rather the medium for transmitting other forms of information.

But if this narrative frame reacts against the postmodern fusion of medium and subject, what follows complicates such an apparently straightforward algorithm. Chapter 1 begins, "Word came today" (Powers 1991: 11), but these three words resonate on at least two levels. On a basic level, this beginning suggests that, whatever complications follow, everything is instigated and driven by the word, by language. On a secondary level, by beginning with "word," Powers is also echoing John Verse 1 Chapter 1, "In the beginning was the Word," which is quoted directly later in the novel (Powers 1991: 568). With such sacred overtones, we seem to be witnessing a restatement of literature's power, yet the word that has arrived turns out to be the announcement of Ressler's death. The message reads: "It's all over with our mutual friend. I've just this instant heard. The attendant at the testing center assures me that all the instruments agree: Dr. Ressler went down admirably" (Powers 1991: 14). The allusion to Dickens apparently confirms the primacy of the word, but that primacy is modified by the third sentence's echo of a refrain from Auden's "In Memory of W. B. Yeats" ("What instruments we have agree / The day of his death was a dark cold day"). Auden's poem is relevant, not just because *The Gold Bug Variations* is suffused with Yeats, or because it, too, is about the death of an older man, but principally because it contains Auden's famous pronouncement on literature's limitations: "poetry makes nothing happen" (Auden 1979: 82). This implicit diminishment of literature does not take place in a vacuum. The power of all of the arts is called into question: Powers links music to literature, by echoing Auden on poetry later in the novel when he announces that "Music was no use for anything" (Powers 1991: 574), and its lack of efficacy stems in part from that fact that it, too, is cursed by self-reference. Music, Powers tells us, was "not condemned to be *about* anything else. It was about itself" (1991: 574). Todd's fascination with painting is similarly dubious, because the turmoil of "current events shamed panel and oil" (Powers 1991: 68).

This account initially seems pretty gloomy for the arts. Each assertion of the power of art is immediately qualified by a reminder of art's impotence. But, on closer examination, the novel actually articulates an argument about what art *can* achieve. Although the postmodern artist is commonly stereotyped as fascinated only with narcissistic works of increasing irrelevance to the rest of society, Powers is concerned with developing a conception of art that is predicated upon collaboration and human connection. To take painting, the focus of Todd's art-history thesis, Herri met de Bles, is immediately presented as an artist who created by working with others: He cooperates by drawing inspiration from more gifted painters—Todd tells us his paintings are "undeniable Patinir derivatives" (Powers 1991: 341)—but Todd also argues that there's reason to believe that he "was actually … a composite of student panelists from Patinir's workshop" (1991: 340). Similarly, Bach's *Goldberg Variations*, which provide the novel with a title, structure, and much else, is revealed to have collaborative foundations: the "germ aria, a heavily ornamented period piece, was not even Bach's own" (Powers 1991: 578). Even the work's original title, the *Clavier-Übung*, had already been used by Bach's predecessor as *Thomaskantor* in Leipzig, Johann Kuhnau. So, just as poetry collaborates with, say, music or science to produce the opening aria, so music and painting are revealed throughout the rest of the novel to be themselves an opportunity for collaboration, for human connection. There are "joint solutions everywhere" in this novel (Powers 1991: 324).

Powers is working not just to untangle the image of the artist as isolated genius but also to counter the idea that Siegel parodies. Both writers are engaged with the idea that writing is a narcissistic undertaking that merely reduplicates, or mirrors, the self. There are echoes, too, of Wallace's insistence on art as a means of human connection. But Powers' critique of artistic isolation, as well as his parallel construction of a model of collaborative creation, climaxes in the final pages of *The Gold Bug Variations* when he reveals that the novel has been a collaboration between Jan and Todd. While it has been obvious to the reader that the text is partly drawn from Jan's attempt to console herself with an account of her year of solitary learning and memories of her relationship with Todd and Ressler, it is only upon rereading the novel that the clues to Todd's authorship of the sections covering Ressler in the 1950s becomes apparent.

In retrospectively revealing the grounds of the novel's creation, however, Powers has—crucially—introduced a metafictional element into his text, and it is the self-referring aspect of these final pages that suggests how Powers has transformed the metafictional postmodern novel. By basing the novel upon a relatively traditional foundation, and then relying upon the codes of realism until the final pages, Powers attempts a synthesis of two apparently opposed modes of rendering the world. The realist dimension to his novels elicits the traditional effects of fiction—understanding, empathy with another's perspective—while the metafictional element draws the reader's attention outside the book, to recognize the way her own life story is constructed. The appeal of such a novel where realism shades into metafiction, resides, as Powers argues in "Being and Seeming," in its ability:

> to interrupt our imaginary continuities and put us head to head with a maker who is not us. Story is a denuding, laying the reader bare, and the force of that denuding lies not in our entering into a perfect representation, but in our coming back out. It lies in that moment ... when we come to remember how finely narrated is the life outside this constructed frame, a story needing only some other minds' pale analogies to resensitize us to everything in it that we've grown habituated to.
>
> (Powers 2000: 17)

For Powers, then, fiction is, as he writes in *Prisoner's Dilemma*, "a place to hide out in long enough to learn how to come back" (1988: 345), and the crucial element is the re-emergence that metafiction prompts. In Powers' synthesis of realism and postmodernism, fiction provides an alternate map of reality, parallel to the world. He knows that "the map is not the place," but he insists that "we can use the map to navigate the place" (Powers 2002–3: 138).

Powers' efforts at the start of the 1990s to reconcile postmodernism and realism and escape the narcissistic inward spiral of self-referring fiction represent one of the most important articulations of what might be called post-postmodernism, a genuine illustration of how the techniques of postmodern fiction could be redirected toward alternate ends. At the end of the decade, Jonathan Franzen published his third novel, *The Corrections* (2001), which, in its own way, suggested a different route that fiction might take after postmodern metafiction.

Franzen had theorized, more or less in public, about the evolution of his third novel throughout the 1990s, wrestling with the question of how a writer shaped by postmodernism might relate to a culture that no longer seemed to listen to the movement. But when *The Corrections* appeared, there had been a radical shift away from the postmodern. Principally this involved character, which Franzen argued postmodern fiction had neglected. He complained that "postmodern fiction wasn't supposed to be about sympathetic characters. Characters, properly speaking, weren't even supposed to exist. Characters were feeble, suspect constructs" (Franzen 2003: 247). The exact targets prompting Franzen's shift are difficult to determine, but William H. Gass, who Franzen accuses of "sophistry" in this essay (2003: 260), might be the focus of Franzen's ire.

In his influential essay collection, *Fiction and the Figures of Life* (1970), Gass attacked misconceptions that he felt lay at the root of our experience of fiction, and several of these concerned the notion of character. Gass stressed the fact that books are made out of language and urged the reader not to mistake a linguistic construct for a mysterious reality: "although no one wonders, of a painted peach, whether the tree it grew on was watered properly, we are happily witness, week after week, to further examination of Hamlet or Madame Bovary, quite as if they were real" (Gass 1970: 31). *The Corrections* seems, on first inspection, to totally reject Gass's idea that novelistic language must not draw attention away from itself. The novel is a kind of dysfunctional family drama, concentrating on the lives of the various members of the Lambert family: the repressed father Alfred, the overbearing mother Enid, the financially aggressive son Gary, the wayward intellectual son Chip, and the superficially normal daughter Denise. In responding to these characters, the majority of reviews greeted the novel as a reaction against the postmodern conception of character propounded by critics such as Gass. James Wood, for example, argued that *The Corrections* could be understood as basically a DeLillo novel with the addition of "human beings" at its center (2001). But such descriptions actually obscure the way Franzen has incorporated (albeit diluted) elements of the self-referential postmodern conception of character that Gass outlines.

A character, Gass writes, is "a proper name" not a person (1970: 44), but, as if to parody this process of reduction, Franzen's novel suggests a further refinement by reminding the reader that the word *character* denotes an alphabetical letter, as well as a personality. Subjecting the Lambert family to the process of "alphabetical ... sorting" that Denise undertakes when she works in an office (Franzen 2001: 355), a significant pattern begins to emerge.

Laid out in order, *A*lfred, *C*hip, *D*enise, *E*nid, and *G*ary, suggest a pattern that, rather than undermining the story, actually recapitulates the family dynamic that *The Corrections* explores. Beginning with the alphafather, Franzen appears to have laid out a neat set of A, B, Cs to demonstrate the flow of patriarchal power. On closer examination, however, it becomes clear that Franzen has deliberately fractured this scheme, so that the two father figures in the family—Alfred and Gary (who, like Alfred, has three children)—are isolated from the rest of their family. This schematic basically encodes one of the stories that Franzen is telling in his novel: The structure of the family has changed, and the patriarch is now in exile.

Embedded within this A-C-D-E-G schematic, however, is also a neat arrangement of the family's relationships. Just as *A* is next to *C*, so Chip is the character who is closest to Alfred's affections, because as Denise observes, "if there was anybody in the world whom Alfred did love purely for his own sake, it was Chip" (Franzen 2001: 526). In parallel, *G* is next to

E, because Gary cares most about his mother. Denise, of course, lies in the centre of this arrangement, as throughout the book she is torn between the needs of the other family members. Taken together, these first letters of the family members' names also offer a pertinent anagram: *caged*. This is another of the techniques Franzen uses to stress that familial inheritance is a kind of prison for these characters, and the inescapability of the family unit is reinscribed a further level down, in the names of the female characters. The letters for Enid's name are embedded within Denise, but just as Denise insists upon how different she is from her mother, it is significant that Denise is an anagram of *denies*.

Like Powers' incorporation of metafictional strategies, Franzen's word games suggest his continued affinities with the earlier program of post-modernism, but there is a notable difference between the avenues explored by the two younger writers. Powers' self-reflexivity is a crucial dimension of his novel, which is clearly wedded to an overarching plan for his fiction. Franzen's linguistic games, by contrast, are optional extras that a reader might play with, should they choose to, rather than an organic element of the text itself. Both writers, however, have clearly taken the self-reflexive aspects of postmodernism as their starting point.

In 1979, Robert Scholes argued in *Fabulation and Metafiction* that "self-reflection in fiction" was "essentially a short-term trend ... nearing its end" (1979: 212). The larger arc of the novel in the 1990s suggests that Scholes was wrong but that he was wrong for interesting, perhaps prescient, reasons. The postmodern novel in its last days, as well as the novel that seeks to move beyond postmodernism, could not escape the tangled complications of self-reference, even when it wanted to.

Notes

1 A significant sub-genre of male postmodernism in the 1990s was the development of books by aging male writers about aging male writers: to add to *Coming Soon!!!*, there are at least William Gaddis's *A Frolic of His Own* (1994), Don DeLillo's *Mao II* (1991), William Gass's *The Tunnel* (1995), David Markson's *Reader's Block* (1996), and Joseph Heller's *Portrait of an Artist, as an Old Man* (2000).

2 As a further indication of postmodernism's desire to spiral criticism back into fiction, note that Jameson's phrase "the end of this or that" is incorporated in Barth's discussion in "The End: An Introduction" ("the end of this, the end of that") quoted earlier in this essay.

3 Wallace's big novel, *Infinite Jest* (1996), had been accompanied by a widely reprinted photograph of Wallace in which, sure enough, he had a scruffy beard and a bandana.

4 Joseph Tabbi argues that Powers' fiction "is ecological in a wider sense, opening connective possibilities" (2002: 61).

5 It is not a coincidence that the poem's four sections mirror the four bases of the gene. For more on such patterns, see Labinger (1995).

References

Auden, W. H. (1979) *Selected Poems*, London: Faber.

Barth, J. (1984) *The Friday Book: Essays and Other Nonfiction*, Baltimore, Md.: Johns Hopkins University Press.

—— (1996) *On with the Story*, Boston, Mass.: Little, Brown.

—— (2001) *Coming Soon!!!*, Boston, Mass.: Houghton Mifflin.

Coover, R. (1996) *John's Wife*, New York: Scribner.

—— (2002) *The Adventures of Lucky Pierre: Directors' Cut*, New York: Grove.

Foster, H. (1996) *The Return of the Real: The Avant-Garde at the End of the Century*, Cambridge, Mass.: MIT Press.

Franzen, J. (2001) *The Corrections*, New York: Farrar.

—— (2003) *How to Be Alone*, 2nd edn, New York: Farrar.

Gass, W. H. (1970) *Fiction and the Figures of Life*, New York: Knopf.

Harris, C. B. (2002) "PoMo's Wake, I," *American Book Review* 23 (2): 1–3.

Jameson, F. (1991) *Postmodernism, or, The Cultural Logic of Late Capitalism*, London: Verso.

Labinger, J. A. (1995) "Encoding an Infinite Message: Richard Powers's *Gold Bug Variations*," *Configurations* 3: 79–93.

Leyner, Mark (1997) "Geraldo, Eat Your Avant-Pop Heart Out," *New York Times* December 21, section 4, p. 11.

Maso, C. (1993) *AVA*, Normal, Ill.: Dalkey.

—— (1996) "Rupture, Verge, and Precipice/Precipice, Verge, and Hurt Not," *Review of Contemporary Fiction* 16 (1): 54–75.

McCaffery, L. (1993) "An Interview with David Foster Wallace," *Review of Contemporary Fiction*, 13 (2): 127–50.

—— (1995) "Avant-Pop: Still Life After Yesterday's Crash," in L. McCaffery (ed.), *After Yesterday's Crash: The Avant-Pop Anthology*, Harmondsworth: Penguin.

Olsen, L. and Amerika, M. (1995) "Smells Like Avant-Pop: An Introduction, of Sorts," in L. Olsen and M. Amerika (eds) *In Memoriam to Postmodernism: Essays on the Avant-Pop*, San Diego, Calif.: San Diego State University Press, pp. 1–31.

Powers, R. (1985) *Three Farmers on Their Way to a Dance*, New York: William Morrow.

—— (1988) *Prisoner's Dilemma*, New York: William Morrow.

—— (1991) *The Gold Bug Variations*, New York: William Morrow.

—— (2000) "Being and Seeming: The Technology of Representation," *Context* 3: 15–17.

—— (2002–3) "The Art of Fiction CLXXV: Richard Powers," Interview with Kevin Berger, *Paris Review* 164: 106–38.

—— (2003) "John Barth: An Introduction," *Paris Review* 167: 292–94.

—— (2005) Unpublished interview with Stephen J. Burn.

Rorty, R. et al. (1997) "Lofty Ideas that May Be Losing Altitude," *New York Times*, November 1, Section B, p. 13.

234 *Stephen J. Burn*

Scholes, R. (1979) *Fabulation and Metafiction*, Urbana, Ill.: University of Illinois Press.
Siegel, L. (1999) *Love in a Dead Language*, Chicago, Ill.: University of Chicago Press.
Tabbi, J. (2002) *Cognitive Fictions*, Minneapolis, Minn.: University of Minnesota Press.
Turner, T. (1996) *City as Landscape: A Post-Postmodern View of Design and Planning*, London: Spon.
Vollmann, W. T. (1990) "American Writing Today: A Diagnosis of the Disease," *Conjunctions* 15: 355–8.
Wallace, D. F. (1989) *Girl with Curious Hair*, New York: Norton.
—— (1993) "E Unibus Pluram: Television and US Fiction," *Review of Contemporary Fiction*, 13 (2): 151–94.
Wood, J. (2001) "What the Dickens?" *The Guardian*, November 9. Online. Available at http://books.guardian.co.uk/reviews/generalfiction/0,590800,00.html (accessed June 16, 2006).
Ziegler, H. (1993) "The End of Postmodernism: New Directions," in H. Ziegler (ed.), *The End of Postmodernism: New Directions*. Stuttgart: Verlag, pp. 5–10.

Index

244   *Index*